FANCINESS IS A MINDSET. It's realizing that you can make everyday food feel special using what you likely already have on hand. It's about seeing the act of cooking not as just another chore but as a nourishing ritual to help ease away the day's stress.

In *We Fancy*, Jerrelle Guy teaches you how to use pantry staples such as canned beans, crackers, or a pint of vanilla ice cream and tools like sheet pans and your air fryer to transform typical weeknight dinners into something easy but memorable. Chapters and recipes include:

FAST 'N' FANCY: Spring Noodle Salad, Five-Spice Maple-Glazed Salmon, Nearly Instantaneous Black Garlic Risotto

DINNER SNACKS: Ritzy "Meatballs," Sky-High Avocado Deviled Eggs

BREAKFAST FOR DINNER: Sheet Pan Rummy French Toast Bites, Pearl Sugar Cornbread Waffles with Crispy Hot Honey Mushrooms

LAVISH LEFTOVERS: Mango & Miso Salmon Grain Bowls, Tomato & Ginger Curry

WEEKNIGHT DESSERTS: Sticky Date Cakes, Olive Oil Brownie Pudding

We Fancy shows that cooking is both a creative and a practical act. In these pages with beautiful and wise writing that is meant to heal, guide, and inspire, Jerrelle Guy gives us new recipes and reasons to look forward to dinner.

WE FANCY

Overnight Lasagna Terrine
(page 120)

SIMPLE RECIPES TO MAKE THE EVERYDAY SPECIAL

WE FANCY

JERRELLE GUY

SIMON ELEMENT

NEW YORK AMSTERDAM/ANTWERP LONDON TORONTO SYDNEY/MELBOURNE NEW DELHI

Atlas 150

for whenever
I've strayed,
a compass back
to my happy place

CONTENTS

PROLOGUE:

PROLOGUE

HER

WHEN I STEP INTO THE KITCHEN, my inner child comes out to play. I can feel her zealous, feisty, and focused energy. Her eyes painted with determination; she is sure of herself, as if she were on a mission to oversee a handful of teddy bears cahooting over tea or caping up to soar between flipped furniture masquerading as skyscrapers. Boy does she thrive when it's time to improvise. I love this fearless, heart-pounding, untamed, spirited little girl.

The kitchen was a place for her to relish the comfort of delicious food. It was a place to build a rich inner reality barricaded from the chaos of the world, from the naysayers and the bubble-bursters. It was a place where her creativity and imagination could thrive.

Somewhere along the way of chasing my dreams, that inner child and I lost touch, and I desperately needed a reminder to reclaim my life with her same whimsy and wonder.

I'm writing this book for her and anyone else looking to bring a little sparkle back into their homes and into their everyday.

PART

1

INTRODUCTION

This is not your typical weeknight cookbook.

WHILE I HOPE it becomes a collection of recipes you make your own and come to cherish for years to come, I also want it to gently shift how you *feel* about the act of cooking, that you see it not just as a task to complete at the end of the day, but also as a tool to help you unwind and find some peace of mind. My wish is that your kitchen will become your refuge, a sanctuary from the world, where the practice of cooking becomes one of healing and restoration.

For my family and me, this practice involves always being mindful to sprinkle a little something extra into our meals. I call it "being fancy," though it has nothing to do with wealth or status, and more to do with being free to be imaginative. Fanciness, as I see it, is a way to savor what we have right in front of us. It's our philosophy, one where mindfulness and play meet with just enough practicality to bring deeper meaning to our dinners and our days.

Although for many years I made a living developing recipes and cooking for other people, I actually struggled to find motivation to make dinner for myself. Once I reframed cooking as a mindfulness exercise and invited more reverence into the kitchen, things changed. By focusing my thoughts on the small details I could control, I was able to regulate my nervous system and shift from the constant frazzled and anxious state I had grown accustomed to into a more calm and hopeful one.

In writing and cooking my way through this book, I found balance and joy in my day and in my diet. I stopped putting time and energy into external things that didn't nourish me, and instead, I poured that energy back into my family, my body, and my home. **That's when things began to re-blossom around me.**

The Crash : The End and the Beginning

By the end of 2020, I was burnt-out, and a fog of depression enclosed me. It was as if someone's thumb smudged the writing on my timeline, and I was stuck sitting in the blur. I could see, faintly, the people and the world shifting past, but I was too sunken inside myself, too lethargic to pierce the haze. Existing like that, I wondered why I was even alive at all.

Less than two years before, already running on fumes after earning a master's in the same year I finished writing and photographing my first cookbook, I got an email from an art director who wanted to know if I'd be open to photographing other authors' cookbooks. I didn't hesitate—I was going to turn my passion for food and my art into a business. I grabbed my now husband by the hand, and with all the energy I had, packed a van with four years' worth of stuff and made the trek from Boston to Dallas to open our own photography studio and get to work chasing our dream.

Dallas promised a better pace than the Northeast: It was a calm place to regroup after the busy year of studying and promoting my book. Plus both of our families were there, and I knew it to be a place where I could tuck away and do my art in peace. And for a while that's what I did. I shot and styled cookbooks and developed and photographed recipes for magazines. As a side gig, I developed dessert recipes for different publications, and I even agreed to write and shoot another cookbook in a three-month sliver of time.

It all looked amazing on paper, but in truth, my body was overworked. I was in survival mode, hustling to pay the next bill, to run a studio with an inconsistent budget, to wear every hat imaginable while learning on the spot, all while living on a terrible sugar diet of recipe spoils and leftover food from our photoshoots. As my schedule and inbox filled, my anxieties increased and my health declined, but I was dismissing the cues so I could maintain false optimism and keep moving with the rest of the world's grind.

What began as a romantic notion of aspirational entrepreneurship with all the signs of a hopeful new beginning quickly devolved into a path that ultimately put me at war against my health, my art, and our rent. It was a lifestyle that left me oscillating between motivational grinding and self-protective child's pose.

After we moved into our new home studio, a Black man was shot in our neighborhood, just 400 feet from our window. The tragedy split the city in half and ignited an insurrection at the foot of our building that spread across the state. The tension on the streets and in the whispers was thick.

And then, soon after the shooting, I was carjacked while leaving a late-night concert downtown. Two men threw me out of my vehicle in the middle of nowhere.

Later, as I sat in the police station, the police officer, with eyes cold and numb, treated the transgression with indifference; I felt that to him my body and case were insignificant among the slew of other problems he had sifted through, and it was in that moment that my last bit of childlike wonder for the world left me, because there was nothing in place to protect it. I no longer felt safe—in my body or out in the chaotic world. In the following months, my body ballooned up like its own shield, and I lost my desire for adventure. The way I understood myself began to collapse. My sense of autonomy and my ability to confidently step through the world slipped away. For a while I lived deep inside myself, barely wanting to leave my bed, burying myself in work, holding tightly to my grief and the loss of faith I had in a just, compassionate, and trustworthy world.

At the start of 2021, around the same time a winter storm disabled the Texas power grid and about a year after the country succumbed to the pandemic, we downsized our studio to a small condo north of the city. We had to renovate it in patches due to limited power and a shortage of building supplies. We were living in a construction zone for months and my usual way of handling things, by pushing forward and grinding harder, wasn't working like it had in the past. The life that I had dreamt about and achieved was beginning to show its holes. I was out of sync with the natural rhythms of my body and ultimately living out of alignment with my truest desires.

Cooking has always made me feel peaceful, like a Mary Poppins–esque fairy doing cabrioles through the kitchen with a platter of snacks, tasked only with making everyone's day feel brighter with food. But I was so run-down, I wasn't happy cooking myself. Something in me was tangled, pretending. I'd let the magic of what brought me joy get swallowed by the seriousness of the world, rushed by deadlines and competition, filtered by fear, poisoned by struggle.

The thing that put me out faster than the fire demon flickering on the hearth of Howl's castle was failing to protect the spark of my inner child by letting her play and create in peace just for the sake of playing and creating.

One night, with our home construction indefinitely on pause, the floors ripped up, and the water cut off, I stood on the bare cement in our kitchen and just snapped. The feelings I tried to bury bubbled up, clouding my vision with resentment and rage.

My lifestyle was depleting me, and the structures I put in place were weak, built on shifting sands. There was nothing for me in rushing to some illusory finish line. I needed to stop the momentum of what I was building, including my idea of who I was supposed to be, and retrace my steps back to the foundation so that I could redevote my energy to the things that truly supported me.

I wouldn't make any sudden moves until the fog cleared and I could sort through the confusion and rubble with clarity. I dropped all my doingness and surrendered into just being. As Katherine May coined it, I had entered my phase of "wintering."

This was my greatest test—to sit in the space of what felt like a dead end and be okay with it. To be okay with starting over from scratch.

Surprisingly, I felt relieved and at peace there in the darkest part of nothingness, in the present moment where there was really nothing on earth to do, except maybe, eventually, cook *myself* something good to eat.

Resting and Reassesing

We've all faced trauma, provoked suddenly or built up over time, that has caused us to disassociate from our bodies, believing them to be unsafe spaces. This disconnection doesn't just fade; it lingers, the fear stuck in the body, shaping how we move through the world long after the initial wound. To live fully and joyfully—without becoming prisoner to our fears and wounds—we have to relearn to trust our bodies and the world around us again, but we can't rebuild a trusting relationship with either or even feel grounded and safe inside ourselves if we keep overriding our intuition, numbing ourselves to rush toward the next distraction, checkbox on our to-do list, and hit of dopamine. We make true progress in the moments when we allow ourselves to slow down, sit with ourselves, and feel deeply into our bodies.

Thanks to my mom's influence, I've always been a voracious consumer of self-help and personal development books. But looking back, I can't help but think that my ambition and constant "doingness" came from a fear of never being good enough. While the wisdom within those books has given me amazing willpower and the ability to shift into empowered action, to slap myself out of moments of self-pity, they've also taught me to gloss over moments that call for greater pause, patience, and self-compassion. I've been trained to constantly chase more material success, more validation, and more productivity, believing those things would provide me a sense of safety and belonging out in the world, not realizing what I actually needed was to cultivate a feeling of "home" within myself.

The Rebuild

Yesterday I was clever, so I wanted to change the world. Today I am wise, so I am changing myself.

—RUMI

It didn't take me long to learn my burnout wasn't just a me problem. I heard similar cries echoing throughout my community, from friends on the internet, friends in real life, family, people feeling worn and weary, wanting to slow down, to find a better way forward. Almost everyone, it seemed, was apprehensive about what a successful life truly was, especially after peering into the curated versions of other people's worlds on social media.

Most people just want to love themselves and their lives, but we're backlogged with information on how to do it or get there, overstimulated by a digital environment of excess, trying to find true value in an arena concerned only with bravado, material results, expansion, speed, competition, mass production, and who can outperform the last.

I wanted to give my body a break from my mind's incessant seeking and striving after being worn down by the different tiny but crushing distractions, comparisons, and expectations. I wanted to stop polluting the air with unnecessary noise. I wanted to create art I believed in and I wanted to make the kind of food I wanted to consume. I wanted to learn to enjoy my life again and I wanted to empower myself by actively creating a life I was happy to live.

We each get to define our own meaning of success, and mine means curating a lifestyle that promotes well-being. It is building a nourishing and sustainable system that supports my mental health and emotional balance, where peace, joy, and play are mainstays . . . and I decided I was going to get serious about this refined definition of *success*.

Of course, the foundation of a sustainable, nourishing system starts with how I feed myself. If I was going to truly learn to care for my body, cooking dinner felt like the most practical next step. So, I set out to find a project that would reignite my passion for living and one that might even remind me that my joy for cooking hadn't truly been snuffed out.

I WOULD WRITE THIS BOOK—a collection of the recipes I craved, the ones that made me excited to cook and eat. I would dive in, using what I already had in my kitchen. That meant starting from scratch—with a half-empty fridge (really just a dormant sourdough starter and a spotted head of cauliflower) and a pantry full of random odds and ends.

HOW TO BE FANCY

A Guidebook

BEING FANCY IS A LIFESTYLE. It is a mindset, a way of interacting with and moving through the world. At its core, it's when you realize that you already have much of what you need to live a rich and fulfilling life. You don't have to try the latest trendy meal at the hottest new restaurant, quit your job, leave your marriage, or move to another country to live a better life. Being fancy is an internal journey that requires training your mind and alchemizing your perception to transform what's already in front of you into something otherworldly. It's the art of seeing the abundance available to you in every moment. Of using your environment (and in this case, your kitchen and the ingredients at your fingertips), for making the ordinary more *extraordinary* until it becomes so. What follows are ten basic principles to keep in mind to help you embody your own "fancy" in the kitchen.

1

GET OUT OF YOUR HEAD

Remove the rules about how your food needs to be. Do your best to get out of your head and into the moment. Spontaneity, and play in the process, will heal you. Humble yourself to the pleasant surprises that happen when you're curious and not clinging tightly to how a recipe and reality must unfold. If tonight's dinner doesn't go as planned, there's always tomorrow's dinner to set your sights on.

TIP

Curiosity is the antithesis of fear and it will unlock pathways in your brain for finding new solutions to old problems. Keeping an eclectic pantry can spark curiosity, creativity, and play, helping you to be more daring.

2

CLEAR, CLEAN, DECLUTTER

A messy kitchen can flare anxiety and disrupt flow, so if you enter a disorganized, unclean kitchen, prioritize cleaning. The cooking can always wait.

Clean Before You Start, and Clean as You Cook: Build the self-loving habit of cleaning during downtime in a recipe, and before you leave the kitchen. It will allow you to reset the space quickly for the next time you enter.

The Dishes: The dishes are the main culprit to a dysfunctional kitchen space. If there's no space to wash your hands or clean your veggies, it can send you over the top. Whether you have a dishwasher or do them by hand, find a way to enjoy the process.

TIP

Learning to master mindfulness during the most mundane activities, like washing the dishes or chopping onions, can be the most practical place to begin. Eventually you'll become practiced at regulating your overall mental state and emotional well-being no matter where you are or what you're doing.

Embrace the Magic of Distilled White Vinegar: Buy a big jug. It's a natural and cost-effective kitchen cleaner and deodorizer with an acidity that cuts through grease, grime, and bacteria (not to mention it's one of the main ingredients in my caramelized Adobo Onions, page 208).

- To make a great, streak-free **all purpose cleaner**: In a large spray bottle combine 1 cup distilled vinegar, 1 cup distilled water, 1 cup rubbing alcohol, a few drops of dish soap, and a few drops of your favorite essential oil (to temper the vinegary smell), and use this on your stove top, appliances, windows, stainless steel, floor and baseboards, and any non-stone counter tops.
- Spray pure distilled vinegar onto greasy, non-porous surfaces, let it sit for 5 to 10 minutes, then wipe clean. For tough spots, like turmeric or red wine stains, sprinkle on baking soda first, then spray with vinegar to create foam. Scrub gently and rinse.
- Clean a stinky sink drain by pouring ½ cup of baking soda followed by 1 cup of vinegar down the drain. Let it bubble and sit for 5 minutes, then rinse with hot water.

- Boil old dish towels on the stove in a large pot of water with a splash of vinegar, a drop of dish soap, and a couple tablespoons of baking soda for 10 minutes to return them to their original freshness.
- Wipe wooden or plastic cutting boards with undiluted vinegar to disinfect and deodorize, then rinse with warm water.

Declutter: The less you keep, the less you have to clean, and keep cleaning. Only hold space for what you value. Retire old objects you don't use. Organize your pantry in a way that makes sense to you, so your body can navigate easier through the space. Wipe down sticky bottles and relabel jars. Put away large countertop appliances. And last, clean the fridge and throw away any old, expired food to refresh the energy everywhere.

Stock Up on Storage Containers: Find containers that you like and that help you function optimally. Deli containers make our kitchen feel like an efficient restaurant kitchen. They're lightweight, stackable, and come in a variety of volumes, yet they all use the same-sized lid, so I'm not left searching for any particular size. I get the ones that are BPA-free and dishwasher and freezer safe. If you prefer glass storage, IKEA's 365+ collection have containers that are just as versatile.

3
DESIGN YOUR INNER WORLD (& KITCHEN)

Our outer reality is a reflection of what is going on inside, so it follows that our homes are a reflection of our energy and mental state. Be mindful of how your environment, home, and kitchen make you feel. Take it in. Then tweak it to make it optimal. Maybe you want your kitchen to feel quiet, nurturing, and calm. Or maybe vibrant, communal. Whatever the case, it should be a welcoming safe haven that supports you mentally and physiologically. Make your kitchen feel like a teeny pocket of the world you can actually control. Make it beautiful: hang pictures, place heirlooms on a shelf, grow herbs on the windowsill. Put your favorite cookbook (like this one!) on a stand. We thrive in aesthetically beautiful places, and when we prioritize making them, it sends signals to the brain that we are safe and abundant.

TIP

UPGRADE YOUR SERVEWARE:
Similar to that saying about the clothes you wear, life's too short to eat on boring plates. Get rid of joyless dinnerware like plastic and paper plates, and choose tableware and utensils that make you feel good, that have personality, heft, and color. It may seem trivial, but when it's time to serve your food, you'll notice an elevation in your mood and a shift in your mental presence.

DRESS THE PART:
Simply throwing on a clean apron will not only protect your clothes but will also work as a sort of costume. Any clothing designated specifically for cooking will become one part ritual, one part mental trick that will switch you into your most confident cooking character.

Establish Some Kitchen Rules: It's okay to communicate what you need to thrive in the space to anyone else who plans to use it, too. Maybe you want dinner to be a community task. Have someone chop veggies while you sauté. Maybe you want to clear everyone away from the kitchen and claim the space to focus. Or maybe you want everyone to wash their own dishes and put them back into the cupboard after dinner. When it comes to your kitchen sanctuary, you have to be mindful of how you and your kitchen operate best.

TIP

Do not allow negativity into your kitchen. If someone is criticizing your food, it is okay to ask them to prepare their own meals—anyway, it's empowering for people to learn how to cook for themselves, and it's important for you to let them.

4

HONE YOUR KITCHEN INTUITION

Your intuition serves as a compass. It helps you move through life with more ease, and confidence in yourself and your choices. As you strengthen it in the kitchen, you'll learn to experiment with new ingredients, adapt to what you have on hand, and trust your instincts to balance flavors and textures. As you develop a closer bond among your body, external environment, and your mind, you will gain access to the intuitive messages that are always speaking, such as the smell of almost-burning food telling you to remove it from the oven, or the quiet whisper to pair two disparate ingredients.

TIP

If you struggle with feelings of anxiety, or whenever your nervous system is dysregulated, slowing down and tuning into each of your five senses and your body's interpretation of them is a helpful somatic practice that can ground you into your body and settle any irrational fears arising.

5

FIND YOUR FLOW

When cooking is a part of your lifestyle, it will become a body-based practice. You will stumble less and flow more. Like with any exercise, repetition is essential for finding a comfortable rhythm and flow. Select kitchen tools that give you confidence: sharpened knives, heavy-bottomed pans (I'm a fangirl for Caraway cookware!), sturdy cutting boards. And don't overlook the power of process-heavy recipes where the process becomes its own therapy. Recipes with long steps leave you no choice but to be present, your brain consumed only with the task of carefully kneading or folding or chopping, and suddenly your worries of dinner stress have dissolved in the most paradoxical way.

6

TRUST YOUR GUT

This will happen naturally over time as you learn to listen to your internal wisdom, mute the external noise, carve your own way, and stop adhering strictly to a recipe's rules from a fear of failure.

TIP

Let your hunger lead the way. If you're feeling lost and uninspired, confused about where to begin, hunger is the perfect motivator—use it to propel you into inspired cooking. Cook what you crave. Make ingredient swaps whenever you feel called or curious, and always adapt recipes to your preferences, pantry, and mood.

7
LEARN TO MASTER TIME

Make time be in service to your joy. While I love the idea of languishing in the kitchen, this is, after all, a weeknight cookbook, and I love a good shortcut to speed along the parts of cooking that don't speak to me. Learning to make time work for you is the ultimate freedom. It's possible to make life work on your timeline, orchestrating dinner, grocery shopping, and the systemization of your kitchen at your own speed. Consider what exactly you feel inspired to do, tasks that you will gladly focus on and immerse yourself into, and then delegate, or speed along the parts you don't care for using these tips:

SLOW DOWN TO SPEED UP

The freezer is a godsend for the overwhelmed user's mind and cluttered schedule. It is literally a *time stopper*.

- **Freeze Homemade Toppings: (page 272)** and other sauces throughout the book so they're always at the ready.
- **Freeze Smaller Portions:** Instead of putting big batches of food away, divide leftovers into portions in meal prep containers (like those Souper Cubes silicone freezer trays) or airtight pouches for eating later. This applies to frozen pizzas, too—defrost frozen pizza slightly, then cut into individual slices and refreeze.
- **Freeze Herbs:** Use herbs when they're fresh, vibrant, and perky but don't toss them when they wilt. Instead, chop them and pack them into ice cube trays, covered with oil or water. Frozen, they will lose some of their color, but you'll still get all their flavor when you melt them into soups or marinades or wherever else you use them.
- **And Then, Freeze Everything Else:** While we're on the subject, you can freeze almost anything with good results: mushrooms, berries, bread, blocks of cheese, shredded cheese, chopped avocados, onions, peppers, and peeled ginger. Par-freeze delicate ingredients or ones that may stick together in a single layer on a sheet pan for at least an hour to firm, then transfer them to larger air-tight bags or containers to freeze indefinitely.
- **Strategize:** Make lists to unburden your mind of all its to-dos. Get good at breaking a recipe into parts and sectioning the tasks. Make fillings, sauces, and compound butters at the top of the week. Defrost some tofu, feed your sourdough starter, put your butters out on the counter overnight so they soften. Make Wednesday Sauce (page 113) or a Jazzy Rice (page 158) to freeze for later. Do whatever will assist your future self.
- **Read and Visualize It:** Walk yourself through the steps before you start cooking and imagine the finished dinner in hand. Instead of casually stumbling through your next steps, play the steps like a movie in your head, so once you start cooking you don't have to continually interrupt the flow to refer back to the recipe from the top. Like

an actor on set, you'll get into character when you know the main points and purpose of your role, and then you can improvise the details.

- **All Ingredients on Deck:** I've organized the recipe list so the ingredients come before the amount you need. I think it's helpful for gathering all the ingredients onto a small sheet tray and making sure you have everything first. You can worry about the exact amounts once you've pooled them all together. If you want to go a step further you can even measure the ingredient amounts into individual vessels.

AND TO SPEED UP, USE THESE "TIME MACHINES":

- **The Instant Pot:** Obviously this machine is the weeknight cook's time machine into the future. Use it to make foolproof rice; modernize the archaic method of cooking risotto (page 72); steam these Sticky Date Cakes (page 246); and even make the best homemade ketchup (page 276) to rival Heinz.
- **(Lots of) Sheet Pans:** Sheet pans have become the loyal mule for multitask roasting and baking. Make little mounds of different things that need to roast at the same time, pairing things that take relatively similar times so they roast together and remove them from the oven just as they're ready. Also, make this mini chocolate sheet cake (page 264).
- **An Immersion Blender:** While the food processor is amazing for quickly shredding veggies, and the Vitamix is great for emulsifying sauces, the immersion blender still beats them all in the speed category because it's essentially your basic blender without the bowl. Having one of these will save on cleanup and eliminate the time it takes to transfer food in and out of a blender.
- **The Air-Fryer:** Besides the obvious of making foods supremely crispy with minimal oil, I think of it as a little oven I secretly never preheat. It hurriedly cooks small batches of things, even surprising recipes like single, home-alone cookie (page 262).
- **A Panini Press or Waffle Iron:** Because they get hot fast and provide even, direct contact heat, other than making elevated sandwiches and weeknight waffles on a whim, you can use these plug-in tools to easily grill halved heads of romaine (page 172) and bread for Solo Toasts (page 202), crisp hash browns (page 240), and quesadillas, or even "bake" store-bought cookie dough in minutes.
- **A Scale:** Start weighing ingredients directly into your mixing bowl. It eliminates the need for measuring cups and spoons, reduces cleanup, speeds prep time, and ensures consistency in baking recipes, where accuracy matters. Try it out to speed along recipes like In-the-Blender Coconut Honeydew Mojito (page 34) or Sticky Date Cake (page 246).
- **The "Meanwhile":** While something else is cooking, knock out other parts of the recipe. Before you start, take a moment to consider what might take the longest, what can be done while something else is in the oven, if something could go in the microwave or air-fryer.
- **Store-Bought Ingredients:** This is nothing to be ashamed of. If they make your life more effortless, and therefore more enjoyable, embrace them. Just give them new life by adding a fresh version of one of the key ingredients already inside to freshen them up. For instance, adding freshly grated ginger to jarred green curry paste, grated garlic or lemon juice to store-bought marinara sauce, and fresh herbs to bottled dressings or vinaigrettes.

TIPS

ON BOILING TOFU:

Giving tofu a quick boil in salted water firms the texture, removes excess moisture, and helps the tofu absorb marinades or sauces well. Use this secret method for stir-fries or braised dishes where you want juicy tofu that holds its shape instead of crumbling. Add 5 teaspoons of salt to 4 cups of boiling water. Add the cut tofu and cook for at least 5 minutes, then drain and pat dry with paper towels before using.

ON FREEZING TOFU:

Freezing tofu helps break down the cellular structure, resulting in a denser, spongier tofu. Use this method for deep-fried tofu, breaded tofu, or tofu that wants a meatier bite. When you get home throw the entire container of tofu into the freezer. Once it's completely frozen, thaw the container on the counter overnight. Remove the tofu from the container, hold the block over the sink between your palms, and press down gently and steadily, until the liquid drains from the block. Alternatively use a tofu press or just wrap the block in paper towels and place a heavy pan on top for 10 to 15 minutes.

Build a Pantry of Time-Hacking Ingredients: Using even a small amount of these ingredients contributes powerful flavor and/or shaves off cook time:

- **Better Than Bouillon Base:** Whisk 1 teaspoon of paste into 1 cup of warm water to make veggie broth on the spot. *This is how I make all the "vegetable broth" I call for throughout the book.*
- **Pre-peeled whole garlic cloves:** I'd never suggest getting the pre-chopped garlic that comes in liquid which has an off taste, but if you want to make garlic prep a little easier, get the pre-peeled garlic in vacuum seals so they stay fresh, and cut the hard stems off garlic cloves so they're easier to smash. Speaking of flavor bombs, buy some black garlic while you're at it.
- **Red or white miso paste:** This paste, with its saltiness, is a little milder than soy sauce and can be used in place of salt but with lots of extra umami flavor.
- **Coconut aminos:** (Just a few dashes take dressing and sauces to the next level).
- **Quick-Cooking Proteins:** Ground beef, sliced mushrooms, and seafood cook in minutes, making them perfect for weeknight meals. Keep them stocked so dinner comes together fast. Tofu is another great option if you know how to prep it (see Tips) and it lasts forever in the fridge, ready whenever you finally decide what to do with it. For even faster shortcuts, turn to proteins like canned beans, tinned fish, or even nuts which don't require thawing or cooking at all.
- **Tomato paste:** A little bit of concentrated tomato paste makes your red sauces taste as if an Italian nonna has been simmering them all day. If you buy the cans instead of the tubes, put the rest in a deli container or transfer to a sandwich bag and cut the tip, and dispense as you need it for up to a week, or freeze in ice cube trays to last months.
- **Sun-dried tomatoes (in oil):** These are miracle makers in a jar, and work wonders even more than tomato paste, offering a deep meaty flavor to pasta sauces, soups, and other recipes.
- **Chipotles in adobo:** A single pepper from a can will completely transform a dish into a smokey, spicy, Tex-Mex wonder.

- **Balsamic vinegar:** I love to have a big bottle on hand for the tangy, slightly sweet, and deeply complex flavor they add to dressings, sauces, and mocktails.
- **Frozen vegetables:** Have packs of pre-cut and pre-cooked frozen vegetables on hand to supplement your dinner in an instant and meet your daily veggie quota. Corn, bell peppers, or entire veggie blends can be thrown into stir-frys, and peas or spinach can be added to soups or pastas just as they're coming off the heat.
- **Wine, sake, liquor, liqueurs, extracts, and water essences:** These add complexity to simmering liquids, drinks, dressings, and desserts.
- **Premixed spice blends:** In a pinch premixed spices like creole seasoning, BBQ rubs, and sour cream and onion soup mix will flavor an entire meal perfectly and save you time on mixing your own.
- **Compound Butters (pages 290 and 291):** Making these in advance will help you elevate everything, including Jazzy Rice (page 158).
- **Liquid sweeteners:** Raw honey, maple syrup, and agave are already in liquid form, so you don't need to waste time dissolving them in liquid, plus they are a little healthier than more refined sugars.
- **Nut and seed butters:** Beyond the obvious like spreading them on toast, you can stir nut butters in cookies (GF-33 Cookies, page 262) to add strucutre and chew, or use them in dressings (Tahini Teriyaki Dressing, page 225) to help emulsify, or cake icings (see page 257) for more nuanced flavors.
- **Jars of pickled veg:** Giardiniera, kimchi, dill pickles, banana peppers, pepperoncini—all make amazing quick additions that cut through fattier foods.
- **Nutritional yeast:** The umami in what some call "nooch" is transformative for building flavorful foundations in food, and, of course, can even add some cheesiness to things without the cheese.
- **High-quality jams and preserves:** Apricot, blueberry, and caramelized onion jams are not just good for smearing on buttered toast, you can also melt them into sauces, like apricot preserves in the sauce for Sweet 'n' Sourdough Coconut Cauliflower Skewers (page 147) and glazes such as Shiny Almond & Peach Cornbread (page 175).
- **Chili pastes, hot sauces, and chili crisps:** Southern hot sauce, Calabrian chili paste, harissa, Sriracha, sambal oelek, gochujang, chili crisp, and red curry paste all pack insane flavor and just enough heat to make simple food sing.
- **Vanilla ice cream:** Round out desserts by making them à la mode, make an easy caramel sauce (see page 245), or whip together one ingredient crème anglaise.

8

GARNISH!

Here's the Truth: We most likely don't need more recipes; we need more ways to enjoy the recipes we have. Luckily there's always something around that can add a little sparkle to what's already on your plate. Garnishes are the fairy dust we all need when life is feeling lackluster. A garnish here and there adds layers of flavor, color, and texture.

TIP

Garnishes are often hidden in plain sight. Zest citrus before juicing them and garnish whatever you're making with that zest at the very end. If you're cooking the whites of scallions, garnish with their green tips; when you're adding celery to something, save the tender center leaves for garnish.

Spot the **golden sprinkles** to see where you can add an extra ingredient or garnish or two. Depending on your current mood and capacity, you can confidently "make things fancy" or keep things simple.

The trick is to see your pantry as a trove of opportunity; almost anything in there that can be drizzled, poured, or sprinkled has garnish potential. Think chili crisp, nuts, balsamic glaze, truffle oil, crushed chips, and so on. These are some of my favorite garnishes—but know that this is not a complete list.

- **Crushed or chopped nuts and seeds:** Raw, toasted, salted, unsalted, or smoked nuts and seeds (all versions of almonds, poppy seeds, sesame seeds, pumpkin seeds, and hemp seeds) make for a light crunch and eye-catching topping.
- **Spices:** Whole spices (like star anise), roughly crushed or chopped spices (like dehydrated onion and garlic flakes), ground spices (like cinnamon and paprika), and spice blends (like za'atar, Pecan Dukkah (page 57), everything bagel seasoning, and Arrabbiata Flakes (page 286) are as special on top of a dish as they are inside.
- **Shaved cheese:** Snow drifts of parmesan and all other cheese incite wide-eyed anticipation and joy.
- **Crushed snacks:** Grab your favorite chips, cookies, croutons, crackers, cereal, candied popcorn, roasted seaweed, kale chips, beet chips, carrot chips, cauliflower chips, crispy chickpeas, crunchy corn nuts—whatever you can find to add texture and creativity to a dish.
- **Panko or breadcrumbs:** (seasoned and plain) Extra crunchy breading at your fingertips.
- **Dried, candied, dehydrated, or freeze-dried fruit:** I always keep raisins and dried cherries on hand to add to snacking boards, homemade trail mixes, syrups (page 172), and carrot cakes (page 257); candied ginger to use in my Orange Tofu with Star Anise (page 134); and dehydrated citrus wheels to elevate drinks in a pinch.
- **Chocolate shavings/chips/cacao nibs:** A touch of chocolate or chocolate crunch at the end of a dessert is always welcomed.
- **Powdered sugar and cocoa:** A very pretty way to cover imperfections.
- **Flaky salt and turbinado/sanding sugar:** Sanding sugar stands up to heat so it doesn't melt. Its crystals bring crunch and shimmer in the light.

- **Herbs/microgreens/fresh (and dried) flowers:** These herbs elevate any dish by adding freshness, color, and aroma, bringing life and instantly lifting any vibe. Find the herbs that grow best in your climate and keep some around on your windowsill so you can pluck them fresh.

TIP

Basil, parsley, mint, and thyme usually thrive well indoors. Choose a sunny windowsill that gets at least 4 to 6 hours of light daily, use well-draining pots with nutrient-rich soil, and water them as soon as the top inch of soil feels dry to the touch.

Growing your own microgreens on your windowsill is insanely easy, too. Repurpose old tuna tins or plastic tofu, strawberry, or tomato containers: clean them and poke a few small drainage holes in the bottom if they don't have them already. Fill them loosely with 1 to 2 inches of potting mix or rehydrated coconut coir, then sprinkle microgreen seeds—radish, broccoli, mustard seeds, or sunflower seeds—evenly over the surface. Gently press the seeds down and mist with water to moisten. Cover the containers loosely with plastic wrap 2 to 3 days to help the seeds germinate, and once they begin to sprout, place the containers on a sunny windowsill and water lightly each day. Within 7 to 14 days, watch your fresh microgreens blossom, then just snip and sprinkle!

- **Parsley dust:** Of course you can always just chop some parsley and sprinkle it over your food, but why not take it a step further and make thoughtful, dainty "dust" for an even spritz of herb where the bits don't clump together? Using a sharp knife, gather a bundle of parsley leaves (some stems are fine) in a tight ball on a cutting board, and then roughly chop to make thin shreds. Go over the leaves as needed until minced, making "dust." Roll the finely minced parsley in a paper towel and squeeze it tight to remove extra water, then sprinkle away.
- **Diamond scallions:** For the classic diamond-shaped scallions: cut the stem of the scallion at a 45-degree diagonal and continue up the leaf in about ¼-inch increments. Anything cut on a heavy bias just looks fancy.
- **Haystack scallions:** Shred scallions into wispy threads: Trim the whites and cut the green parts in 2- to 3-inch pieces. Then, using your fingers, peel the pieces into thin strips. Submerge the strips into a small bowl of ice water and set aside for a few minutes to curl. Remove them from the water, pat dry, and then pile the shreds into the center of soups or grain bowls or use them to garnish any stir-fry.
- **Herb confetti:** For mint and basil, roll up the leaves into a tight cigar shape, and cut them thinly, or use a pair of kitchen scissors to snip thin confetti shreds overtop of your finished dishes. Reserve the smaller, more dainty leaves in the center of the bundle for garnishing cocktails and desserts.

- **Sturdy herbs such as rosemary, thyme, bay leaves, and sage** are great for garnishing cocktails (like the Andrica Calmer, page 40). The bay leaves in the Overnight Bitter-ish Bay Leaf Lemonade (page 37) impart flavor over time but don't break down. Any inedible bits can be removed before serving, but I usually leave them in as a garnish for color and visual contrast.

- **Air-fried herbs:** Dehydrate herbs in your air-fryer and use them whole for cocktail toppers or to garnish any dish. Line the basket of your air fryer with parchment to prevent any smaller pieces from falling through the cracks. Grab a handful of whole leaves from soft herbs such as parsley, sage, dill, (or others) and pat them dry between a couple of paper towels. Place them in the air fryer and cook at 350°F for 2 to 4 minutes until completely dried out. (This trick also works with dehydrating minced garlic and onions, which can be expensive to purchase at the store.)

9

PRACTICE GRATITUDE

Remember to have reverence for your food, for the farmers who grew it, for the truckers who shipped it, for the people who work at the stores where you picked up last-minute things on your way home. It's humbling to think how these different hands and your own efforts worked in tandem to realize your meal. Hover over your plate and take a moment to breathe deeply and acknowledge the wonder that it is to eat and be a part of such an elaborate system. How loved you are to have food. Even if it's only you at the table, speak your gratitude aloud into the open space.

10

USE THAT PINKY FINGER!

Do it to remind yourself to loosen up and not take dinner and life so seriously.

PART

2

RECIPES

Cook What You Crave

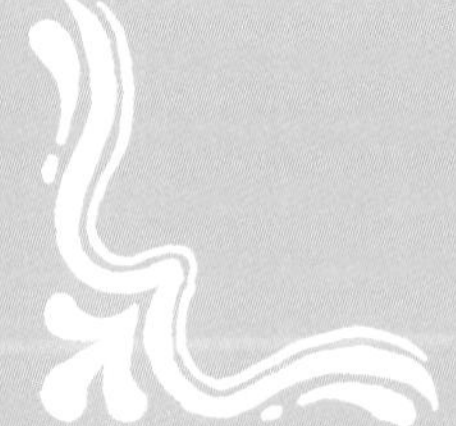

IT'S YOUR KITCHEN. IT'S YOUR WORLD. Keep in mind that most of these recipes were tested with **Diamond Crystal kosher salt**, which is notoriously lighter and less salty than other salts. So use less if you're using another kind. And if you're watching your sodium intake, treat the amount listed in the recipe as a starting point. Keep it in a small bowl nearby and sprinkle as you go. You'll get better layers of flavor that way. I've also dropped in markers for other dietary needs and time-savers. Look for these tags to help you cook and eat intuitively as you work through the book:

df = dairy free

ef = egg free

gf = gluten free

nf = nut free

rsf = refined sugar free

≤5 = 5 ingredients or fewer

≤30 = 30 minutes or less

CHAPTER 1

POUR YOURSELF A DRINK

Pause & Refill your Cup

ONCE YOU STEP INTO THE kitchen and officially commit yourself to the act of cooking there is no better way to christen the moment than to pour yourself a drink. Take this second to inhale, recalibrate, and step into the proper state of mind. Then, try one of the recipes that follow, and remember that a good drink fancies a garnish.

In-the-Blender Coconut & Honeydew Mojito

SERVES
2
(DF, GF, NF, ≤30)

ripe, sweet honeydew ½ pound, peeled and chopped or sub another melon

turbinado sugar *or sweetener of choice* 1 ounce (2 tablespoons)

mint leaves 0.2 ounces (¼ cup), plus more for garnish ← or sub basil

fresh lime juice 1 ounce (2 tablespoons)

canned cream of coconut *or unsweetened coconut cream* 2 ounces (¼ cup) at room temp, shaken before measured

kosher salt *or Himalayan pink salt* a pinch

white rum 4 ounces (½ cup) (optional) ← or try Lyre's white rum alternative

crushed ice, for serving

sparkling mineral water *or seltzer water*, for topping

I've made one of my favorite cocktails as effortless as possible. You don't need a litter of jiggers or measuring cups, just place your blender cup or pitcher directly on the scale and start pouring from there to make this creamy, fizzy, frothy drink. Even the sugar, which would usually be boiled into syrup on the stove, goes straight in with all the other ingredients. And while the alcohol goes well in this drink, it won't bring any less joy if it's left out.

MIX THE DRINK: Place a blender pitcher on a scale and the honeydew, turbinado sugar, mint, lime juice, cream of coconut, kosher salt, and rum (if using), then place the pitcher on the base and blend on high until completely smooth, about a full minute.

STRAIN: Hold a small mesh strainer (if you have one) a few inches over a Tom Collins glass (or glass tumbler) filled with ice. Pour the blended mixture over top. If you don't have a strainer, it will just be a little thicker.

FINISH AND GARNISH: Top with sparkling mineral water and garnish with a bushy sprig of mint.

TIP Sprigs of bushy herbs like mint or lemon verbena, or spikes on a pineapple trimmed along the edges, or even the leafy parts of celery stalks (for a Bloody Mary, perhaps?) are "statement greens"—I find that the bushier or gaudier the leaf, the more playful and loosened up I get, so don't hold back.

Infuse Your Water

Don't let the looming task of dinner cause you to skip the calming benefits of the drink ritual.

Even if you're sticking to water, you can always peel a few thin, wide ribbons from a seedless cucumber and drop them into your glass. Then, take a moment to watch the ribbons slowly unfurl and bloom in the water. And, almost as if you're taking cues from the cucumber, slowly drop your shoulders away from your neck and allow yourself to unwind and ease into a calmer cooking rhythm (see page 33).

SERVES
1

(DF, EF, GF, NF, ≤5, ≤30)

aquafaba (liquid from a can of white beans, butter beans, or chickpeas) ¼ cup

Bitter-ish Bay Leaf Lemonade (recipe follows) *or favorite lemonade* 6 ounces

alcohol-free gin (such as Monday or Ritual) 1 ounce (optional)

ice cubes a handful

MAKE IT FANCY

Foam is the perfect backdrop for **a dehydrated lemon wheel** or **a marinated bay leaf** leftover from the Bitter-ish Bay Leaf Lemonade.

Honey Bay Chassé

Serve lemonade in a cute coupe glass and top it with a fluffy foam topper, and suddenly you can call it a fancy mocktail (see Tip). Experiment with the influx of spiritless spirits arriving on the scene right now. For this recipe I like Monday (an alcohol-free botanical gin with a nose of sweet lemon) paired with lemonade, or even better, my Bitter-ish Bay Leaf Lemonade Or, for a sharper experience, try replacing the gin with ½ ounce sambuca (licorice liqueur).

CHILL THE GLASSES: Fill a coupe glass (or a martini-style glass) to the top with ice water and allow it to sit for 5 to 10 minutes to chill.

MEANWHILE, MAKE THE FOAM TOPPER: Add the bean liquid to a small measuring cup and, using a milk frother, immersion blender, or hand beater, blitz the liquid until it foams and doubles in size. Set aside.

SHAKE: Into a shaker put the bay leaf lemonade, gin (if using), and a large handful of ice. Shake vigorously until cold.

SERVE: Working quickly, empty the ice water from the coupe glass, and then strain the shaken lemonade into the cold glass. Spoon over the white bean foam and serve.

TIP Foam immediately makes food feel otherworldly. Sometimes egg foam feels aggressively viscous and sulfuric to me, but the liquid from a can of white beans or chickpeas has a pleasant saltiness that brings some cocktails to life while also softening them, and then the leftover beans can be added to dinner.

Overnight Bitter-ish Bay Leaf Lemonade

MAKES 6 CUPS

Adding bay leaves to anything makes me feel like I'm channeling my inner Sean Brock. It's a magical leaf that adds a hint of something you can't totally put your finger on, and what it does subtly in every soup or stew, it also does to this lemonade. The flavors really bloom after steeping for 24 hours. The lemonade is slightly bitter from blending the whole lemon, piths and all, but that is precisely why it makes a good cocktail shrub.

whole lemons 1 pound (3 to 4 medium), preferably organic, rinsed and scrubbed

bay leaves 6 to 8, fresh or dried

honey *or agave* ½ cup

CUT THE LEMONS: Quarter the lemons and remove the seeds.

STEEP THE BAY LEAVES: In a large pot, bring the lemon quarters, bay leaves, **6 CUPS WATER**, and the honey to a gentle boil over medium heat and cook for about 15 minutes, or until the lemons soften and their white piths become transparent, then remove from the heat and allow the mixture to cool slightly.

BLEND THE LEMONS: Remove the bay leaves and set aside. Blend the cooled mixture in a high-powered blender until liquefied. Strain through a sieve to remove any residual pulp.

MARINATE FOR 24 HOURS: Divide the lemonade between two quart containers, add the bay leaves back to the lemonade, cover, and chill in the fridge for at least 24 hours before enjoying.

Wind-Down Drinks

You've built this wonderful climax up to and during dinner; why should the fun end so abruptly? I've always appreciated the ritual of a drink after the tables have cleared, something intended to help with digestion and fully relish in all that has occurred.

Digestifs are traditionally liqueurs taken straight, no shooter, but because they exist to help settle your stomach, they could also include something as simple as a hot, dairy-free cacao drink, or even warm water with lemon or vinegar. However, I prefer drinks like kombucha or chamomile tea that I then dress up into something a little more fun.

SERVES
4
(DF, EF, GF, NF, ≤30)

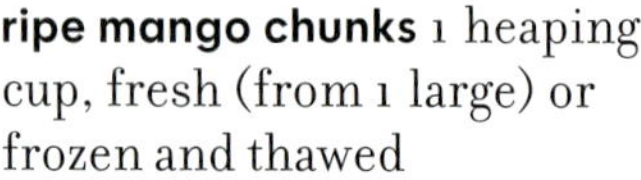

Smokey Mango Kombucha Spritz

ripe mango chunks 1 heaping cup, fresh (from 1 large) or frozen and thawed

navel oranges 2, juiced (about 1/2 cup)

limes 2, juiced (about 1/4 cup)

honey *or agave* 2 tablespoons

ice cubes (preferably 2 x 2-inch large-format ice cubes if you have them)

kombucha (flavor of the day) *or citrusy seltzer water* 1 (16-ounce) bottle

smoked paprika, for sprinkling

kosher salt a pinch

Kombucha settles my stomach after dinner. I make this mocktail to mimic the thrill of the Dallas patio date nights my husband and I shared early in our romance. With our bistro table stacked with emptied chip baskets and little saucers of salsa, we sipped smokey mezcal margaritas and talked for hours. I can't separate those drinks from the happy glimmers of my early twenties. Thankfully, these are much gentler on my body and come without the side of morning migraine, which I consider a generous act of self-love. Doubly so, because this recipe only calls for things that are already on my standard grocery store haul.

PUREE THE FRUIT: In a high-powered blender, blend the mango chunks, orange juice, lime juice, honey, and **1 CUP WATER** on high until smooth. Transfer the puree to a lidded container and chill until ready to use or use immediately.

TO MAKE THE DRINK: Fill four glasses with ice (preferably large format, so it melts slowly) and pour 4 ounces of the puree over top of each glass. Top with kombucha and sprinkle with paprika and salt and serve.

MAKE IT FANCY

Before filling the glasses, roll the edges in more **paprika and/or salt** (see Tip) and top with **a dehydrated wheel of citrus.**

TIP Garnish the rims of your cocktail: Brush the rim or side of the glass with water, juice, honey, or something else edible that will help dry "debris" stick. Sprinkle over things like citrus zest; flavored or coarse salt; spices; crushed, freeze-dried fruit; flavored sugars; or anything else finely ground and fitting for the drink, even ingredients like fine cookie crumbs or espresso powder—think chocolate martinis!

Andrica Calmer

SERVES
2

(DF, EF, GF, NF, ≤5)

fresh ginger 1 (1-inch) knob, sliced

chamomile *or valerian root tea* 2 satchels or 1 tablespoon loose leaf

raw honey *or sweetener of choice* 1 tablespoon, plus more as needed

lemon juice 1 tablespoon

ice cubes a handful

dry red wine *or tart cherry juice* 1 to 2 ounces

MAKE IT FANCY

Grab **a rosemary sprig** at the base, and using a torch or match, carefully light the tip of the rosemary until it catches fire. Immediately blow out the fire and watch as the smoke drifts and swirls. Add the sprig to your drink. This should make you feel calm (see Tip).

My middle name, Andrica, has become an incantation for my alter ego and higher self, and I call out to her on days when I need something to dissolve my anxiety and slip into a state of peace. Say hello to my timeless pandemic drink—named after me and inspired by an Arnold Palmer. The drink has a base of calming tea made visually dazzling with a bobbing floater of bright red cherry juice or red wine, both of which contain melatonin.

STEEP THE TEA: In a small saucepan, bring **1½ CUPS WATER** and the ginger slices to a boil. Remove the pan from the heat and add the chamomile tea. Allow it to steep for 15 to 20 minutes, until the water is at room temperature. Strain the ginger, then stir in the honey and lemon juice. Add more honey to taste, if desired.

MAKE THE DRINK: Fill wineglasses halfway with ice cubes. Pour over the tea mixture. Hover a teaspoon directly over the top of the tea, and slowly pour the wine (from the spout) into the center of the spoon to prevent the juice from sinking to the bottom of the glass with force. This will create that lovely layered ombre look.

TIP

Set herbs (or citrus) ablaze to help release their natural oils and add a little essence to the air.

All-Nighter Dragon Iced Lattes

SERVES

1

(DF, EF, GF, NF, ≤30)

matcha powder 1½ to 2 teaspoons

vanilla syrup *or agave syrup* 1 tablespoon

fresh mint *or lemon verbena* 1 teaspoon chopped, plus sprigs for garnish (optional)

oat milk *or milk of choice* 1¼ cups, divided

frozen wild blueberries ¼ cup

lavender syrup 1 tablespoon (see Tip)

taro powder 2 tablespoons (optional)

broken ice 1 cup ← add ice to a zip-top bag and smash with a rolling pin to break into shards

MAKE IT FANCY

Turn the floater into a Cold Cream Matcha Floater by swapping the ¼ cup oat milk with **3 tablespoons heavy whipping cream + 2 tablespoons of whole milk** and whisking with the matcha until thick.

But maybe the night is not yet over for you? Make a wild blueberry lavender latte with just-enough-to-keep-you-up-to-finish-chasing-your-dreams caffeine. The matcha in this mint floater packs a powerful punch, and, unlike coffee, its energy feels more steady and less erratic, like it won't give you a crash. This drink resembles majestic dragon scales once you add the shards of broken ice. Use frozen wild blueberries, because as they begin to thaw, they'll release a brilliantly colored juice.

MAKE THE MATCHA FLOATER: Sift the matcha powder into a small bowl, then whisk in the vanilla syrup, mint, if using, and ¼ cup of the oak milk until smooth. Set aside.

MUDDLE THE BERRIES: Into a 16-ounce tumbler add the blueberries, lavender syrup, and taro powder, if using. Using the handle of a wooden spoon, muddle and mash the berries to mix and help the berries release their juices and color.

MIX: Top the berries with the broken ice, about half of the way up the glass. (The ice will also help keep the layers separated for as long as possible for slow sipping.) Fill the glass with the remaining 1 cup of oat milk, and then pour the matcha floater over the top.

SERVE: Using a straw, cocktail spoon, or just by gently spinning the glass in a circular motion, swirl the latte to begin blending the layers. Garnish with a sprig of mint (if using) and serve.

TIP **FOR HOMEMADE LAVENDER SYRUP:** Steep 2 tablespoons **organic dried culinary lavender** in 1 cup **hot water**. Strain, and sweeten with ⅓ to ½ cup raw agave or honey to taste. Cool and store in an airtight container in the fridge for up to 2 weeks.

Le Sirop
Lavender
Gourmet Syrup
25.4 fl

CHAPTER 2

DINNER SNACKS

The Rebel Meal

DINNER SNACKS allow flexibility and freedom. They're a quick solution to your hunger while something heartier cooks, or simply a loophole from the pressure of making a "real dinner" with an official main and side.

Some nights when you're not tied to any plan and can't quite name what you're craving, let your curiosity and resources guide you. Make a smorgasbord to turn casual snacking into an impromptu tasting.

Start by gathering the odds and ends from the pantry and fridge: the last bits of cheese, a spoonful of dip, a handful of nuts, maybe something pickled, some fresh or dried fruit, and definitely easy, homemade snacks like Smoked Almond Queso (page 197) or Baklava Honey (page 50). Arrange everything on a cutting board to look pretty, and once it's all together, the scraps will start to feel like an intentional meal. Will everything pair perfectly? Maybe not. But each bite will be an unplanned surprise, its own little adventure.

For practicality, add some crackers or toasted bread, and to make things feel even more special, pour a glass of wine or shake up a mocktail or two.

SERVES
8
(MAKES 16 CHEESE STICKS)

(NF, RSF, ≤30)

firm feta cheese 2 (8-ounce) blocks

all-purpose flour ¼ cup, for dusting, plus more as needed

eggs 3 large

Dijon mustard 1½ tablespoons

Italian-style seasoned panko breadcrumbs *or seasoned breadcrumbs* 2 cups, plus more as needed

cooking spray *or neutral oil* (like avocado, canola, or grapeseed), for frying

Effortless Marinara (page 112) *or jarred marinara*, warmed for serving

Double-Crusted Feta Sticks

After having a plate of breaded feta that melts into a pocket of gooey, tangy cream as it fries, I could never go back to flavorless mozzarella sticks. Once I bread these, I like to cook only the amount I'll eat, and freeze the rest. I just place the breaded sticks I don't plan to eat on a sheet pan in a single layer, place the tray in the freezer to "flash freeze" for 1 to 2 hours, then transfer them to a zip-top bag and back into the freezer until I'm ready to eat more of them.

CUT THE FETA: Using a sharp knife, carefully cut each block of feta in half lengthwise, and then into 4 strips widthwise to make a total of 16 fingers.

PREPARE THE COATING: On a plate, spread out the flour and set it aside. In a shallow bowl, whisk together the eggs, mustard, and **A SPLASH OF WATER**, then set aside. On a rimmed plate, spread out the seasoned panko breadcrumbs and set aside.

COAT THE FETA: Have an extra sheet pan nearby. Place a feta stick into the flour to dust. Transfer the stick to the egg mixture, turning to coat. Shake off any excess egg, then roll it through the breadcrumbs, pressing the crumbs into the cheese to help it adhere. Dip the stick back into the egg mixture, then back into the breadcrumbs a final time to make a double-crusted coating. Transfer the stick to the sheet pan, and continue with the remaining feta sticks.

AIR FRY: Preheat the air fryer to 400°F. Spray the cheese sticks generously all over with cooking spray and transfer them to the bottom basket of the fryer. Cook for 7 to 9 minutes (11 minutes if they're frozen), until the coating is crispy and golden brown; just make sure they're cooked all the way through.

OR BAKE: Preheat the oven to 450°F. Arrange the cheese sticks on a sheet pan fitted with a wire rack (to help create airflow), spray the cheese sticks with cooking spray,and bake for 15 to 18 minutes (2 to 3 minutes longer if frozen), flipping them halfway through, until the crust is golden brown all over and the center is soft.

OR SHALLOW FRY: For the crispest shell, fry these in oil. I like to fry smaller items like these cheese sticks in a medium heavy-bottomed pan or a wok (in batches if needed) to save on oil and space. Heat ½ inch of neutral oil to 325°F. Once hot, fry the sticks in batches, for 2 to 3 minutes per side, until deep golden brown on the crust and gooey and soft on the inside.

SERVE: Transfer the feta sticks to a platter and serve with marinara sauce.

MAKE IT FANCY

Decorate the plate by grating over some fresh **Parmesan cheese** and serving it with **a bundle of parsley** and **a few lemon wedges** for that elegant sports bar feel.

Sour Cream & Onion Edamame

SERVES 4

(DF, EF, GF, NF, RSF, ≤30)

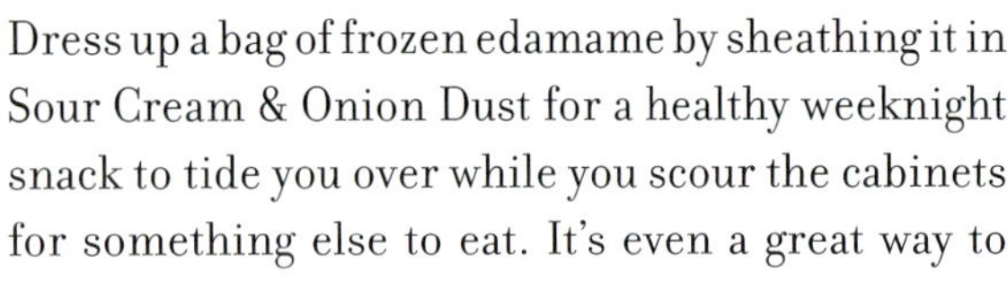

Dress up a bag of frozen edamame by sheathing it in Sour Cream & Onion Dust for a healthy weeknight snack to tide you over while you scour the cabinets for something else to eat. It's even a great way to spruce up your cashews or water crackers, too.

frozen unshelled edamame
1 (12-ounce) bag

avocado oil *or olive oil*, for drizzling

frozen unshelled edamame
1 (12-ounce) bag

Sour Cream & Onion Dust (recipe follows)
or your favorite dry onion soup & dip mix, crushed into a fine powder
¼ cup, divided

PREHEAT THE OVEN to 425°F and have a sheet pan nearby.

BAKE: On the sheet pan, spread the frozen edamame in a single layer. Drizzle with enough avocado oil to coat and sprinkle 2 tablespoons of the sour cream and onion dust overtop, tossing everything together with your hands to evenly coat the edamame. Bake for about 20 minutes, tossing them halfway through, until their skins are lightly crispy and golden brown in spots.

SERVE: Remove from the oven, toss with the remaining 2 tablespoons of dust, transfer to a bowl, and enjoy warm.

Sour Cream & Onion Dust

MAKES ABOUT ⅓ CUP

If you're a sour cream and onion fan, you'll love having this seasoning dust around. Sprinkle it over popcorn, or use it as a dry rub for anything from homemade potato chips to chicken wings. Stir it into yogurt or sour cream to dip your carrots, or use it to top smoked salmon or a baked potato. Thankfully the seasoning will keep in an airtight container for up to 3 months, so you have time to play around with it on other things.

sour cream powder
or buttermilk powder
¼ cup ← find it online!

nutritional yeast
2 tablespoons

onion powder
2 teaspoons

garlic powder
2 teaspoons

kosher salt
2 teaspoons

mustard powder
½ teaspoon

sweet paprika
¼ teaspoon

MIX THE DUST: In a small bowl, combine the sour cream powder, nutritional yeast, onion powder, garlic powder, salt, mustard powder, and paprika and using clean, dry hands, rub the spices together to crush the nutritional yeast flakes and disperse the spices evenly. Alternatively, do this in a mortar and pestle.

Baklava Honey

MAKES ABOUT
1
CUP

(EF)

Here's the recipe for one of my favorite charcuterie board additions—jazzed-up honey. Outside of just eating it from a spoon along with toasted bread and pita chips, it can be drizzled inside a peanut butter sandwich for an elevated PB & honey experience, over a baked block of gooey brie or feta, or even a grilled cheese for a late-night autumn spin. The nutty honey will keep, covered, in the fridge for up to 2 months.

raw hazelnuts, *walnut halves, or almonds* ¼ cup

shelled roasted and salted pistachios, *cashews, or pumpkin seeds* ¼ cup

light brown sugar *or coconut sugar* ½ tablespoon

unsalted butter 1 tablespoon, softened

honey ½ cup

ground cinnamon ¼ teaspoon

ground cardamom ⅛ teaspoon

rose water *or orange blossom water* 1 tablespoon

pita chips, crusty bread, cheese, and/or fruit (dried or fresh), for building out your spread

PREHEAT THE OVEN to 325°F and have a small sheet pan lined with parchment paper nearby.

TOAST THE NUTS: Using a chef's knife, cut the hazelnuts in half (or break them up with the back of the knife), discarding any flaking skins. Skip this step if using other nuts. Spread them on the prepared sheet pan along with the pistachios, brown sugar, and butter. Using your hands, massage everything together to coat the nuts evenly in the butter, then bake for 12 to 15 minutes, until the nuts are golden brown and you begin to smell the toasty butter. Remove from the oven and set aside.

MAKE THE HONEY SYRUP: In a small saucepan, whisk the honey, cinnamon, cardamom, rose water, and **1 TABLESPOON WATER** together and heat over medium-low heat, until it's warm and fragrant. Remove from the heat and stir in the toasted nuts. Into an 8-ounce mason jar with lid, pour in the honey and allow to cool.

SERVE the honey on a board with pita chips or crusty bread, your favorite cheeses, and dried or fresh fruits.

MAKE IT FANCY

For extra texture, use honey that comes with a piece of honeycomb. Cut **a small piece of honeycomb** into smaller pieces and add it to the mason jar along with the other ingredients.

Peanut Butter Cracker Brittle

MAKES ABOUT
40
CRACKERS

(DF, EF, ≤30)

saltine crackers 35 to 40 (1 sleeve)

creamy peanut butter *or nut or seed butter of choice* 2 tablespoons (33 grams)

virgin coconut oil 2 tablespoons (33 grams), melted

unsweetened applesauce 2 tablespoons (33 grams)

light brown sugar ½ cup (100 grams) packed

baking soda ¼ teaspoon

kosher salt ½ teaspoon

regular or mini semisweet chocolate chips ½ cup ← use dairy-free, if you like

MAKE IT FANCY

Add **1 tablespoon Sriracha** to the batter for a little extra flavor and heat.

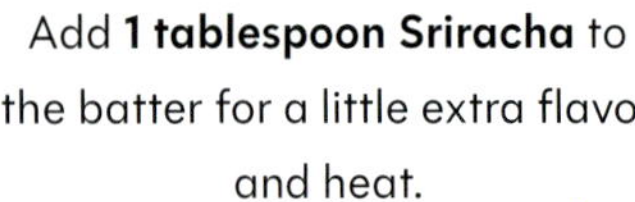

When I'm fumbling through the cabinets looking for a snack, I always seem to have a sleeve or two of saltine crackers in there. Of course, I could just smear some peanut butter on them and call it a day, but what kind of humdrum day would that be? Instead, I make a superfast, mixed-entirely-in-one-bowl, nuttier knockoff of chocolate coated matzo—no boiling of caramel required.

PREHEAT THE OVEN to 325°F, line a large sheet pan with parchment paper, and arrange the crackers in a single layer with some space between them. Set it aside.

MAKE THE BATTER: In a small mixing bowl, whisk together the peanut butter, coconut oil, applesauce, brown sugar, baking soda, and salt until smooth.

COAT THE CRACKERS: Using a butter knife or the back of a spoon, spread a thin layer of the peanut butter mixture over each cracker. Then sprinkle over the chocolate chips.

BAKE AND COOL: Bake the crackers for 10 to 12 minutes, until they are a dark amber brown color and the sugar has mostly ceased bubbling. Remove them from the oven and allow them to cool completely to harden, at least 20 minutes.

STORE: Place them in a lidded container or zip-top bag and keep in the fridge or freezer to intensify their crunch.

Hot Pickle Dip

SERVES
6 TO 8

(EF, GF, NF, RSF, ≤30)

plain cream cheese 2 cups (16 ounces) softened

mayo ¼ cup

giardiniera *hot or mild* 1 (16-ounce) jar roughly chopped, plus ¼ cup brine reserved from the jar

garlic powder ½ teaspoon

onion powder ½ teaspoon

shredded mozzarella cheese ½ cup

shredded Parmesan cheese ½ cup

panko breadcrumbs, for sprinkling

olive oil, for drizzling

crudite, *chips*, *crackers*, *or warm bread*, for serving

As a pickle addict, I love to make homemade giardiniera—it's the best excuse to clean the fridge of any stray or going vegetables—but I'm also no stranger to store-bought jars when I can't find the time to pickle my own. This dip is my way of repurposing my collection of half-eaten jars of fridge pickles. Again, I prefer the array of colors and crunch in giardiniera, but you could try this with banana peppers, dill pickles, kimchi . . . Arguably, everything works in this steamy, tangy dip.

PREHEAT THE OVEN to 400°F and have a shallow 1-quart baking dish nearby.

MIX: In a mixing bowl, combine the cream cheese, mayo, reserved brine, garlic powder, onion powder, mozzarella cheese, and Parmesan, then fold in the giardiniera.

BAKE: Spoon the mixture into the baking dish, smoothing in an even layer. Sprinkle the top with the panko and drizzle over some olive oil. Bake for 18 to 20 minutes or until hot and gooey.

SERVE: Remove from the oven and serve with your favorite dippers.

MAKE IT FANCY

Turn this into a Charcuterie Dip by topping the dip with **½ cup chopped hot soppressata**, your favorite charcuterie meat, or **plant-based salami** before you sprinkle over the breadcrumbs.

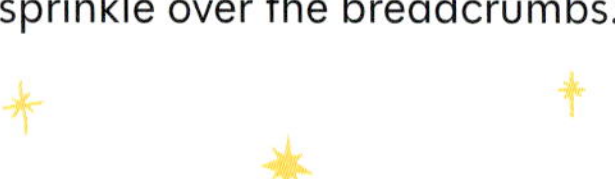

Sky-High Avocado Deviled Eggs

SERVES
6
(MAKES 1 DOZEN HALVES)

(DF, GF, RSF, ≤5, ≤30)

hard-boiled eggs 8 large (see Tip for air frying your eggs)

mashed avocado 1/4 cup (from 1 small avocado)

lemon juice *or lime juice* 1 tablespoon, plus more as needed

kosher salt and **freshly ground black pepper**

Pecan Dukkah (page 57), for sprinkling (optional)

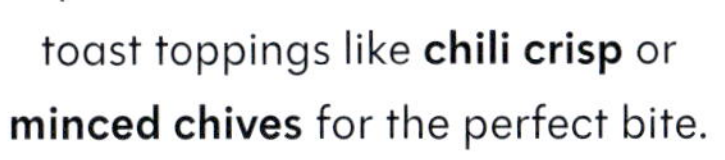

MAKE IT FANCY

Sprinkle over other favorite avo-toast toppings like **chili crisp** or **minced chives** for the perfect bite.

Deviled eggs (or even halved jammy eggs) are an easy, elegant snack that can be as embellished or casual as needed to flex to any occasion. Here, I've swapped the mayo with avocado to create a gorgeous green filling and topped them with Pecan Dukkah (page 57), so now they're sort of like bites of avocado toast without the toast. Use whatever leftover deviled eggs you have in my Smashed Curry Egg Tea Sandwiches (page 218).

MAKE THE FILLING: Into the bowl of a mini food processor fitted with a steel blade, place 2 whole eggs (sacrifice the ugly eggs to the food processor; see Tip), the avocado, lemon juice, and a pinch each of salt and pepper and set aside.

Using a sharp knife, cut the remaining eggs in half across the center lengthwise. Add the yolks to the processor bowl with the other ingredients, and arrange the emptied egg whites on the platter. (Using your knife, trim a small piece off the bottom of the egg white halves so they sit up straight.) Blend the ingredients on high until everything is completely smooth, stopping to scrape down the sides of the processor bowl as needed. Taste and season with more lemon juice, salt, and pepper as desired.

STUFF THE EGGS: Fill the eggs carefully using a couple small spoons or transfer the filling to a zip-top or pastry bag fitted with a star tip, and pipe the mixture into the center of the egg whites. Sprinkle with the Pecan Dukkah (if using). Serve, or cover loosely, and chill for up to 4 days, until ready to serve.

(recipe continues)

TIP Try air-frying your eggs: Preheat a canister air fryer to 270° or 275°F, and have a large bowl of ice water nearby. Once the fryer is preheated, put as many eggs as will fit into the basket with space between each egg so they don't crack into one another, and cook the eggs for 13 to 15 minutes for hard-boiled, or 10 to 12 minutes for a more jammy egg. With tongs, remove the eggs from the fryer, and immediately submerge them into the water to stop the cooking and allow to cool enough to peel. I credit this trick for the prettiest deviled eggs to my mom: Boil a couple more eggs than you need, and blend them, whole, into the filling mixture so you have an abundance of filling for piling or piping your eggs extra high.

Pecan Dukkah

MAKES ABOUT ¾ CUP
(EF, GF, RSF, ≤30)

This is my take on the Egyptian spice dukkah, but with a Southern twist. You'll probably want to sprinkle this over everything, like I do: Sky-High Avocado Deviled Eggs (page 55), flatbread (see page 92), salads, hummus, salmon filets, and even cream cheese bagels.

fennel seeds 2 teaspoons

star anise 1 whole

ground cumin 1 teaspoon

ground coriander 1 teaspoon

light brown sugar 1 teaspoon

ground cayenne ¼ teaspoon

raw pecan pieces or halves ½ cup

sesame seeds ¼ cup

kosher salt

GRIND THE SPICES: Using a mortar and pestle (see Tip), grind the fennel seeds, star anise, cumin, coriander, brown sugar, and cayenne until no large pieces of spice remain.

ADD IN THE PECANS and continue grinding until they break down into small chunks, then add the sesame seeds and season with salt to taste.

TIP Breaking everything up in a mortar and pestle is the way to go for dukkah (which literally translates to "to crush" or "to pound" in Arabic). It releases the oils from the spices and nuts and marries all the notes. I prefer this method to a spice grinder, or toasting the nuts, which can make the flavors too overpowering. Store this blend in an airtight container in the cabinet for up to 1 month.

Ritzy "Meatballs"

SERVES

4

(MAKES ABOUT 2 DOZEN MEATBALLS)

(DF, EF, NF)

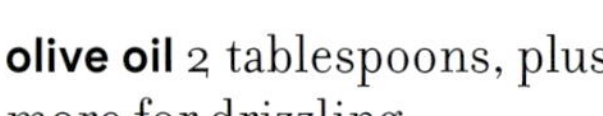

olive oil 2 tablespoons, plus more for drizzling

dried fennel seeds 1 tablespoon

crushed red pepper flakes ½ teaspoon

garlic cloves 4, minced

dried lentils (green or brown) ½ pound (heaping cup)

sweet potato 1 medium (½ pound), peeled and cut into bite-size chunks

kosher salt ½ teaspoon

white miso paste 1 tablespoon

Ritz crackers *or other butter crackers* 1 cup crushed (from about 28 or 30 crackers)

flat-leaf parsley leaves large handful, finely chopped (or other combination of herbs)

Wild Blueberry BBQ Sauce (recipe follows) *and/or five-spice glaze (see page 94) or sauce of choice*, for coating

These anytime, anywhere baked sweet potato lentil meatballs can slip gracefully into many recipes—soups, pasta bakes, toasted hoagies (see Tip). They're simple, versatile, and, if you're not counting the fresh herbs, made entirely with pantry things. Here, I treat them as a party snack, bathed in Wild Blueberry BBQ Sauce (recipe follows) and our favorite sticky five-spice glaze (see page 94). They are easy and improvisational and, even when eaten as a snack, still manage to make me feel elegant, especially once poked with cocktail forks or frilly-topped toothpicks.

COOK THE LENTILS AND POTATOES: In a medium saucepan over medium-high heat, heat the olive oil. Once the oil starts to shimmer, add the fennel seeds, red pepper flakes, and garlic and cook, stirring constantly, for about a minute until the fennel seeds are fragrant and lightly toasted.

Stir in the lentils, sweet potato, and salt, and cover with 2 cups water. Bring to a boil. Reduce the heat to a simmer, and cook, until both the lentils and sweet potato are tender and all the liquid has absorbed, about 15 to 20 minutes. Transfer the lentils and sweet potatoes to a large bowl.

PREHEAT THE OVEN to 450°F and have a well-oiled sheet pan nearby. Alternatively preheat your air fryer (or toaster oven on the air fryer setting) to 400°F.

MIX THE MEATBALL MIXTURE: In the bowl with the lentils and sweet potato, add the miso paste, Ritz crackers, and parsley. Using clean hands, mix everything together until thoroughly combined.

ROLL: Using a medium ice cream scoop or your hands, scoop golf ball–size chunks of the mixture and drop them onto the prepared sheet pan. Oil your hands, and then roll the mounds lightly between your palms to make balls, and place them back on the sheet pan or in the basket of the air fryer (or toaster oven).

(recipe continues)

BAKE OR AIR-FRY: Drizzle their tops with a little more olive oil, and cook them for 18 to 20 minutes (7 to 10 minutes in the air fryer), flipping them over with tongs halfway through, until they're crunchy on the sides, deeply golden brown, and cooked through. Remove from the oven and allow to cool for 10 minutes to firm.

SERVE: Once cool and firm, using a pastry brush, generously brush the tops and sides with the Wild Blueberry BBQ Sauce. Transfer the meatballs to a platter and serve with cocktail forks or frilly-topped toothpicks.

NOTES ON WHAT TO DO WITH THESE "MEATBALLS"

- Swap the fennel with lemongrass and ginger, and replace the parsley with cilantro for a meatball ready for a vegetarian banh mi.
- Serve them as is, laid out on a pretty platter surfing along a smear of hummus and more herbs.
- Serve them over a bed of green cabbage or in a toasted hoagie topped with Effortless Marinara sauce (page 112)
- Stuff them into soft, split potato rolls with a crunchy slaw (classic or Asian style).

Wild Blueberry BBQ Sauce

MAKES ABOUT 1 CUP
(DF, EF, GF, NF, ≤30)

frozen wild blueberries *or regular fresh blueberries* 1 cup (5 ounces)

light brown sugar *or coconut sugar* ½ cup packed

tomato paste ¼ cup

grated fresh ginger 1 teaspoon

yellow mustard 1 teaspoon

kosher salt ½ teaspoon

freshly ground black pepper ½ teaspoon

garlic powder ½ teaspoon

apple cider vinegar 2 tablespoons

COOK THE SAUCE: In a medium saucepan, combine the blueberries, brown sugar, tomato paste, ginger, mustard, salt, black pepper, garlic powder, vinegar, and **½ CUP WATER**. Cook for 15 to 20 minutes over medium heat until thick, stirring occasionally.

PUREE: Remove the pan from the heat and, using an immersion blender, puree the sauce until completely smooth. Alternatively, you can puree the sauce in a blender or food processor, placing a clean dish towel over the lid to prevent hot liquid from splattering.

STORE: Allow to cool and transfer to a squeeze bottle or jar with a lid and keep refrigerated for up to 3 weeks.

MAKES
1
QUART DIP/SPREAD

(≤30)

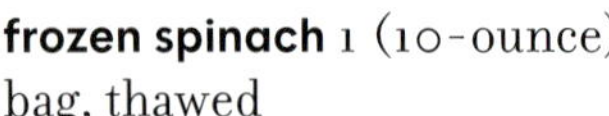

Goat Cheese with Honey & Spinach Spread

frozen spinach 1 (10-ounce) bag, thawed

plain cream cheese 1 (8-ounce) block, softened

plain goat cheese 1 (4-ounce) log, softened

honey 2 teaspoons

olive oil 2 tablespoons, plus more for drizzling

Dijon mustard 1 teaspoon

garlic cloves 3

onion powder 2 teaspoons

lemon 1 large, zested and juiced

hot sauce (such as RedHot) *or Buffalo sauce* 2 to 3 teaspoons

kosher salt ½ teaspoon

crushed red pepper flakes ½ teaspoon

shredded Parmesan cheese *or Pecorino Romano* ½ cup (2 ounces), plus more for sprinkling

Whenever I make any version of spinach dip for a family gathering or game night, nothing in the pantry is spared. Everything from the bottled horseradish to the Worcestershire sauce gets added. I think of it like a big pot of soup—a little of this and a little of that—and suddenly it all melds together into an irresistible topping for crisp crostini or even the beginnings of the easiest weeknight pasta. For your sake and time, I've shared a more tempered ingredient list, a more approachable cousin to that dip, but keep in mind, the hot sauce is not optional. I like to make a batch of this spread up to a week ahead of time and chill it until a snack fit strikes.

SQUEEZE THE SPINACH TO REMOVE ALL THE WATER: In a clean kitchen cloth or a few stacked sheets of paper towels, wrap the thawed spinach and squeeze it tightly over the sink to remove any excess water. Set aside.

BLEND THE SPREAD/DIP: In a food processor fitted with a steel blade, blend the cream cheese, goat cheese, honey, olive oil, mustard, garlic, onion powder, lemon zest and juice, hot sauce, and salt on high until smooth. Remove the lid and add the spinach, red pepper flakes, and Parmesan and pulse until just combined. Transfer the mixture to a lidded container and refrigerate until ready to use.

NOTES ON WHAT TO DO WITH THIS SPREAD

- **MAKE CROSTINI:** Slice a **French baguette** on a heavy diagonal to make long, thin pieces. (Freeze extra slices you won't be eating for another time.) Pile some spread onto the bread, spreading to the edges. Place on a sheet pan, drizzle with **olive oil**, sprinkle over **Parmesan cheese**, if you like, and bake for 10 to 12 minutes at 425°F until the bread is crispy and the cheese is melted.

- **STUFF MUSHROOMS:** Clean **1 pound of baby bella** or button mushrooms of debris, remove their stems, and arrange them in a casserole dish cap-side down. Fill the bellies of the mushrooms with the dip, then drizzle their tops lightly with **olive oil**. Add **a splash of water** to the bottom of the dish and cover the dish with a lid (or foil) so the mushrooms slowly steam as you roast them in the oven at 375°F for 20 to 25 minutes, until the mushrooms are tender and the tops are browned.

- **BAKE AS IS:** Transfer the spread to a casserole dish, smoothing to the edges. Sprinkle over more **Parmesan**, and bake in a 425°F oven for 15 to 17 minutes or until bubbly and browned on top. Serve with **warm pita bread** or **apple slices**.

- **MAKE CREAMY PASTA:** For an easy weeknight pasta, toss together **1 pound cooked pasta noodles** with 1½ cups of the spread, 1 cup hot starchy pasta water, **½ cup chopped sun-dried tomatoes**, and 1 cup drained, roughly-chopped **quartered artichoke hearts** in brine or oil or a handful of chopped **kalamata olives**. Season with fresh **lemon juice** and **salt and pepper** as needed.

CHAPTER 3

FAST 'N' FANCY

Sheet Pans, Shiitake Mushrooms, and Other Shameless Shortcuts

REST ASSURED, THERE IS HOPE that you can make dinner quickly without compromising your fancy.

The following recipes, like quesadillas (Salmon, Kimchi & Corn Quesadillas, page 89), are naturally effortless. Other recipes will encourage you to lean on those trusty time machines like the Instant Pot (for Nearly Instantaneous Black Garlic Risotto, page 72), the handy half sheet pan (for recipes like Sheet Pan Shiitake Jerk Tacos (page 86) or for BBQ Roasted Tomato Bread Salad, page 73), or the miraculous panini press.

Here, you'll also find reminders on using store-bought, time-shaving ingredients for the base of entire meals and, in some cases, other convenient ingredients, like frozen peas, added at the end of a soup's simmering for a sweet and easy pop of green. Canned beans, frozen artichokes, fresh mushrooms (which cook so quickly!), and tinned seafood are also time-saving ingredients, and you'll see these unsung heroes sprinkled throughout.

SERVES

4

(NF, RSF, ≤30)

Sun-Dried Tomato Soup *with Jalapeño Popper "Breadsticks"*

With the help of jarred sun-dried tomatoes, here's an entirely from-the-pantry tomato soup that's rich and red and will coat your belly with warmth. It's probably the easiest tomato soup you'll find. When you use a high-powered blender, it emulsifies the oil from the jarred tomatoes to make a velvety soup. Save a couple cups of soup, or double the recipe for leftovers to make an easy Tomato & Ginger Curry (page 222) later in the week.

JALAPEÑO POPPER BREADSTICKS

plain cream cheese *or soft goat cheese* 1/2 cup (4 ounces), at room temperature

shredded cheddar cheese 1/2 cup

pickled jalapeños slices 1/4 cup (2 ounces), roughly chopped

garlic powder 1/2 teaspoon

kosher salt and **freshly ground black pepper**

sourdough sandwich bread 4 slices

unsalted butter, softened for spreading

shredded Parmesan cheese 3/4 to 1 cup

SUN-DRIED TOMATO SOUP

sun-dried tomatoes in oil 1 (8- to 10-ounce) jar (see Tip)

crushed tomatoes 1 (28-ounce) can

kosher salt

crushed red pepper flakes (optional)

PREHEAT THE OVEN to 400°F and have a large parchment-lined sheet pan nearby.

MAKE THE BREADSTICKS FILLING: In a small bowl, stir together the cream cheese, cheddar cheese, jalapeños, and garlic powder. Season with salt and pepper to taste.

BUILD THE BREADSTICKS: On a clean work surface, arrange 2 slices of bread. Spread the filling in a generous layer over the bread right to the edges and top with the remaining slices of bread. Generously butter both outer sides of the bread.

On the sheet pan, sprinkle two piles of Parmesan in the shape of the bread. Carefully place the buttered breadsticks on each pile and slightly press them into place, then sprinkle more Parmesan over the top so that both sides are covered completely with cheese.

TOAST THE BREADSTICKS: Bake the breadsticks in the oven for 12 to 14 minutes, until the cheese is golden brown and crispy on both the tops and bottoms of the sandwiches and the inner cheese is gooey.

MEANWHILE, MAKE THE SOUP: In a high-powered blender, place the sun-dried tomatoes and crushed tomatoes and blend on high until you have a smooth and creamy puree. Taste and add the salt and red pepper flakes (if using), as desired.

WARM THE SOUP: In a medium saucepan, bring the blended soup to a boil over high heat, then reduce the heat to low and cover to keep warm.

SERVE: Remove the breadsticks from the oven, allow to cool for a few minutes to harden, then cut into strips. Spoon the warm soup into bowls and serve alongside the breadsticks.

MAKE IT FANCY

Drizzle **Basil Oil (page 294)** or another herb-infused oil over the soup for a pop of color.

TIP For soup with extra flavor, buy the jars of sun-dried tomatoes that are already marinated in herbs and spices. If you can't find them, just throw in a handful of fresh herbs like basil or thyme and save a sprig of the herb for topping the soup in the end.

SERVES

2 TO 4

(MAKES 8 SKEWERS)

(NF, ≤30)

unsalted butter 4 tablespoons, melted

minced garlic 1 tablespoon (from 3 cloves)

fresh rosemary 1 teaspoon minced, plus 8 long, sturdy stalks

Worcestershire sauce *or coconut aminos* 1 teaspoon

light brown sugar *or maple syrup or honey* 1 teaspoon

onion powder ¼ teaspoon

kosher salt 1 teaspoon

lion's mane mushrooms ½ pound, torn into small chunks ← or sub 1 pound cubed chicken breast

lemon wedges, for serving

MAKE IT FANCY

Whisk in **1½ teaspoons cumin seeds or 1 teaspoon ground cumin** to the butter sauce for extra earthiness.

Lion's Mane Rosemary Kebabs

Chunks of lion's mane mushrooms pave the way to a quick and clever dinner. Beaded onto sturdy rosemary stems, dry seared, then basted with a simple rosemary and garlic butter, they make bold, succulent kebabs. Serve these skewers with Baked & Bejeweled Yellow Rice (page 163) or stuff them into a pita with Iceberg Tzatziki (page 211) after removing their stems.

MAKE THE BUTTER SAUCE: In a small bowl, whisk together the butter, garlic, minced rosemary, Worcestershire sauce, brown sugar, onion powder, and salt and set aside.

BUILD THE SKEWERS: Strip the rosemary stalks of their leaves to expose the woody stem, while still leaving a couple inches of green leaves at the top for decoration. Working from the bottom of the stalk up, pierce the mushrooms, beading them along the stem and nestling each mushroom against the last (see Tip). You'll need about ¼ cup (1 ounce) mushrooms per rosemary stalk.

SEAR THE SKEWERS: Heat a large cast-iron skillet over medium heat. Once hot, carefully place the skewers in the dry pan, and sear the mushrooms without disturbing them for 3 to 5 minutes, until they're wonderfully golden brown on one side, then rotate and cook the other sides. When the mushrooms are almost finished, use a pastry brush and begin basting the skewers generously with the butter sauce. Allow the mushrooms and rosemary to cook for a final minute for the garlic in the butter to release its fragrance.

REMOVE the skewers from the pan and arrange them on a platter. Serve with the remaining butter sauce and lemon wedges for a squeeze of fresh lemon juice over top.

TIP If your rosemary stems are on the flimsier side, use wooden skewers to pierce through the mushrooms first, then cut a rosemary stalk in half, and through the holes created in the mushrooms, insert a stalk in the top and bottom to give the illusion that it's going all the way through. No one has to know.

Shiitake & Broccoli Stir-Fry

SERVES
4
(DF, EF, NF, ≤30)

soy sauce *or tamari* 1/4 cup, preferably 1/2 dark, 1/2 light

rice vinegar 2 tablespoons

coconut aminos *or Worcestershire sauce* 4 teaspoons

toasted sesame oil 1 teaspoon

light brown sugar *or coconut sugar* 2 packed teaspoons

garlic clove 1, grated or minced

fresh ginger 2-inch knob, peeled and grated (2 packed teaspoons)

cornstarch *or arrowroot powder* 1/2 teaspoon ← 1 teaspoon for a thicker sauce

avocado oil, *or grapeseed oil, or canola oil* 3 tablespoons for frying, plus more as needed

broccoli florets 1/2 pound (about 3 packed cups) from a 1- to 1 1/2-pound head

white onion 1 small, halved and sliced

shiitake mushrooms 1/2 pound, sliced 1/4 inch thick

freshly ground black pepper 1/2 teaspoon

Sticky Stovetop Coconut Rice (page 162) *or warm rice*, for serving

Here's an easy mushroom stir-fry to serve with Sticky Stovetop Coconut Rice. If you don't have broccoli or crave something else, you can swap it with absolutely any hearty, green vegetable—bok choy, broccolini, or even lacinato kale. You could even trade the mushrooms for thinly sliced chicken or steak, tossed with just enough cornstarch, about a teaspoon to coat, so they cook quickly and stay tender.

MAKE THE STIR-FRY SAUCE: In a small bowl, combine the soy sauce, vinegar, coconut aminos, sesame oil, brown sugar, garlic, ginger, cornstarch, and **2 TABLESPOONS WATER** and whisk together. Set aside.

SAUTÉ THE VEGGIES: Have a large bowl or plate nearby. Heat a wok or large cast-iron skillet over high heat. Once it's hot, drizzle in 1 tablespoon of the avocado oil. Add the broccoli, tossing for a minute, then add a few tablespoons water to help it steam. Continue cooking for 2 to 3 minutes, tossing, until the water has evaporated and the broccoli has reached the desired doneness. Remove the broccoli and set aside in the bowl. Add another tablespoon of oil and then the onion and cook for 2 to 3 minutes, until it is tender and charred a bit. Remove the onion and set aside in the bowl with the broccoli.

COOK THE MUSHROOMS: Add the remaining tablespoon of oil to the same pan, and cook the mushrooms in batches for 1 to 2 minutes, adding more oil if the pan seems dry, watching closely as you go to avoid burning.

COMBINE AND FINISH: Add all the veggies back to the pan and pour the sauce over them, stirring rapidly as they cook, about 1 minute, or until the sauce thickens and coats the vegetables. Sprinkle over the pepper, tossing to incorporate. Remove the pan from the heat. Serve over coconut rice.

MAKE IT FANCY
Top your bowl with Haystack Scallions (page 27) for a simple, wispy garnish.

SERVES
4
(EF, GF, NF, RSF, ≤30)

arborio rice 1 cup

vegetable broth 3 cups (3½, if you prefer a thinner risotto)

unsalted butter 2 tablespoons

black garlic 1 ounce, peeled and mashed into a paste

kosher salt ½ teaspoon

freshly ground black pepper ¼ teaspoon

lemon juice 2 teaspoons

heavy cream 2 tablespoons, plus more for thinning

grated Parmesan cheese 2 tablespoons, plus more for topping

MAKE IT FANCY

For more protein, stir in **1 (5-ounce) can albacore tuna (in water or in oil)** along with its juices before pressure cooking, or once the risotto has finished cooking, stir in **½ cup frozen peas** or an easy-wilting green like **a handful of spinach** for extra color and brightness.

Nearly Instantaneous Black Garlic Risotto

Let's have no more stirring over the stove for hours to achieve that coveted creamy risotto texture you've had in restaurants. You can make this dreamy dish entirely in the Instant Pot or pressure cooker. The secret to hands-off risotto is to rinse the grains thoroughly and to collect their starchy rinsing water to add *back* to the cooking pot to thicken. For this recipe I used black garlic, which is practically umami in a bulb. It instantly elevates a dish into something pungent and powerful, so a little goes far. Double this recipe or use the left-over risotto to make an irresistible Black Garlic Suppli (page 220).

RINSE THE RICE AND RESERVE THE WATER: In a large bowl, combine the rice and vegetable broth, using your hands to agitate the kernels vigorously in the broth to shake off their starches. Drain all the (now very starchy) liquid into a separate bowl and set aside.

TOAST THE RICE: Place the butter into the pot of an Instant Pot or multicooker, set to sauté. Once it's melted, bubbling, and foamy, add the rice and cook for 2 to 4 minutes, stirring often, until the rice is completely coated in the butter and is translucent and smells lightly toasted. Add the garlic and, using a wooden spoon, break it up to help disperse it throughout the rice (smaller chunks are totally fine). Add the reserved starchy broth, the salt, and pepper and stir to combine, submerging any straggling kernels on the side of the pot back into the broth.

COOK THE RISOTTO: Turn off the Instant Pot, secure the lid, and pressure cook on high for 6 minutes, allowing for a 5-minute natural release followed by a quick release at the end.

SERVE: Once the rice has finished cooking, remove the lid and stir in the lemon juice, heavy cream, and Parmesan cheese. If you want a thinner risotto, add more heavy cream as desired. Serve in bowls with Parmesan cheese, if desired.

SERVES

4

(EF, NF)

BBQ Roasted Tomato Bread Salad

with Halloumi Frico

SHERRY DRESSING

Basil Oil (page 294) *or extra-virgin olive oil* (see Tip) 2 tablespoons

sherry vinegar *or red wine vinegar* 4 teaspoons

crushed red pepper flakes ¼ teaspoon

light brown sugar *or coconut sugar* ½ teaspoon

ground celery seeds ¼ teaspoon

kosher salt

ripe tomatoes (such as Roma, beefsteak, Campari, cherry) 1 pound, cut into large chunks (leave smaller tomatoes whole)

red onion ½ small, halved and thinly sliced

olive oil, for drizzling

BBQ rub seasoning (I used Bludso's Pork Rub) 2 tablespoons

crusty bread ½ pound, torn into about 1½- to 2-inch chunks (about 6 to 7 cups)

garlic clove 1

halloumi 4 ounces

tender salad greens a handful

This is just a warm panzanella playing coy and underselling itself as a "bread salad." Usually, when you make panzanella, you have to wait a little for the bread to soak up the macerated tomato juice, but this is a recipe you can enjoy immediately. The tomatoes are roasted first, so they give up their juice straight away, and the toasted bread graciously accepts it with open arms.

PREHEAT THE OVEN to 425°F and have two large sheet pans nearby.

MAKE THE DRESSING: In a small bowl, whisk together the basil oil, vinegar, red pepper flakes, brown sugar, celery seeds, and salt to taste. Set aside.

ROAST THE TOMATOES: Place tomatoes and onion on one sheet pan. Drizzle them generously with the olive oil and sprinkle with the BBQ rub and salt to taste, tossing everything together to coat. Bake in the oven for 15 to 18 minutes, until the tomatoes begin to break down.

MEANWHILE, TOAST THE BREAD: On one side of the second sheet pan, spread out the bread. Using a Microplane, grate the garlic clove over the bread. Drizzle generously with olive oil and season with salt to taste, then toss everything together to coat.

MAKE THE FRICO HALLOUMI (SEE TIP): Using a box grater, shred the halloumi into medium shreds. On the other side of the sheet pan with the bread, add the shredded halloumi in a thin pile and drizzle with olive oil.

(recipe continues)

BAKE the second sheet pan on the bottom rack for 12 to 15 minutes, until the bread is golden brown and crispy on the outside but still slightly springy to the touch and the halloumi has crisped on the bottom. Remove both pans from the oven and set aside to cool and allow the cheese to fully crisp.

SERVE: Put the roasted tomatoes along with their juices and the onion into a large serving bowl. Pour over the sherry dressing, tossing to combine. Taste and add more salt, if desired. Add the bread and greens and toss to coat, then top with chunks of the cooled halloumi and serve immediately.

TIP

If you don't have Basil Oil already made, use **extra-virgin olive oil**, and add **2 to 3 tablespoons freshly chopped basil** to the dressing instead.

•

The trick for making frico, or "fried cheese," is to cook low-moisture cheeses like Parmesan, cheddar, or halloumi into thin sheets so they become like crispy, salty crackers. Play with this technique to decorate and add extra texture to food. You can also use frico as a gluten-free alternative to salad croutons, to make a crunchy shell for low-carb tacos, or to give your grilled cheese extra crispy edges.

Coconut Saffron Salmon Soup

SERVES

4

(DF, EF, GF, NF, RSF, ≤30)

vegetable broth 5 cups

saffron threads ½ teaspoon

salted butter 2 tablespoons

yellow onion 1 cup diced

celery ½ cup diced

kosher salt

uncooked long grain rice ½ cup, rinsed

garlic cloves 3, minced or grated

full-fat coconut milk 1 (13.5-ounce) can

bay leaves 2, fresh or dried

skinless salmon filets 1 pound ← add more for a chunkier chowder

frozen sweet peas ½ cup

MAKE IT FANCY

Top the chowder with **fresh dill fronds.**

Salmon filets poached in rich coconut milk create perfectly tender fish and make this dish truly the salmon chowder of my dreams. The rice adds heartiness, and the floral and fragrant saffron brings luxury and a beautifully golden hue. I also love this dish because it calls for frozen peas, which require no investment at all; they're literally a vegetable afterthought, thawing instantly in the hot broth at the last minute and still allowing you to check your veggie serving off the list.

STEEP THE SAFFRON: In a large bowl or liquid measuring cup, combine the vegetable broth and saffron. Set aside and allow the saffron to steep while you prepare the soup.

MAKE THE SOUP BASE: In a large pot over medium-high heat, melt the butter. When the butter begins to foam, add the onion, celery, and a pinch of salt and cook for 10 minutes. Add the rice, garlic, and another pinch of salt and toast the rice for 2 to 3 minutes, until it begins to take on some color.

POACH THE SALMON: To the rice, stir in the steeped saffron broth, coconut milk, bay leaves, and another pinch of salt, making sure to push any grains of rice caught on the side of the pot into the liquid. Bring the liquid to a boil, reduce the heat to a simmer, and add the salmon filets. Cover and cook on low for about 25 minutes, or until the rice is tender and the salmon is opaque.

SERVE: Remove the lid and, using two forks, flake the salmon into chunks, then add in the peas. Taste the soup and season with more salt if desired. Spoon the soup into serving bowls.

Artichokes in the Perfect Butter-Wine Sauce
(page 80)

SERVES

4 TO 6

(EF, NF, RSF, ≤30)

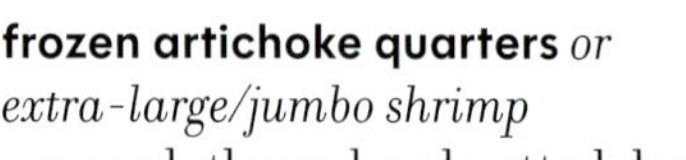

frozen artichoke quarters *or extra-large/jumbo shrimp* 1 pound, thawed and patted dry

cornstarch *or arrowroot starch* 3 tablespoons for dusting, plus more as needed

creole seasoning (such as Tony Chachere's) ½ teaspoon, plus more as needed

olive oil, for frying

Pizza Butter (page 291) 4 ounces (½ cup), plus more as needed

dry white wine ½ cup, plus more as needed

crusty baguette *or cooked linguine, rice, or orzo*, for serving

Parsley Dust (page 27) *or chopped parsley*, for sprinkling

Artichokes in the Perfect Butter & Wine Sauce

It's like shrimp scampi but with a bag of frozen artichokes instead. This quick skillet recipe makes good use of the Pizza Butter you hopefully already have stashed in the freezer. It's one of those "a little bit of this and a little of that" recipes where you'll need to taste as you go and get the flow. And if you're not feeling bread is the ideal carb option, serve this over hot pasta (of course, the extra butter will varnish the noodles) or a colorful rice pilaf instead.

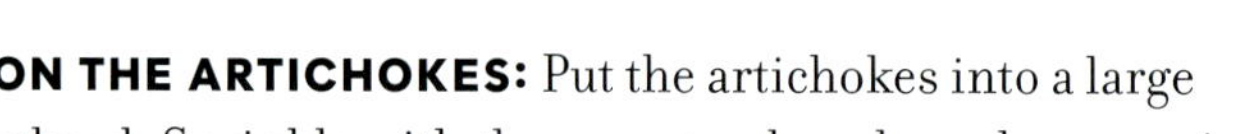

SEASON THE ARTICHOKES: Put the artichokes into a large mixing bowl. Sprinkle with the cornstarch and creole seasoning and toss to coat.

SEAR THE ARTICHOKES: Heat a large stainless steel skillet over medium-high heat. Once hot, drizzle the pan with the olive oil to coat. Place the artichokes in a single layer (depending on the size of your pan, you may need to do this in batches) and cook, flipping occasionally until the artichokes are crisp and lightly golden brown all over, 2 to 3 minutes per side (6 to 7 minutes if you're searing shrimp, being careful not to overcook). Remove from the pan and set aside on a plate.

MAKE THE BUTTER SAUCE: Back in the hot skillet, add the butter and wine and cook, whisking, until a silky sauce comes together. Taste and adjust, adding more creole seasoning, butter, or wine as desired.

SERVE: Add the artichokes back into the pan to coat them in the sauce and warm them through, then transfer to a serving platter along with torn chunks of baguette. Sprinkle over Parsley Dust and serve immediately, using the bread to help sponge up all the buttery winey goodness from the plate and into your mouth.

SERVES

4

(EF, NF, RSF)

Pumpkin & Cauliflower-Cream Pasta *with Shiitake Lardons*

Shiitake Lardons (recipe follows)

kosher salt

dried linguine noodles *or spaghetti noodles* ¾ pound

pumpkin puree ¼ cup

cauliflower florets 1 cup (5 ounces), frozen and thawed ← sub freshly steamed or boiled cauliflower florets

white miso paste 2 tablespoons

nutritional yeast ¼ cup

Porcini Butter (page 290; see Tip) *or salted butter* 2 to 3 tablespoons

freshly ground black pepper lots ← at least 1 teaspoon

Parsley Dust (page 27) *or fresh chopped parsley*, for sprinkling

TIP

If you'd like to make this vegan-friendly, just make your Porcini Butter (page 290) using dairy-free butter.

In the midst of all your autumnal baking, does it ever disturb you to find orphaned, half-used cans of pumpkin puree in your fridge after a recipe didn't call for its entirety? I now consider it a blessing because of all the inventive things I can do with it. It's so mild in flavor you can stir the extra into chilis, risotto, the custard base of my Sweet Potato Challah Bread Rolls (page 250), or make my favorite late-night pasta dish—this addictive vegetarian-friendly carbonara. Thanks to the squash (and the extra cauliflower I snuck in, too) it manages to be eggless, despite being quite eggy, and cheesy without an ounce of cheese.

MAKE THE SHIITAKE LARDONS and set aside.

BOIL THE NOODLES: Bring a large pot of salted water to a boil. Add the linguini and cook according to the package instructions, stirring occasionally so the noodles don't stick.

MEANWHILE, MAKE THE CAULIFLOWER SAUCE: Place the pumpkin puree, cauliflower, miso paste, and nutritional yeast in a blender and set aside. Once the pasta water is semiopaque and starchy, skim ½ cup of the boiling foamy pasta water and add it to the blender. Blend on high until the sauce is smooth.

FINISH THE PASTA: Heat a large saucepan over medium-high heat. Melt the butter, and as soon as it begins to bubble and brown, use a pair of tongs to transfer the cooked noodles to the butter, tossing to coat. Pour over the cauliflower mixture, tossing again to coat the noodles. Remove from the heat and add the pepper. Transfer to plates and top with the lardons and Parsley Dust and serve.

Shiitake Lardons

MAKES ABOUT 1 CUP
(DF, EF, GF, NF, RSF, <5)

These blow my mind as incredible bacon bit replacers. Serve them on a baked potato (see page 210), a vegetarian cobb salad, my spin on carbonara (Pumpkin & Cauliflower-Cream Pasta, page 81), or on Crispy Buffalo Brussels Sprouts (page 182). Don't be alarmed that the dehydrated mushrooms soak in oil; I mean they *are* trying to mimic bacon after all.

whole dried shiitake mushrooms 8 to 10

olive oil *or avocado oil* 1/3 to 1/2 cup, for soaking

kosher salt

PREHEAT THE OVEN TO 350°F and have a sheet pan nearby.

SOAK THE MUSHROOMS: In a small bowl, cover the dried mushrooms with the olive oil, making sure every inch is completely submerged. Let the mushrooms soak for 15 to 20 minutes to soften.

CUT THE MUSHROOMS: Remove the mushrooms from the oil and transfer them to a cutting board. Using a sharp knife, cut them into 1/4-inch strips. Sprinkle the mushrooms with salt to taste. (Adding the salt on it before it goes in the oven or air fryer, makes it easier for the salt to adhere.)

BAKE IN THE OVEN for 8 to 12 minutes, checking toward the end so they don't burn. (See Tip for air-fryer instructions.) They shrink slightly while cooking and are best enjoyed immediately.

TIP To make these in an air fryer, cook at 325°F for 10 minutes. Use a small baking dish that fits in the air fryer or fit the bottom of the air fryer rack with parchment or foil so the pieces don't fall through the cracks.

SERVES
6 TO 8
(EF, NF, RSF, ≤30)

One-Pot Penne alla Fennel-y Vodka Sauce

olive oil 2 tablespoons

chopped garlic 3 tablespoons (from 8 to 10 cloves)

crushed red pepper flakes ½ teaspoon

fennel seeds 1 tablespoon

dried oregano 2 teaspoons

tomato paste ¼ cup

crushed tomatoes 1 (28-ounce) can

vodka ¼ cup

pure maple syrup 2 tablespoons

kosher salt 1 tablespoon, plus more as needed

dried penne pasta *or other sturdy medium-length pasta such as farfalle or jumbo fusilli* 1 pound

heavy cream *or half-and-half* ½ cup

lemon juice 1 tablespoon, plus more as needed

Parmesan cheese ¼ cup grated, plus more for serving

Parsley Dust (page 27) *or chopped parsley*, for sprinkling

Punchy vodka is obviously the star in any vodka sauce. But with the mound of garlic and fennel seeds, the ease of one-pot cooking, plus the fact that I get to pour maple syrup into my spaghetti sauce like Buddy the Elf, I'm not sure which of these subtle upgrades should get most of my praise.

NOTE: Depending on the brand you use, one 28-ounce can of crushed tomatoes typically only contains about 1½ to 1¾ cups of actual liquid; the rest is just tomato solids. Keep this in mind when experimenting with the ratios of one-pot pastas.

SAUTÉ THE AROMATICS: Heat a large Dutch oven or heavy-bottomed pot over medium high-heat. Once hot, drizzle in the oil, then add the garlic, red pepper flakes, fennel seeds, and oregano. Sauté, stirring constantly, for 1 to 2 minutes, until the garlic and fennel seeds are toasted and fragrant. Be careful not to burn them.

MAKE THE SAUCE: Add the tomato paste, and cook for 1 more minute, breaking it up to incorporate the spices. Then add in the crushed tomatoes, **1½ CUPS WATER**, the vodka, syrup, and salt, stirring after each addition.

ADD THE PASTA: Bring the pot to a boil and stir in the penne, submerging the noodles completely in the sauce. Reduce the heat to a simmer, cover the pot, and cook the pasta until the noodles are tender and have absorbed most of the liquid and you're left with a thick tomato sauce that's rich and sweet, about 20 minutes. Be sure to stir the pasta occasionally so it doesn't stick to the bottom of the pan.

SERVE: Remove the pan from the heat and stir in the heavy cream, lemon juice, and Parmesan. Taste and add more salt or lemon juice as desired. Spoon the pasta into bowls and top with Parmesan and Parsley Dust.

The Wonders of One-Pot Pasta

One-pot pastas are a dinnertime blessing and a canvas for creativity once you get your head wrapped around the ratios. Instead of boiling pasta in large quarts of water, you cook the noodles in just enough sauce or broth so you never have to take the time to drain the noodles and add them to a separate sauce. It also makes especially flavorful noodles.

The key is to double the weight of liquid to the weight of dried pasta—for instance, 3½ to 4 cups liquid (or more for a saucier dish) to 1 pound pasta with slight variations based on the brand and type of pasta you use. Gluten-free pastas made from legumes or vegetables will absorb a little more liquid, so the liquid ratios increase.

SERVES

4

(DF, EF, NF, RSF)

Sheet Pan Shiitake Jerk Tacos

with Roasted Pineapple Salsa

avocado oil *or olive oil*, for oiling the pans and drizzling

scallions 4, green and white parts, roots trimmed and cut into chunks

Scotch bonnet pepper *or habanero pepper* 1, seeds and stem discarded

garlic cloves 6 large

fresh ginger 1 (2-inch) knob, peeled

soy sauce *or tamari* 2 tablespoons

coconut sugar *or packed light brown sugar* 2 to 3 tablespoons

dried thyme leaves 1 tablespoon (or 2 tablespoons fresh thyme leaves)

ground cinnamon 1 tablespoon

ground allspice 2 tablespoons

ground nutmeg 1½ teaspoons

vegetable bouillon paste 2 teaspoons

shiitake mushrooms ¾ pound, sliced

kosher salt

fresh or frozen sweet juicy pineapple chunks *or mango chunks* 2 ounces, chopped (2 cups)

red onion 1 small, chopped

corn *or flour tortillas* 10 to 12 (6 inch)

Meaty shiitakes are a fast weeknight protein, and here they soak up a fiery, aromatic jerk paste—made with hints of allspice, thyme, and citrus—like a happy sponge. The spicy mushrooms get tucked into warm tortillas topped with pineapple chunks also roasted in the oven, which helps them break down into the juiciest, sweetest salsa. Everything gets made on a couple of sheet pans for ease; even the tortillas use the handy sheet pan technology to get warm and ready.

PREHEAT THE OVEN to 400°F and position two racks in the center of the oven. Oil two sheet pans and set aside.

BLEND THE JERK PASTE: In a high-powered blender, combine the scallions, Scotch bonnet pepper, garlic, ginger, soy sauce, coconut sugar, thyme, cinnamon, allspice, nutmeg, and bouillon paste and blend on high, adding **1 TABLESPOON WATER** at a time until a smooth paste is formed.

BAKE THE VEGGIES: Transfer the shiitakes to one of the prepared sheet pans. Pour over the jerk paste and, using tongs, toss everything together well to evenly coat. Spread the mushrooms in an even layer and drizzle generously with more oil and season with salt to taste. To the second prepared sheet pan, add the pineapple chunks and red onion in a single layer and drizzle with oil and season with salt to taste. Bake both pans in the oven for 25 to 30 minutes, until the mushrooms are tender and the pineapples and onions are juicy and browned on their tips, rotating the pans halfway through.

(recipe continues)

6% ALC/VOL

cilantro a large handful, chopped

fresh orange juice 1 tablespoon, plus more as needed

MAKE IT FANCY

Make an **Orange Crema** by mixing together **⅓ cup plain Greek yogurt** (or sour cream) with **a splash of fresh orange juice**. Drizzle it over the tacos to cool down the extra heat.

WARM THE TORTILLAS: Five minutes before the mushrooms are done cooking, wrap the tortillas in foil and place on the sheet pan with the mushrooms to warm through. Remove the pans from the oven and set aside.

MAKE THE SALSA: Transfer the roasted pineapple and onion to a medium bowl along with the cilantro, orange juice, and a pinch of salt, tossing to coat. Taste and add more orange juice, if needed. Set aside.

BUILD THE TACOS: Divide the roasted mushrooms among the tortillas (a little goes a long way), topping with some of the pineapple salsa, and serve.

SERVES
4
(EF, NF, ≤30)

gochujang sauce 2 tablespoons

soy sauce 2 tablespoons

lime juice 1 tablespoon, plus more for serving

onion powder 1 teaspoon

garlic powder 1 teaspoon

ground ginger 1 teaspoon

dry mustard powder ½ teaspoon

kosher salt ½ teaspoon

freshly ground black pepper ¼ teaspoon

sour cream (full-fat or light) *or Greek yogurt* ½ cup

salmon (preferably skin on) ½ pound (see Tip)

avocado oil *or olive oil*, for frying

kimchi 1 cup, lightly drained and roughly chopped

sweet corn kernels ½ cup, fresh or frozen and thawed

diced scallions ¼ cup, both green and white parts, plus more for serving

cilantro 2 tablespoons roughly chopped, plus more for serving

shredded cheese (like sharp cheddar, Gouda, Monterey Jack, or mozzarella) 1½ to 2 cups

flour tortillas 4 (8 inch) ← or sub 8 (6-inch) corn tortillas

Salmon, Kimchi & Corn Quesadillas

When we were kids, and my mom was too overwhelmed to cook, she would fry quesadillas for dinner to feed my brother, my sister, and me. She kept her version simple with just chicken and cheese, but I've always appreciated how quesadillas can be anything you want them to be. This is my favorite version of a quesadilla because it has pickled kimchi and cheddar cheese, as you can probably tell from my Frico Kimchi Hash (page 240).

MAKE THE MARINADE: In a small bowl, whisk together the gochujang, soy sauce, lime juice, onion powder, garlic powder, ginger, mustard powder, salt, and pepper.

MAKE THE CREAM SAUCE: In a separate small bowl, whisk together half the gochujang mixture and the sour cream to combine. Cover and refrigerate until it's time to serve. Reserve the remaining gochujang mixture.

SEASON THE SALMON: Pat the salmon dry. Then with your fingers or using a pastry brush, rub the entire surface of the salmon, including the skin, with the rest of the gochujang mixture, being sure to coat well. Allow the salmon to marinate on the counter for 10 minutes.

SEAR THE SALMON: Heat a large cast-iron skillet over medium-high heat. Drizzle in enough avocado oil to coat the pan, and tilt the pan to spread the oil evenly. Add the salmon, skin side down, then reduce the heat slightly to medium and cook for 4 to 5 minutes, until the skin is dark and crispy. Carefully flip and cook on the other side for another 3 to 4 minutes, until just cooked through and the sides are completely opaque. Remove from the pan and place on a plate. Allow to cool slightly before sliding a thin, sharp knife between the flesh and skin to separate, then discard the skin. With a couple of forks gently shred the salmon into chunks.

(recipe continues)

MAKE IT FANCY

Add **2 teaspoons light brown sugar** (or coconut sugar) and **¼ teaspoon toasted sesame oil** to the cream sauce for more flavor.

FILL THE QUESADILLAS: In a large mixing bowl, toss the flaked salmon, kimchi, corn, scallions, cilantro, and cheese to combine. On a clean counter surface, lay out the tortillas, and divide the salmon filling (about 1 cup) among the tortillas, placing the mixture on the bottom half of each tortilla in an even layer. Flip the tortillas closed to create half-moon shapes.

FRY THE QUESADILLAS: Heat a large cast-iron skillet over medium heat and lightly coat the pan with avocado oil. Add the quesadillas in batches and fry for 3 to 5 minutes per side, until the cheese has melted and the tortilla is a deep golden brown. Alternatively you can cook them in a hot, oiled panini press or waffle iron. Remove from the skillet and, using a sharp knife, cut each quesadilla into 3 triangles.

SERVE: Transfer the quesadillas to a serving plate and dollop with the dipping sauce (or transfer the sauce to a squeeze bottle and drizzle over top). Squeeze over more lime juice, sprinkle over more scallions and cilantro, and enjoy.

TIP Consider keeping the skin on the salmon because it helps seal in the juices and prevents overcooking. Plus, once the salmon is cooked, the skin will peel away effortlessly.

SERVES

4

(RSF, ≤30)

Carrot & Feta Flatbread

with Pecan Dukkah

flatbread (such as *store-bought naan, lavash*, or *flour tortillas*) 4, roughly 8-inch pieces

feta cheese 4 ounces

whole-milk mozzarella cheese 4 ounces (1 cup shredded)

Parmesan cheese 1½ ounces (½ cup shredded)

full-fat Greek yogurt *or heavy cream* ¼ cup

carrots 1 to 2 large, peeled

red onion ¼ small, thinly sliced

olive oil, for drizzling

honey, for drizzling

Pecan Dukkah (page 57) *or store-bought dukkah*, for sprinkling (optional)

MAKE IT FANCY

Add **a handful of Thai (or regular) basil confetti (page 27)** to the flatbreads once they're out of the oven.

I used to think store-bought and homemade pitas, flatbreads, and tortillas were just a vehicle for shoveling hummus or curries into my mouth, or as a way to hold hearty sandwich ingredients together. Once it clicked in my mind that they can also be a substitute for great thin-crust pizza, I always make (or buy) extra, because it makes dinner planning a cinch, which in turn makes it more fun.

PREHEAT THE OVEN to 425°F. Place the flatbread on two sheet pans and set aside.

MAKE THE CHEESE SPREAD: In a mini food processor, crumble in the feta and add the mozzarella, Parmesan, and yogurt. Pulse until combined into a sticky paste, stopping to scrape down the sides of the bowl if needed; some chunks of cheese remaining is fine. Divide the cheese spread among the flatbreads and, using the back of a spoon, spread it close to the edges in an even layer.

ROLL THE CARROTS: Using a vegetable peeler, thinly peel the carrots into long thin strips. Roll the strips between your fingers into a loose Fruit Roll-Up shape and nestle them into the cheese mixture. It doesn't need to be perfect; in fact, abstract is more fun. Sprinkle over the red onion slices and drizzle the flatbreads with olive oil and a little honey.

BAKE THE FLATBREADS: Bake for 7 to 12 minutes, until the onion and carrots have softened, the cheese is golden brown, and the flatbread is crispy. Remove from the oven and sprinkle over the dukkah. Cut the flatbread into pieces and serve.

SERVES

4

(DF, NF, ≤30)

Five-Spice Maple-Glazed Salmon

Salmon and rice is a default dinner in our home. It's the perfect unplanned, last-minute meal that feels complete and satisfying. But when the cycle becomes too repetitive, I trick my brain by switching up my serving vessel and making the addictive Mango & Miso Salmon Grain Bowls (page 224), or I pull out our five-spice blend and make this sticky, complex sauce packed with warm spices and fresh ginger to snap us out of the funk. Serve this glazed salmon with mashed potatoes spiced with a hint of nutmeg or stick with steamed rice, just be sure to drizzle that sauce all over when it's time to eat.

FIVE-SPICE GLAZE

pure maple syrup 1/4 cup

soy sauce *or tamari* 1/4 cup

rice vinegar 1/4 cup

five-spice powder 2 teaspoons

fresh ginger 2 1/2-inch knob (15 grams), grated

garlic cloves 5 to 6 (15 grams), grated

Sriracha 1 teaspoon

cornstarch *or potato starch* 1 teaspoon

skin-on salmon 4 (4- to 6-ounce) filets

kosher salt

avocado oil *or light oil olive*, for searing

hot cooked rice *or mashed potatoes*, for serving

veggies (julienned carrots, scallions, cucumber, and/or shredded purple or green cabbage), for topping

MIX THE GLAZE: In a medium bowl, whisk together the maple syrup, soy sauce, vinegar, five-spice powder, ginger, garlic, Sriracha, and cornstarch to combine. Set aside.

SEAR THE SALMON: Using paper towels, pat the salmon dry and season it all over with salt. Heat a large stainless steel skillet over medium-high heat for 2 to 3 minutes, then use enough avocado oil to coat the bottom of the pan, tilting the pan to spread the oil evenly. Add the salmon skin side down and cook for 3 to 5 minutes, until the skin is deeply charred and crispy and the salmon is cooked two-thirds of the way up the flesh.

ADD THE GLAZE: Using a metal spatula, carefully flip the salmon over and continue cooking for another 30 to 45 seconds, then pour the glaze over the filets. Be careful, it may splatter. Shake the pan to allow the glaze to get underneath the salmon, and allow it to bubble away and thicken and the salmon to finish cooking through, another 2 to 3 minutes depending on the size of the filets. Spoon the glaze over the top of the filets as they finish cooking. Remove from the heat and set aside.

SERVE the salmon with rice, spooning more glaze over everything, and top with the veggies for crunch and color.

MAKE IT FANCY

Sprinkle **toasted sesame seeds** over the salmon for a little extra crunch.

TIP

Practice cooking with your nose: This glaze is a good place to practice using your sense of smell to build on flavors as you cook. As you're making the glaze, add one ingredient at a time, close your eyes to take in the aromas, sniffing after each addition to understand how flavors balance out in the nose first.

A Magical Peanut Sauce

SERVES
4
(DF, EF, GF, RSF, ≤30)

natural unsweetened peanut butter 1/4 cup, stirred in the jar before measuring

medjool dates 4, pitted ← or sub 2 tablespoons maple syrup or honey, plus more as needed

tamari *or soy sauce* 2 tablespoons, plus more as needed

chili garlic sauce *or Sriracha* 1 tablespoon, plus more as needed

garlic cloves 2

lime juice *or lemon juice* 2 tablespoons, plus more as needed

A good peanut sauce can be drizzled over nearly anything—from a juicy, seared rib eye or even a bacon cheeseburger, to the lightest, most refreshing spring veggie salad. It's so versatile it borders on heroic, not to mention it's one of those recipes that can be tailored to whatever you have on hand. I've made countless variations of it, barely measuring, just tossing things in, and somehow each time it turns out solid, but even if the winds are off that night and the flavors just aren't hitting, it only takes a little tweaking to get things back into balance. This time I added plump dates, but you can sweeten this however you like and even throw in a few dashes of fish sauce for extra depth, a knob of peeled ginger for spice, or 1/2 teaspoon tamarind concentrate for twang—have fun with this!

BLEND THE SAUCE: In a high-powered blender, blend the peanut butter, dates, tamari, chili garlic sauce, garlic gloves, juice, and **½ CUP WATER** on high for about 3 minutes, or until thick, emulsified, and warm. Taste and adjust seasonings as needed and add more water to thin if desired.

SERVE: Drizzle it over anything your heart desires, like one of the easy dishes that follow.

Spring Noodle Salad

SERVES 4
(DF, EF, GF, RSF, ≤5, ≤30)

uncooked rice noodles *or other noodles of choice* 1 pound ← or sub 2 pounds store-bought fresh zucchini or carrot spirals (see Tip for making your own)

shredded purple cabbage *or green cabbage* 1 cup ← for extra crunch

A Magical Peanut Sauce (page 96)

Prepare the noodles according to their package instructions. Drain and add to a large serving bowl along with the cabbage.

Serve: Pour some of the peanut sauce over the noodles and toss to coat, adding more sauce as desired. Divide into bowls and serve.

TIP How to zoodle: Don't sleep on zoodling at home—it's a blast. If you have a spiralizer, spiralize 2 pounds of zucchini and/or carrots according to the manufacturer's instructions, toss with a generous pinch of salt, and place into a colander for about 10 minutes to drain away any excess moisture. If you don't have a spiralizer, you can use a julienne peeler to shave them into ribbons or a regular potato peeler to shave them into long, wide strips.

MAKE IT FANCY

Top with a vibrant and complementary Crispy Herb Salad: Heat a small skillet over medium heat. Once hot, add **¼ cup avocado oil**, then add **¼ cup diced shallots** and **2 teaspoons chile peppers** (such as Thai, serrano, or jalapeño peppers) and cook, stirring occasionally, until the shallots are crisp and golden, about 8 to 10 minutes. Add **1 to 2 tablespoons sesame seeds** and **¼ cup chopped peanuts or cashews**. Let the seeds and nuts cook for 1 to 2 minutes, just until toasted, then remove the pan from the heat. While hot, add **a pinch of salt** and **a pinch of sugar** (coconut, brown, or granulated), and allow the oil to cool. Just before serving, add a **handful of cilantro leaves** and a **handful of Thai basil or fresh mint**, tossing to coat them in the oil. Taste, adjusting with more salt and/or sugar, if needed.

Sheet Pan Tofu with Asparagus

SERVES 4
(DF, EF, GF, RSF)

extra-firm tofu 1 (14-ounce) block, cut into ¾-inch squares (see Tip on page 24 for prepping your tofu)

asparagus ½ pound (½ bunch) woody ends trimmed, and halved through the center ← or sub other chopped veggies like green beans, bok choy, broccolini, or summer squash

white onion ½ large, chopped into chunks

green bell pepper 1 large, cored and chopped into chunks

tamari *or soy sauce* 3 tablespoons ← or sub coconut aminos

sesame oil 2 teaspoons

avocado oil *or light olive oil*, for drizzling

A Magical Peanut Sauce (page 96)

Sticky Stovetop Coconut Rice (page 162) *or cooked brown rice*, for serving

PREHEAT THE OVEN to 400°F.

SEASON: To a sheet pan, add the cubed tofu, asparagus, onion, and bell pepper. Drizzle the tamari and sesame oil over the tofu and vegetables, tossing gently to coat. Allow to sit for 5 to 10 minutes so the tofu absorbs most of the liquid.

COAT AND BAKE: Spread everything out in a single layer and drizzle generously with avocado oil. Bake for 18 to 20 minutes, tossing halfway through, or until the tofu is golden brown and firm on the outside and the veggies are tender.

SERVE: Remove from the oven, pour over peanut sauce to coat, return to the oven to bake for an additional 3 to 5 minutes. Remove from the oven and toss with more sauce as desired. Serve over rice.

Crunchy Peanut Chicken Salad

SERVES 4
(DF, EF, GF, RSF, ≤30)

shredded or pulled chicken *or cooked chickpeas or rehydrated soy curls* 2 cups

shredded cabbage *or broccoli slaw* 4 cups or 2 (8-ounce) bags

celery 2 large stalks, thinly sliced

scallions 4, thinly sliced, both green and white parts

red bell pepper 1, cored and thinly sliced

A Magical Peanut Sauce (page 96)

MIX THE INGREDIENTS: In a large serving bowl, combine the chicken, cabbage, celery, scallions, and bell pepper. Pour over some of the peanut sauce and toss to coat, adding more sauce as desired. Divide into bowls and serve.

MAKE IT FANCY

Add ½ cup of **Rice Croutons (page 81)** or **crunchy chow mein noodles, shelled edamame, mandarin segments, cashews, golden raisins, chopped apples**, or all of the above!

CHAPTER 4

WHAT'S THE RUSH?

Comfort, Cravings & Labors of Love

ON DAYS WHEN MY MIND feels stuck in a vicious head loop, throwing myself into the act of making dinner becomes its own salve. Cooking gives my hands and mind a physical task that pulls me out of my thoughts and anchors me firmly in the present, forcing me to slow my movements down.

Carve out time for at least one process-driven recipe each week. These recipes—the slow, deliberate ones—are labors of love. They invite us to immerse fully in the act of creating and often impact us the most.

You could try your hand at homemade pasta dough (page 110), or dive into the magic of bread making, watching sourdough starter (page 148) rise under your care. Tackle "Tidy" Joe Milk Buns (page 128), a play on weeknight sloppy Joes, or simply cook something nostalgic that feels hearty and coats your belly well.

The recipes that follow bring us back to ourselves. They build stores of comfort within our bodies. They require you to linger in the kitchen just a little longer, and embrace the journey as much as the end result. Wherever the process leads you, let it become a grounding ritual, a small act of creation that carries you away from the external chaos of the world and gently back home into your body.

SERVES
6 TO 8
(DF, NF, ≤30)

dried ancho chiles 2 large (1 ounce)

dried guajillo chiles 2 large (1 ounce)

onion 1 medium, peeled and chopped into chunks (about 1 cup)

garlic cloves 5

tomato paste 2 tablespoons

ground cumin 2 teaspoons

dried oregano 2 teaspoons

cayenne pepper 1/4 teaspoon (optional)

vegetable bouillon paste 1 teaspoon

kosher salt 2 teaspoons, plus more as needed

avocado oil *or olive oil* 2 tablespoons

Mexican lager (Dos Equis, Modelo, Corona, etc.) 1 (12-ounce) bottle

crushed tomatoes 1 (28-ounce) can

light brown sugar *or coconut sugar* 1 tablespoon packed, plus more as needed

apple cider vinegar *or distilled white vinegar* 1 tablespoon, plus more as needed

Jumbo Chili Mac

I love to hover over a wide bowl of hot chili mac, my face steaming from the earthy peppers; the warmth comforts me and momentarily clears away my troubles. At a glance this recipe ingredient list would seem like a lot, but I enjoy taking my time collecting the condiments and cans, measuring the spices, and toasting the whole chiles. It's like a steady, slow dance that I then pass off to my partner, The Pot, to simmer everything together into a rich and layered dinner.

TOAST THE CHILES: Preheat the oven to 375°F. Clean the ancho and guajillo chiles with a damp kitchen towel and place them on a sheet pan. Toast them in the oven for 3 to 4 minutes, or just until they release their fragrance into the kitchen. They will be a couple shades darker on the surface and puffed. You don't want to over toast them or they'll turn bitter. Remove the chiles from the oven and allow them to cool enough to handle.

SOAK THE CHILES: Discard the stems and seeds from the chiles and put them into a medium heatproof bowl. Cover the chiles with boiling water to submerge. Soak them for 15 to 20 minutes, until softened, then drain and set them aside.

MAKE THE CHILE PASTE: Blend the chiles, onion, garlic, tomato paste, cumin, oregano, cayenne pepper (if using), bouillon paste, and salt in a mini food processor until you have a smooth paste. Set aside.

COOK THE CHILI MAC: Heat a large Dutch oven over medium-high heat, and once it's hot pour in the avocado oil and the pureed chili paste. Cook for 2 to 3 minutes, until the paste turns a couple shades darker. Stir in the lager, crushed tomatoes, brown sugar, apple cider vinegar, soy sauce, and beans, along with **1 CUP WATER**. Bring the pot to a boil, cover, and reduce the heat to a simmer. Cook the chili for 30 minutes, or closer to an hour to get an even deeper flavor, stirring occasionally.

soy sauce *or tamari*
1 tablespoon, plus more as needed

kidney beans *or other canned beans* 2 (14-ounce) cans, drained and rinsed

dried paccheri pasta (see Tip) *or other favorite medium-length pasta* ¾ pound

MAKE IT FANCY

Top the bowls with **grated white cheddar or Monterey Jack cheese** and **Diamond Scallions (page 27)**.

MEANWHILE, BOIL THE PASTA: Place a colander in a sink. Bring a large pot of salted water to a boil. Cook the pasta according to the package instructions. Drain in the colander, then transfer to the pot of chili, tossing to coat the pasta. Continue cooking for a few more minutes, until the pasta begins to absorb some of the sauce. Taste and adjust with more soy sauce, apple cider vinegar, or sugar, if needed, to balance.

SERVE: Spoon the chili mac into bowls and enjoy.

TIP Consider upgrading from small, everyday kidney bean–size pasta to bulbous and ridged paccheri noodles, so the kidney beans and the rich meaty sauce can nestle themselves into the large tubes like a warm sleeping bag.

Gnocchi with Lobster & Leeks

SERVES

4

(GF, NF, RSF, ≤30)

unsalted butter 4 tablespoons

leek 1 large, dark green top leaves discarded, and the bottom white and light green parts halved, rinsed of all dirt, and sliced into half moons ← or sub 1 diced shallot

celery 1 stalk, thinly sliced

kosher salt and **freshly ground black pepper**

garlic cloves 3, chopped

all-purpose flour 1 tablespoon

evaporated milk 1 (10 ounce) can ← or sub 1¼ cups half and half

dry white wine (such as Pinot Grigio) ½ cup

Creole seasoning (such as Tony Chachere's) 1 teaspoon

potato gnocchi *or cauliflower gnocchi* 1 (16-ounce) package

pre-cooked frozen lobster meat 4 ounces (about 1 cup), or more if you're ballin' like that

shredded Gruyère *or Swiss cheese*, ½ cup

nutmeg freshly grated

When you're wrestling with a craving for something as decadent as lobster gratin but lack the the will to peel and cube potatoes, consider a package of store-bought gnocchi to be a fluffier, low-maintenance version of a boiled potato ready to slip into action for you at a moment's notice.

SAUTE THE AROMATICS: In a large skillet, over medium-high heat, melt the butter. Once it begins to foam, add the leek, celery, and a pinch of both the salt and the pepper. Cook for about 5 minutes, or until the veggies soften, tossing frequently. Add the garlic, and sauté for 30 seconds until fragrant, then stir in the flour and cook, tossing for a couple minutes to toast.

SIMMER: Turn the heat to medium, and slowly whisk in the evaporated milk until combined. Add the wine and Creole seasoning, then reduce the heat to medium low and add the gnocchi. Allow the gnocchi to simmer until the sauce thickens, the gnocchi is tender, and the taste of wine cooks from the sauce, about 10 minutes. Stir in the lobster then the Gruyère cheese and cook just until the lobster has thawed and the cheese is melted.

SERVE: Divide across plates and grate over with the nutmeg to give some depth to the cream sauce before serving.

MAKE IT FANCY
Instead of plates, divide the gnocchi across gratin dishes, sprinkle the tops of each dish with **shredded Parmesan cheese** and crushed **saltine crackers**, and bake in a 450°F oven until golden brown and bubbling.

Tuna Furikake Casserole

SERVES
4 to 6
(NF, RSF)

wide egg noodles *or medium-length pasta, such as penne or rigatoni* 1/2 pound

Swiss & Ricotta Lemon Cream (recipe follows) 14 ounces (1 1/2 packed cups)

albacore tuna 1 (5-ounce) can in water or oil, drained ← or use leftover cooked salmon flaked into chunks (see Tip)

lemon juice 2 teaspoons

granulated garlic 1/2 teaspoon

hot sauce a few dashes, plus more for serving

plain panko breadcrumbs 1 cup

furikake 2 to 3 tablespoons (depending on the saltiness of the furikake)

shredded mild cheddar cheese *or sharp cheddar cheese* 1/2 cup (2 ounces)

olive oil 2 tablespoons, plus more as needed

TIP

To keep this casserole vegetarian, omit the tuna and double-check that your furikake doesn't contain dehydrated seafood derivatives. There are numerous varieties out there to choose from.

Here's a tuna casserole I can get behind. Classic egg noodles are folded into Swiss & Ricotta Lemon Cream—essentially just different cheeses mixed together in a bowl—to replace the canned cream of mushroom soup that the old-fashioned tuna casseroles call for. This one gets finished with a crunchy panko topping mixed with furikake, the Japanese sesame and seaweed seasoning that complements the seafood and brings salty, umami notes.

PREHEAT THE OVEN to 425°F.

COOK THE NOODLES: Bring a large pot of salted water to a boil, add the noodles, and cook according to package instructions.

MEANWHILE, PREP THE CASSEROLE: In a 2-quart (8-cup capacity) casserole dish, combine the Swiss & Ricotta Lemon Cream, tuna, lemon juice, granulated garlic, and hot sauce and set it aside.

MAKE THE PANKO TOPPING: In a medium mixing bowl, mixing with your hands, combine the panko, furikake, and cheddar cheese. Drizzle the olive oil over the mixture to dampen the breadcrumbs, tossing to coat, and adding more oil, if needed. Set aside.

MIX EVERYTHING TOGETHER: Once the noodles are done, use a spider or mesh strainer to remove them from the pot and add them directly to the casserole dish, along with **½ CUP OF THE PASTA WATER** and half of the panko topping mixture. Toss everything together to coat and begin melting the cheese, adding more pasta water if desired. Spread the noodles in an even layer to flatten.

BAKE THE CASSEROLE: Sprinkle over the remaining panko topping. Transfer the dish to the oven and bake, uncovered, for 15 to 20 minutes, until the topping is deeply golden brown and crispy and the cheese is gooey. Serve!

MAKE IT FANCY

Before baking, arrange ½ **pound fresh-sliced Roma, beefsteak, or Campari tomatoes** over top. (As the casserole bakes the tomato juices will trickle into the noodles giving them a pleasant sweetness that balances all that savory cheese and salty seaweed.)

Swiss & Ricotta Lemon Cream

MAKES ABOUT 2½ CUPS

I use this spread frequently, and you will find it called for throughout the book, like in the Tuna Furikake Casserole (page 106) and the Overnight Lasagna Terrine (page 116). It comes together easily and is wonderfully versatile. Use it as a filling for homemade ravioli, dollop it over grains or soups to add extra creaminess, spread it liberally on a pizza crust topped with ribbons of zucchini for an amazing white pizza, and if you have any remaining, make yourself a slice or two of cheesy avocado toast for a light dinner.

ricotta cheese (whole-milk or part-skim) 2 cups (16 ounces)

shredded Swiss and Gruyère cheese blend *or all Gruyère or all mozzarella* 1 cup

shredded Parmesan cheese 1 cup

grated lemon zest (from 1 large lemon)

granulated garlic 1 teaspoon

kosher salt 1 teaspoon

ground nutmeg (preferably freshly grated) ¼ teaspoon (see Tip)

freshly ground black pepper ½ teaspoon

COMBINE THE INGREDIENTS: In a large bowl, using a spoon, mix together the ricotta, Swiss cheese, Parmesan cheese, lemon zest, garlic, salt, nutmeg, and black pepper.

TIP Whole nutmeg seeds and whole peppercorns are even more powerful and fruity when they're freshly grated or coarsely cracked.

Eggplant Parm Ravioli

MAKES
25
RAVIOLI
(NF)

Effortless Marinara (page 112) *or a jarred marinara* (such as *Rao's*) 1½ to 2 cups

eggplant 1 pound (2 small or 1 medium), peeled and chopped into ¼-inch pieces (about 4 cups)

kosher salt 2 teaspoons, divided, plus more as needed

unsalted butter 1 tablespoon, plus 4 to 8 tablespoons melted, for serving

panko breadcrumbs *or plain or Italian-style breadcrumbs* 1 cup

olive oil 3 tablespoons, plus more as needed

yellow onion *or white onion* ½ cup diced

garlic cloves 4, chopped

red pepper flakes a pinch

dried oregano ½ teaspoon

lemon juice 2 tablespoons, plus more as needed

turbinado sugar *or granulated sugar* 1 teaspoon, plus more as needed

shredded Parmesan cheese ½ cup, plus more for serving

wonton wrappers 50 pieces (see Tip)

all-purpose flour, for dusting

fresh basil confetti'd, for topping

Some nights, comfort will be rolling out pasta dough from scratch (see Tip). Other nights, store-bought wonton wrappers give you a direct route to ravioli making. Either way when making this playful twist on classic eggplant Parm, you can tailor the total experience to what feels most comforting for you. These "ravioli" are stuffed with tender, cooked eggplant, boiled, then drizzled with melted butter and finished with toasted panko—because eggplant Parm just isn't complete without the crispy breading.

WARM THE MARINARA: Place the marinara sauce in a saucepan on the back burner over low heat to keep warm.

DRAIN THE EGGPLANT: Put the eggplant into a salad spinner and sprinkle over some salt. Allow to sit for 10 minutes, then spin to remove any excess water and bitterness.

MEANWHILE, TOAST THE BREADCRUMBS: Heat a large skillet over medium heat. Once hot, melt the 1 tablespoon butter and toast the breadcrumbs, tossing frequently, for 5 to 6 minutes, until golden brown. Set aside.

COOK THE EGGPLANT FILLING: Back in the same skillet over medium-high heat, drizzle in the olive oil and add the onion, garlic, red pepper flakes, and 1 teaspoon of the salt and cook for about 3 minutes. Add the eggplant, the remaining 1 teaspoon of salt, and the oregano and cook until soft, adding more oil if needed. Add **1 CUP OF WATER** to the mixture and cook for 3 to 5 more minutes, until most of the liquid cooks out. Then add half of the toasted breadcrumbs, the lemon juice, and turbinado sugar. Using the back of a spoon, mash the eggplant mixture until it becomes a chunky paste. Taste and add more sugar and lemon juice as desired. Reduce the heat and let it stew on medium for 10 to 12 minutes, until the eggplant is tender. Add the Parmesan cheese and stir until just melted. Transfer the mixture to a bowl to cool.

(recipe continues)

STUFF THE RAVIOLI: Lay the wonton wrappers on a lightly floured surface and carefully place about 1½ tablespoons of filling in the center of every other wonton wrapper, making sure to leave a border. Using your finger, brush a little water around the edges of the filling and place another wonton square on top to cover. Press around the edges and up to the filling to remove any air pockets to seal the pasta firmly.

COOK THE RAVIOLI: Bring a large pot of salted water to a boil over high heat and add the ravioli one at a time so they don't stick. Cook for 3 to 5 minutes, gently tossing them, being careful not to allow them to stick to the bottom of the pot, yet also being gentle with them so that they don't tear, until all the ravioli are tender and have floated to the surface.

SERVE: Using a slotted spoon or spider, remove the ravioli from the water, tapping away any excess water, and transfer to serving plates. Drizzle with the melted butter and sprinkle over the remaining breadcrumbs and some Parm. Spoon the warm marinara sauce over each and garnish with basil leaves.

TIP
TO MAKE HOMEMADE WHOLE WHEAT PASTA DOUGH FOR RAVIOLI:

Mix 2 cups whole wheat flour (or use all-purpose flour) with **a pinch of salt**, then create a well in the center and add **2 large eggs** and **1 tablespoon olive oil**. Gradually mix the flour into the eggs until a dough forms, then knead for about 10 minutes, or until smooth. Wrap in plastic wrap and let it rest for 30 minutes. After resting, roll the dough out on a lightly floured surface or use a pasta machine, working from the widest setting to the thinnest, until it's about 1/16-inch thick. Lay one sheet flat, spoon small portions of filling evenly spaced apart, then place another sheet on top. Press around the filling to seal, then cut into squares with a knife or pasta cutter. Or skip the ravioli concept altogether: Cut long noodles from the dough and cook them for 1 to 3 minutes in boiling water, until al dente, and pile the filling on top.

Pre-cut wonton wrappers are a brilliant hack for making speedy ravioli but they also make crunchy chips when baked or fried for dips and spreads.

Effortless Marinara

MAKES ABOUT 4 CUPS (32 OUNCES)
(EF, GF, NF, RSF, ≤30)

Because everyone should have their own homemade, simple marinara sauce, here's my 15-minute any-night-of-the-week version. This one is speedy-quick and a solid base recipe that you can tweak with powdered or freshly minced garlic, a leaf or two of basil or dried oregano, red wine, or whatever you think will bring flavor, and let it simmer longer; it's all up to you.

unsalted butter
2 tablespoons

olive oil 2 tablespoons

tomato paste
1 (6-ounce) can

crushed tomatoes
1 (28-ounce) can
(see Tip)

onion powder
1 tablespoon

kosher salt
2 teaspoons, plus more as needed

COOK THE TOMATO PASTE: In a medium saucepan with a lid over medium heat, melt the butter and olive oil. Once the butter begins to bubble and foam, add the tomato paste and let it cook for a few minutes, whisking until incorporated into the fat.

MAKE THE SAUCE: Add the crushed tomatoes. Fill the empty can with about **½ CUP WATER**. Swirl it around to collect any remaining sauce from the sides of the can and add that to the pan as well, along with the onion powder and salt.

SIMMER: Bring to a boil then reduce the heat to medium-low and simmer the sauce, partially covered, for 10 to 15 minutes. Taste and season with more salt, if desired.

TIP

CANS OF PRE-CRUSHED TOMATOES
Crushed tomatoes are just as delicious as some of the more expensive whole canned tomatoes out there and easy to doctor up, plus you won't have to dirty your hands crushing them yourself.

Wednesday Sauce

SERVES
16 to 20
(MAKES 8 CUPS)
(GF, RSF)

onion 1 large, chopped into large chunks

celery sticks 3 medium stalks, chopped into large chunks

carrots 3 medium, peeled and chopped into chunks

garlic cloves 6

roasted red peppers 1 (12-ounce) jar

sun-dried tomatoes packed in oil ½ cup

raw walnuts ½ pound (2¼ cups)

fresh rosemary 1 sprig, chopped

Porcini Butter (page 290) *or salted butter* ¼ cup, divided

olive oil 2 tablespoons

kosher salt 2 teaspoons, divided, plus more as needed

crushed red pepper flakes ½ teaspoon

tomato paste ¼ cup

dry red wine 1 cup ← or sub extra veggie broth plus a splash of balsamic vinegar

crushed tomatoes 1 (28-ounce) can

porcini water (see Porcini Butter, page 290) *or mushroom broth or veggie broth* 1 cup

bay leaves 2, dried or fresh

Here's a slow-simmering vegetarian Bolognese that you can ignore while it bubbles away on the stove. It can give you a foundation for hearty meals throughout the week: a layered lasagna in Overnight Lasagna Terrine (page 116), as a base for poaching eggs in Shakshuka Bolognese (page 226), spooned over a roasted spaghetti squash, or stuffed into cooked pasta shells for a last-minute pasta bake. I nickname this my "Mama Sauce." It can become the backbone for many meals, so it's been rightfully promoted to queen status in the kitchen.

MAKE THE VEGETABLE PASTE: To the bowl of a food processor fitted with a steel blade, blend the onion, celery, carrots, and garlic on high, stopping to scrape down the sides of the bowl as needed, until a coarse paste forms. Transfer the veggie paste to a bowl and set aside.

MAKE THE ROASTED PEPPER PUREE: In the same food processor bowl (no need to wash it), add the roasted red peppers with their brining liquid and blend until completely pureed. Pour the puree back into its original jar or into a separate bowl and set aside.

MAKE THE WALNUT MEAT: Next, in the same food processor bowl, add the sun-dried tomatoes with their oil and blend on high until ground. Remove the top and add the walnuts and rosemary, then pulse a few times until the walnuts are coarsely ground and the mixture looks like ground beef. Transfer the mixture to a bowl and set aside.

(recipe continues)

BUILD THE SAUCE: In a large Dutch oven or heavy-bottomed pot set over medium-high heat, melt 2 tablespoons of the Porcini Butter with the olive oil. Once they begin to bubble and brown, add the veggie paste, 1 teaspoon of the salt, and the crushed red pepper flakes. Cook, stirring occasionally, for 12 to 14 minutes, until the vegetables soften and begin to lightly caramelize. Add the walnut mixture and the remaining teaspoon of salt to the pan and cook, stirring frequently, for another 2 to 3 minutes, until the walnuts start to smell toasty. Push some of the mixture to the side of the pot and add the remaining 2 tablespoons of Porcini Butter and the tomato paste. Fry together for 1 minute to cook the paste before stirring everything together.

DEGLAZE AND SIMMER: Add the wine to deglaze the mixture, scraping up any bits of fond sticking to the bottom of the pan. Then add the pureed red peppers, crushed tomatoes, porcini water, and bay leaves. Taste and season with salt, if needed. Bring the pot to a boil, then reduce the heat to a simmer and cook, covered, stirring occasionally, for 2 hours, or until thickened and deeply flavorful. Taste and season with more salt, if needed.

SERVES
8

Overnight Lasagna Terrine

It's always a shame to layer lasagna only to slice into and watch all the sauce ooze out and the layers collapse. Using up the leftovers of our Wednesday Sauce (page 113) and our Swiss & Ricotta Lemon Cream (page 108), I set out to make lasagna that allowed me to really take in all its layers. I assembled it in a loaf pan, and instead of cutting it hot out of the oven, I patiently waited while it chilled in the fridge, then I cut it cold. The result is a beautiful baby loaf with distinct, alternating layers I can cut and reheat for dinner the next evening or throughout the week.

olive oil

oven-ready (no-boil) flat lasagna sheets 1 (9- or 12-ounce) package

leftover Wednesday Sauce (page 113) 3½ to 4 heaping cups

Swiss & Ricotta Lemon Cream (page 108) 1 recipe

Effortless Marinara (page 112) *or jarred marinara sauce*

MAKE IT FANCY

Stir **1 teaspoon white truffle oil** and **2 tablespoons pesto** (homemade or jarred) into the Swiss & Ricotta Lemon Cream before layering it into the lasagna.

PREHEAT THE OVEN to 375°F.

LAYER THE LASAGNA: Lightly oil a 9 x 5-inch loaf pan, and place two lasagna sheets in a single layer squarely on the bottom of the pan (it's okay if they overlap somewhat). Spoon over a third of the Wednesday Sauce (about 1 heaping cup), to make a ¼-inch-deep layer, smoothing the sauce to the edges and tapping the pan down on the counter to settle any air pockets.

Add another layer of lasagna sheets, breaking pieces as needed so they fit and cover all the sauce; again, it's okay if they overlap a bit. Using a spoon, dollop about a third of the ricotta cream over the top, carefully smoothing it to the edges. Continue alternating layers of sauce, lasagna, and ricotta cream, ending with a final layer of ricotta cream topped with lasagna sheets. Tap the pan down a final time, then brush the top lasagna sheets with olive oil or spoon over a thin amount of marinara to keep the sheets from drying out.

BAKE THE LASAGNA: Cover the loaf pan with foil and bake for 45 minutes. Remove from the oven and cool on a wire rack (while still in the pan).

(recipe continues)

CHILL THE LASAGNA: Refrigerate the lasagna in the pan overnight to allow the layers to set and flavors to build. You can make the lasagna up to 5 days ahead of when you plan to serve it and keep it stored in the fridge, or wrap and freeze for up to 2 months.

SLICE THE LASAGNA: When ready to serve, preheat the oven to 350°F and have a large cutting board ready. Remove the lasagna from the fridge and run a butter knife carefully along the edge of the loaf pan to help loosen it. Flip it over onto the cutting board and lightly tap the bottom of the loaf pan and wiggle it to release it completely. Using a serrated knife, cut the lasagna crosswise to make 8 to 10 equal slices.

RE-BAKE: Spoon a layer of marinara into the bottom of a large casserole dish. Arrange the lasagna slices over top in a flat layer and bake them in the oven for about 25 minutes, or until hot and crisped along the edges.

Shredded Carrot Flautas *with Carrot Top Salsa Verde*

SERVES

4

(EF, GF, NF, RSF)

CARROT FILLING

olive oil, for coating the pans and drizzling

carrots 1 pound, peeled, and green tops saved for serving and for the Carrot Top Salsa Verde (recipe follows) ← or sub 2 chicken breasts (1 pound)

onion 1 medium, thinly sliced

ground cumin 1 tablespoon

kosher salt 2 teaspoons

freshly ground black pepper 2 teaspoons

CARROT TOP SALSA VERDE (MAKES ABOUT 2½ CUPS)

tomatillos 1 pound, papery husks discarded, rinsed of their sticky film, and quartered

onion 1 medium, chopped

jalapeño peppers 2, halved through the stems, seeds and ribs discarded

garlic cloves 3, peeled

olive oil, for drizzling

kosher salt and **freshly ground black pepper**

carrot top leaves *or curly parsley* 1 packed cup, rinsed and drained, plus more for garnish

lime juice 1 tablespoon, plus more as needed

Flautas are my go-to Tex-Mex take-out meal, but they're so insanely easy to make at home that they've actually become my go-to weeknight dinner, too. This recipe encourages me to buy beautiful carrots with bushy tops. I blitz those greens into a simple, fabulous salsa verde I can use throughout the week. For instance, I add some fried tortilla chips to a skillet and smother them with this sauce and add a couple eggs to simmer, or I spoon it over grilled shrimp, veggie enchiladas, or over this migas-inspired Hot Mess Baked Potato (page 210). And because it freezes so well, I stow some in the freezer, until I come up with other tasty things to do with it.

PREHEAT THE OVEN to 450°F, arrange two racks in the center of the oven, and have two oiled sheet pans nearby. Cut the green tops off the carrots and set them aside for the salsa.

MAKE THE CARROT FILLING: Using a box grater, shred the carrots. On one prepared sheet pan, place the shredded carrots (or chicken breast, if using) with the onion. Sprinkle over the cumin, salt, and pepper and drizzle generously with olive oil. Toss everything together to coat, then spread evenly on the pan. Roast the veggies on the lower rack for about 20 minutes, or until the carrots and onion are tender, browned on their edges, but still have a slight bite (or the chicken registers 165° internally). Remove from the oven and set aside. If you're working with chicken, use two forks to shred the meat.

MAKE THE CARROT TOP SALSA VERDE: On the other prepared sheet pan place the tomatillos skin side up, along with the chopped onion, jalapeño halves (skin side up), and garlic. Drizzle everything lightly with olive oil, just to coat, and season lightly with salt and pepper. Roast in the oven on the upper rack for 15 minutes, rotating the pan about halfway through. Remove from the oven and let cool slightly. Set aside.

(recipe continues)

freshly squeezed orange juice 1/4 cup, plus more as needed

cilantro a large handful, some tender stems are fine

corn *or flour tortillas* 12 (6-inch) (see Tip)

avocado oil *or grapeseed or canola*, for frying

Mexican crema *or sour cream*, for serving

cotija cheese *or crumbled feta*, for serving

PUREE THE SALSA VERDE: Into a high-powered blender, place the cleaned carrot tops along with the roasted tomatillos, onion, and jalapeños. (You can just slide everything right off the pan and into the blender.) Add the lime juice, orange juice, and cilantro and blend to combine. Taste and adjust with more lime juice, orange juice, and salt, if needed, and set aside.

ROLL THE FLAUTAS: Have a sheet pan lined with paper towels nearby. Lay the tortillas down on a clean surface, and fill each with about 3 tablespoons of the filling, making a line about an inch from the edge of the tortillas. Roll the tortillas tightly around the filling and place them on the sheet pan seam side down. Repeat with the remaining filling and tortillas.

FRY THE FLAUTAS: Fill a 9-inch cast-iron skillet with about 1/4 inch avocado oil. Working in batches, once the oil starts to shimmer, place the flautas into the skillet seam side down to seal and cook for 3 to 4 minutes, until golden brown on all sides, using tongs to carefully turn them over in the oil. Once they're done, remove the flautas, tilting them to the side and pouring off any excess oil from their tips, before transferring back to the prepared sheet pan.

SERVE: Spoon a puddle of salsa verde into the center of a plate or shallow bowl and arrange 3 flautas on top. Drizzle over the crema, crumble over the Cotija cheese, and garnish with a carrot top leaf.

TIP For easier rolling, wrap the tortillas in a damp paper towel and warm them in the microwave on high for 10 to 15 seconds, so they're pliable and won't tear while rolling. But because tearing is sometimes inevitable, cut up any too-shredded tortillas, and throw them in the air fryer at 280° for 15 to 20 minutes (spritzing with cooking spray, like avocado spray or olive oil spray, and toss with a little salt halfway in) to make tortilla strips to use later on the migas-inspired Hot Mess Baked Potatoes (page 210).

Blackened Palm Stick Tacos

SERVES
4
(EF, NF, RSF)

HOMEMADE BLACKENED SEASONING

chili powder 2 tablespoons

freshly ground black pepper 1½ teaspoons

smoked paprika *or regular paprika* 1 teaspoon

dried oregano 1 teaspoon

garlic powder 1 teaspoon

onion powder 1 teaspoon

cayenne pepper ¼ teaspoon

kosher salt 1½ teaspoons, plus more as needed

PALM STICKS

all-purpose flour ¼ cup, plus more for dusting

milk of choice *or water* ½ cup

Old Bay Seasoning 1 teaspoon

juice of 1 lemon, plus wedges for serving

unseasoned panko breadcrumbs 1½ cups, plus more as needed

hearts of palm 2 (14-ounce jars or cans in water, not brine) drained ← I imagine you could sub ¾ pounds of shrimp

avocado oil *or olive oil*, for drizzling

These tacos were born from an attempt to break the habit of ordering out every other night from the taco joint down the street. Making them at home, complete with all the toppings, has now become its own therapeutic ritual my husband and I share. We carve out extra time, prep everything together, and in the end save ourselves from another takeout run. I recommend serving these with all the listed accoutrements, but don't stop there—throw in some mashed avocado or pico—make it a whole thing.

PREHEAT THE OVEN to 450°F and have a large sheet pan nearby.

MAKE THE BLACKENED SEASONING: In a small, shallow bowl, combine the chili powder, black pepper, smoked paprika, oregano, garlic powder, onion powder, cayenne pepper, and salt and set aside.

BREAD THE PALM STICKS: Place the palm sticks on a plate and dust them lightly with flour to coat. In a medium bowl, combine the remaining ¼ cup flour, the milk, Old Bay Seasoning, and lemon juice and mix together until smooth. In a separate medium bowl, combine the panko and the blackened seasoning and mix to combine. Roll a floured palm stick through the wet batter, shaking off any excess. Then transfer to the bowl of breadcrumbs, pressing the coating into the palm stick to help it adhere. Transfer the stick to the sheet pan and continue with the remaining palm sticks.

BAKE THE PALM STICKS: Drizzle the sticks with avocado oil and bake them for 18 to 20 minutes, until crispy and golden brown all over. Remove from the oven and chop into chunks.

flour tortillas *or corn tortillas* 12 (street-size or 6-inch)

avocado oil *or olive oil*

store-bought shredded cabbage/coleslaw mix 2 cups

frozen corn kernels *or fresh* 1 cup

kosher salt

TOPPINGS:
Whipped Chipotle Feta (recipe follows)

Very Green Ranch (page 277)

Pickled Pink Onions (page 287), for serving

MEANWHILE, CHAR THE TORTILLAS AND CABBAGE: Heat a large cast-iron skillet over high heat. Cook the tortillas on each side, until they begin to blacken and char in spots, about 30 seconds per side. Set aside on a plate and cover with a clean kitchen towel to keep warm. Back in the same pan, pour in a couple tablespoons of oil, then add the cabbage/coleslaw mix, the corn, and a pinch of salt. Cook for 1 or 2 minutes, until the cabbage is slightly charred and wilted and the corn has thawed. Remove the pan from the heat and set aside.

BUILD THE TACOS: Smear the tacos with chipotle feta, and top with the cabbage/corn mixture, pieces of palm, and a drizzle of green ranch. Garnish with Pickled Pink Onions and serve.

Whipped Chipotle Feta

MAKES ½ CUP
(EF, NF, RSF, ≤30)

Canned chipotles are another cabinet wonder that can transform dinner. They show up powerfully and pair well with delicate, sweet vehicles like creamy feta or avocado, which soften the heat. Spread this on Blackened Palm Stick Tacos (page 122), reserve some to smear on a plate beneath Roasted Rainbow Carrots (page 170) and on hot charred pita bread, dollop onto grain bowls, or simply serve it on a veggie tray as a spicy alternative to ranch.

feta cheese 4 ounces, crumbled

heavy cream 1/4 cup

canned chipotles in adobo 1 pepper, seeds removed (depending on spice preference), plus 1 teaspoon of the sauce (see Tip)

garlic powder 1 teaspoon

olive oil 2 tablespoons

lime juice 1 tablespoon

pure maple syrup *or honey* 1 teaspoon

BLEND AND STORE THE SAUCE: In the bowl of a food processor fitted with the steel blade attachment, combine the feta, heavy cream, chipotle peppers and the adobo sauce, the olive oil, lime juice, maple syrup, and garlic powder. Blend on high until smooth. Taste and add more salt as desired. Transfer to a lidded container and store in the fridge for up to 2 weeks.

MAKE IT FANCY

Chill the spread for a couple hours until firm, then shape into small discs, roll the discs in panko breadcrumbs or crushed nuts, freeze until hardened, and pan-fry them until golden brown to serve over a green leaf salad with a fresh citrusy vinaigrette.

Soy-Glazed Lychee Lettuce Wraps

SERVES
2
(OR 4 IF YOU SERVE WITH RICE)

(DF)

canned (no sugar added) peeled and pitted lychees 2 (11-ounce) cans

LYCHEE GINGER DRIZZLE
reserved lychee syrup

fresh ginger 2 tablespoons, peeled and minced

scallions ¼ cup (from about 2), both green and white parts, thinly sliced

soy sauce 4 teaspoons

toasted sesame oil 2 teaspoons

chili garlic sauce (such as sambal oelek or Sriracha) 1 teaspoon

avocado oil *or grapeseed oil* 2 tablespoons

One night, after being highly inspired by the bountiful spirit of David Chang's Bo Ssam—a slow-roasted pork shoulder served with pickled veg—my husband and I made savory glazed lychees. I found some cans in the pantry from a dessert recipe I'd hoped to test, but one thing led to another and I was pleasantly surprised to discover that cooking lychees in a sticky soy glaze turns them into something that resembles juicy bites of pork belly. Pair these lettuce wraps with crisp veggies and warm Sticky Stovetop Coconut Rice (page 162).

DRAIN THE LYCHEES: Place a strainer over a small bowl and drain the canned lychee to collect the syrup and separate the fruit. Put the fruit in a separate bowl and set both bowls aside.

MAKE DRIZZLE (SEE TIP): In a third small bowl, whisk ½ cup of the reserved lychee syrup, the ginger, scallions, soy sauce, sesame oil, sambal oelek, and avocado oil together and set aside for the flavors to come together while you prepare the next steps.

MAKE THE GLAZE: In a fourth small bowl, combine the soy sauce, brown sugar, vinegar, and 1 tablespoon of the reserved lychee syrup and whisk together until the brown sugar has dissolved. Set aside.

SEAR THE LYCHEES: Heat a medium heavy-bottomed pot over medium-high heat. Drizzle in the oil, then add the drained lychee fruit and fry them for about 5 minutes, or until crisp and dark brown in spots, tossing occasionally so all their sides are seared well. Use the lid to protect yourself from any splattering oil.

(recipe continues)

SOY GLAZE

soy sauce 1/4 cup

light brown sugar 3 tablespoons packed

rice vinegar 1 tablespoon

reserved lychee syrup

avocado oil *or grapeseed oil* 1/4 cup, for frying

lettuce cups (from Bibb or butter leaf) 8 to 12

unsalted dry-roasted peanuts crushed, for topping

crunchy veggies (such as sugar snap peas, snow peas, shredded carrots, shredded radishes, shredded purple cabbage, etc.), for serving

cooked rice, for serving

ADD THE GLAZE: Stir the glaze to redistribute any sugar that has settled to the bottom and pour it over the lychees, tossing to coat. Cook for about another 5 minutes, tossing every 30 seconds or so, until the sauce has thickened, the soy sauce is beginning to caramelize, and the lychees are dark brown and glazed all over. Remove the pot from the heat.

SERVE: Transfer the lychees to a serving bowl and serve alongside lettuce cups, crushed roasted peanuts, crunchy veggies, the ginger drizzle, and cooked rice.

TIP This recipe makes extra lychee ginger drizzle. You can put the sumptuous sauce on nearly anything—a juicy, chopped tomato and avocado salad (!); cheesy scrambled eggs; a steamy bowl of congee/creamy rice soup (simmer 1 cup of short- or medium-grain rice with 8 cups water or broth over low heat for 1 to 2 hours until creamy, stirring occasionally); or even use it to marinate tofu.

MAKE IT FANCY
Shake yourself a Lychee Martini while you cook: Combine 2 ounces vodka (or favorite nonalcoholic vodka or gin) with 2 ounces leftover lychee syrup and a handful of ice in a cocktail shaker. Shake well, strain into a chilled martini glass, and serve.

MAKES

8

BUNS

(NF, RSF)

"Tidy" Joe Milk Buns

Japanese milk buns are a special weekday baking project that can give your mind something to settle on, and your teeth something to *literally* sink into with great pleasure. They're gaining popularity here in the States because of their cushiony body that sets them far apart from ordinary dinner rolls. The whole milk in the dough creates a rich flavor and a touch of sweetness, and the tangzhong, a gel-like paste made of cooked milk, water, and flour, helps the buns retain moisture, resulting in the ultimate steamy and feathery bread pull. I fill these with a sloppy joe mix (which you can make up to 3 days in advance) but, of course, you can fill them with absolutely anything, from leftover Walnut Chili (page 194) to peanut butter and jelly, or simply leave them empty.

TIDY JOE FILLING

olive oil 2 tablespoons

onion ½ cup diced

red bell pepper ¼ cup diced (from about ½ a bell pepper)

kosher salt 1 teaspoon, plus more as needed

lean ground beef *or beef substitute* ½ pound

tomato paste ¼ cup

vegetable bouillon paste ½ teaspoon

light brown sugar 2 tablespoons packed

Worcestershire sauce *or smokey coconut amino acids* 2 teaspoons

chili powder 2 teaspoons

garlic powder ½ teaspoon

distilled white vinegar ¼ cup

shredded cheddar cheese ½ cup (8 tablespoons) (optional)

MILK BUNS

TANGZHONG

bread flour 2 tablespoons (8 grams)

whole milk 3 tablespoons (15 grams)

MAKE THE FILLING: In a large skillet over medium heat, heat the oil. Once it starts to shimmer, add the onion, bell pepper, and a pinch of salt. Cook for several minutes, tossing occasionally, until the onion has softened. Add the meat and a pinch of the salt and break up with a wooden spoon. Cook for about 5 minutes, or until browned. Move the beef to the side of the pan, add the tomato paste to the pan, and cook for a minute before stirring into the meat. Then add the bouillon paste, sugar, Worcestershire sauce, chili powder, garlic powder, and another pinch of salt and cook for 1 to 2 more minutes. Deglaze the pan with the vinegar and **¼ CUP WATER**, stirring to thin the mixture. Remove the pan from the heat and set it aside to cool completely and let the flavors meld.

MAKE THE MILK BUNS: In a small saucepan, off the heat, whisk the flour and **3 TABLESPOONS WATER** until smooth and then whisk in the milk. Place the pan over medium-low heat and cook, whisking continuously, until the mixture thickens after a couple minutes. Remove the pan from the heat and set aside to cool. This is the tangzhong.

(recipe continues)

DOUGH

bread flour 2½ cups (325 grams), plus more for dusting

granulated sugar ¼ cup (50 grams)

kosher salt 1 teaspoon (3 grams)

instant yeast 1 tablespoon (9 grams)

whole milk ½ cup (120 grams)

egg 1 large

unsalted butter 4 tablespoons, melted and cooled slightly

GOLDEN EGG WASH (SEE TIP)

egg yolk 1 large

whole milk *or heavy cream* 2 tablespoons

kosher salt a pinch

sesame seeds, for sprinkling (optional)

TIP

To make your baked goods more attractive, brush them with a rich Golden Egg Wash before baking. This mixture will produce the glossiest, most golden and stunning crusts every. Single. Time.

KNEAD THE DOUGH: In the bowl of a stand mixer, place the cooled tangzhong, the flour, sugar, salt, yeast, milk, egg, and butter. Combine roughly with your hands, then knead for about 10 minutes on medium speed with the dough hook attachment, scraping down the sides of the bowl as needed, until the dough becomes smooth and elastic and stops sticking to the sides of the bowl. You can do this by hand as well, but it takes a while. (A good way to tell it's ready is to stretch a piece of the dough between your fingers. You should be able to stretch it and almost see through it without it tearing.)

SHAPE AND RISE THE DOUGH: On a lightly floured countertop, shape the dough into a ball and transfer it to a large lightly greased bowl. Cover the bowl and let it rise for 1 hour to 1½ hours, until doubled in size.

FILL THE BUNS: Have a greased 9-inch cake pan nearby. Gently deflate the dough and, using a bench scraper or knife, separate the dough into 8 equal pieces. Lightly oil your hands and, on a clean work surface, working one piece at a time, while keeping the remaining dough still covered, shape each piece into a 4-inch disk. Into the center of the dough, add about 1 tablespoon cheese (if using) and top with one-eighth of the filling (about ⅓ cup). Gently stretch the dough around the filling and pinch the ends closed to seal well. Flip the ball over and arrange it in the cake pan seam side down. Continue with the rest of the dough.

SECOND RISE: Cover the rolls with a damp cloth and let them rest for another 25 to 30 minutes until puffed. Toward the end of the second rise, preheat the oven to 350°F.

MAKE THE EGG WASH: In a small bowl, whisk the egg yolk, milk, and salt together and set it aside.

BAKE: Once the buns have risen, brush them lightly with the egg wash and sprinkle with sesame seeds (if using). Bake them for 28 to 30 minutes, until golden brown. Remove the pan from the oven and allow to rest on the counter for a few minutes before carefully transfering to a platter and allowing to cool for another 10 to 15 minutes. Serve warm, allowing people to pull at the rolls at will.

Crunchy-Bottom Cast Iron Fried Rice *with "Egg Rolls"*

SERVES
4 to 6
(NF)

uncooked sushi rice (such as Botan Calrose) 1½ cups (see Tip)

kosher salt

unsalted butter 2 tablespoons

avocado oil *or other neutral oil* 2 tablespoons, plus more as needed

soy sauce ¼ cup ← preferably 1 tablespoon dark soy sauce + 3 tablespoons light soy sauce

toasted sesame oil 2 teaspoons

rice vinegar 1½ tablespoons

granulated sugar 1 teaspoon

onion (*white or yellow*) ½ cup diced

carrots *or red or yellow bell pepper* ½ cup diced

celery ½ cup diced

garlic cloves 1 tablespoon chopped

fresh ginger 1 tablespoon chopped

frozen peas *or frozen corn* ½ cup

"EGG ROLLS"
eggs 2 large

toasted sesame oil ½ to 1 teaspoon

scallion (the green parts) 1 tablespoon finely chopped

kosher salt

butter or oil ½ tablespoon, for frying

When I make fried rice at home, I tailor it to my preferences and pantry; I always add whatever protein or chopped/diced veggies I have on hand. I'm highly addicted to adding kimchi and finishing it off with Thai basil and chili crisp for a bit of punch. I also cook the eggs in a separate pan, splash them with a little sesame oil, and roll them up into little bites to serve on the side. This way, I still enjoy the delicate flavors of the rice and as a bonus, I have unmuddled, pillowy eggs that happen to look pretty and bright yellow.

COOK THE RICE: Into a medium pot with a lid, combine the sushi rice along with **2 CUPS WATER**, and a pinch of salt. Bring the pot to a boil, then cover with the lid slightly ajar and reduce the heat to medium-low. Cook for about 20 minutes, or until the rice is tender and all the liquid has absorbed. Transfer the rice to a large mixing bowl and set aside.

MELT THE BUTTER: Heat a well-seasoned 10-inch cast-iron skillet over medium-high heat and melt the butter until it begins to foam. Pour the butter over the rice. Add the soy sauce, sesame oil, vinegar, and sugar and fluff everything together with a fork to coat each grain. Set aside.

SAUTÉ THE VEGGIES: Back in the buttery skillet, add the onion, carrots, celery, garlic, ginger, and a pinch of salt and cook, for 4 to 5 minutes, tossing often and lowering the heat if needed, until the onions begin to soften.

FRY THE RICE: Add the oil to the skillet, then add the rice mixture and the peas. Cook over high heat for 2 to 3 minutes, tossing constantly, then turn the heat to medium low, and spread the rice

(recipe continues)

over the bottom of the skillet, pressing down with the spatula to flatten. Cook for 6 to 8 minutes, this time undisturbed, until the bottom is deep golden brown and sticks together to form a crust.

MEANWHILE, COOK THE "EGG ROLLS": In a small bowl, whisk together the eggs, sesame oil, scallions, and a pinch of salt. Heat a small skillet over medium heat and melt the butter, swirling the pan to coat. Add the egg mixture and swirl the pan to spread in a thin, even layer. Cook until the egg is completely set on the bottom but a little undercooked on top. Using a rubber spatula, scoot the egg out of the pan onto a cutting board. Starting at one end of the egg, roll it over itself to create a tight cigar shape. Using a sharp knife, cut into thin rolls.

SERVE: Place a large plate over the skillet and carefully flip the rice out onto the plate. Scatter the rolled eggs over top, and serve.

MAKE IT FANCY

Build out a full spread and serve this with Orange Tofu with Star Anise (page 134) along with a semidry bubbly wine or champagne.

TIP

The trick to making crispy-bottomed fried rice is to use unrinsed sushi rice, which is super starchy and crisps well in a hot skillet.

SERVES

4

(DF, EF, NF)

navel oranges *or blood oranges* 2 large

firm or extra-firm tofu 1 (14 to 16 ounce) block, drained and patted dry (see Tip page 24)

cornstarch *or arrowroot starch* 1/4 cup plus 1 tablespoon, divided

baking powder 1/2 teaspoon

kosher salt 1/2 teaspoon

freshly ground black pepper *or white pepper* 1/2 teaspoon

neutral oil (such as avocado, grapeseed, or canola), for frying

vegetable broth 1/2 cup

light brown sugar 1/2 cup packed

whole star anise 4

soy sauce (preferably 1/2 dark, 1/2 light) 2 tablespoons

rice wine vinegar 1/4 cup

Orange Tofu with Star Anise

Adding star anise to an orange sauce adds a subtle licorice complexity that cuts through the sometimes too-sweet sauce that accompanies the dish. While you would never eat the star anise whole, they're definitely too beautiful to leave off the plate, and they'll break up the monotony of all that orange color. Serve this with frozen or fresh steamed veggies or Crunchy-Bottom Cast Iron Fried Rice (page 131) for a full dinner spread.

PREP THE ORANGES: Using a citrus zester or Microplane, zest the navel oranges. Using a sharp knife, cut one orange in half and squeeze the juice into a small bowl and set aside. Supreme the other orange by cutting off both the top and bottom of the orange, right where the peel meets the flesh. Then, slowly begin cutting down and around the orange to remove the rest of the peel in strips. With the sharp base of your knife, cut between the white piths to release the segments of the orange. Squeeze the last bit of juice from the scraps over the bowl of orange juice and then discard the innards. Set the segmented oranges aside.

CUT AND BREAD THE TOFU: Using a sharp knife, and with the long end of the tofu block facing you, cut it in half and then cut each half into 4 pieces. Rotate the entire block of tofu 90 degrees, then cut the block in half. You should now have 16 pieces. Cut each piece diagonally across the width to make 32 triangles. In a small bowl, add the 1/4 cup of cornstarch, the baking powder, salt, and black pepper, then sprinkle the tofu pieces with the starch mixture, tossing to coat.

(recipe continues)

FRY THE TOFU: Have a paper towel–lined sheet pan or plate nearby. In a large skillet over high heat, drizzle in enough oil to coat the bottom of the pan. As soon as the oil starts to shimmer, add the tofu pieces in a single layer with a little space between them, working in batches if you need to so you don't overcrowd the pan. Fry for 2 to 3 minutes on each side, until their outsides crisp and turn light golden brown. Remove the tofu from the pan and set aside on the prepared sheet pan. (Alternatively, you can spray the pieces with cooking spray and cook them in batches in the air-fryer at 400°F for 8 to 10 minutes until crisp.)

MAKE THE ORANGE SAUCE: Wipe the skillet down removing any remaining oil. To the pan, add the broth, the brown sugar, the reserved orange juice, the orange zest, and star anise. (Hold off on adding the orange segments until the end so they don't break down in the sauce.) Bring the mixture to a heavy simmer and cook for 5 to 6 minutes, until the star anise becomes very fragrant and the sugar dissolves.

THICKEN THE SAUCE: In a separate bowl, whisk together the remaining 1 tablespoon of cornstarch and the soy sauce to make a smooth slurry, then whisk in the vinegar. Pour the starch mixture into the orange sauce and continue to cook on medium-high heat until the sauce is thick like maple syrup, another 5 to 6 minutes.

FINISH: Add the tofu back into the skillet along with the orange segments, gently tossing everything together to combine. Spoon onto plates over a mound of hot steaming rice and serve.

MAKE IT FANCY

Add **2 tablespoons diced candied ginger** to the mix to take it over the top with chewy pops of spice. Personally, I would say this part is *not* optional.

SERVES
4
(DF, RSF)

shallots 3 to 4 large (½ pound) *or 1 medium white onion (½ pound)*

lean ground beef *or Beyond Meat* 1 pound

panko breadcrumbs *or regular breadcrumbs or almond meal/flour* 1 cup

berbere spice 2½ teaspoons, divided

kosher salt ¼ teaspoon, plus more as needed

freshly ground black pepper ¼ teaspoon, plus more as needed

olive oil 4 tablespoons, divided

unbleached all-purpose flour *or gluten-free all-purpose flour* 3 tablespoons

vegetable bouillon paste 1 teaspoon

fresh sage leaves 4 to 5

Parsnip Puree (recipe follows) *or mashed potatoes*, for serving

Salisbury Steak

with Berbere Gravy and Sage + a Parsnip Puree

Salisbury steak was never truly easy on the eyes, but because it's always been a simple, tasty, and convenient meal, I felt compelled to modernize it by simmering the gravy with sage and Ethiopian berbere spice to add some elegance and life without losing the integrity of the original dish. I love this, especially over a bed of orange peel–infused Parsnip Puree.

CUT THE SHALLOTS: Using a sharp knife, trim the tops of the shallots (not the root), then break the shallot into cloves (if any), discard their skins, and cut them in half lengthwise to expose their layers, leaving the root still intact. If using the onion, trim off the top of the onion, and then cut the onion in half through the root, leaving the root intact. Discard the skin. Cut the halves through the root to make 8 pieces/wedges. Set them aside.

SHAPE THE PATTIES: In a medium mixing bowl, combine the ground beef, panko breadcrumbs, 1 teaspoon of the berbere spice, the salt, and the pepper. Mix with your hands to combine. Divide the mixture into four equal mounds (see Tip) and mold the mounds into oval patties.

COOK THE PATTIES: In a large skillet over medium-high heat, heat 2 tablespoons of the olive oil. Once the oil begins to shimmer, add the patties and fry for 1 to 2 minutes on each side just to brown. Transfer the patties to a plate and set aside.

SEAR THE SHALLOTS: Back in the same hot skillet over medium heat, using another tablespoon of olive oil, add the shallots cut side down and season with a little more salt. Cook the shallots without disturbing for 2 to 3 minutes, until they're deep golden brown and caramelized on one side. Transfer the shallots to the plate with the patties, being careful not to break them apart.

(recipe continues)

MAKE THE GRAVY: Back in the same skillet, with the heat reduced to medium, heat the remaining tablespoon of olive oil. Add the remaining berbere spice, the flour, and bouillon paste and, using a whisk, scrape up any fond (charred bits of food still clinging to the pan) and cook the flour for about a minute to remove its raw taste. Slowly drizzle in about **2 CUPS WATER**, whisking constantly so there are no dry clumps of flour and the liquid is fully incorporated. Add the sage leaves and cook until the gravy thickens, another 2 to 3 minutes.

SIMMER: Transfer the patties (and any juices) along with the shallots (cut side up) back to the skillet with the gravy and simmer for 10 to 12 minutes, until the patties are cooked through and the shallots are tender. Remove from the heat and serve over a bed of Parsnip Puree (see Tip).

TIP Flatten your mixture evenly into the base of the mixing bowl, and using the sides of your hands score it horizontally and vertically, like you're cutting wedges out of a pie to make portions roughly the same size.

For better presentation, hold back the sauce (in this case, the gravy) so that the different elements of the dish don't get buried, then spoon it over the dish at the end in a controlled way.

MAKE IT FANCY

Top the finished dish with a crisped sage leaf: Rinse a handful of fresh sage leaves, pat them dry, and spray them with cooking spray or brush them with oil, then lay them in a single layer in the air fryer and cook at 400°F for 2 to 3 minutes or until completely dehydrated.

Parsnip Puree

SERVES 4
(DF, GF, NF, RSF, ≤5 , ≤30)

It's high time we graduate from potatoes and start turning other veggies like squash or peas into silky smooth purees. Parsnips are one of my favorites to puree. They're just as creamy as potatoes but have notes of anise and citrus that also complement meaty dishes like Salisbury Steak with Berbere Gravy (page 137). Try pureeing celeriac root, peas, or butternut squash, too. Add a splash of cream or a couple pats of cold butter to a puree to make it creamier, if you wish, or keep it simple, like I did here, giving the vegetable all the spotlight.

oranges 2, peel only (optional)

parsnips 2 pounds, peeled and chopped into 1-inch chunks

kosher salt

PEEL THE ORANGES (IF USING): Using a vegetable peeler, peel the oranges, then using a spoon scrape away any bitter white piths from the underside of the zest.

BOIL THE PARSNIPS: Place the parsnips, orange peels, if using, and a generous pinch of salt in a medium saucepan and cover with water. Bring the water to a boil and cook for 10 to 12 minutes, until the parsnips are fork-tender with no resistance. Reserve about ½ cup of the water for blending, then drain the remaining liquid, discarding the orange zest.

PUREE: In a high-powered blender, puree the drained parsnips on high until completely smooth, stopping to scrape down the sides of the bowl as needed. If you prefer a thinner puree, add the reserved water, a little at a time, until it's to your desired consistency. Serve.

Maybe Auntie Nae's Baked Creole Tetrazzini

SERVES
8
(NF)

kosher salt

dried spaghetti noodles 1 pound

unsalted butter *or olive oil* 4 tablespoons

Creole seasoning (such as Tony Chachere's) 2 teaspoons

paprika ½ teaspoon, plus more for sprinkling

garlic powder 2 teaspoons

dried thyme *or oregano* 1 teaspoon

freshly ground black pepper 1 teaspoon

cayenne pepper ½ teaspoon

whole milk *or milk of choice* 3 cups

plain full-fat cream cheese 4 ounces, cubed into pieces

shredded cheddar cheese 2 cups, plus more for sprinkling

Parsley Dust (page 27)

There are a few recipes throughout my life that stick out in my mind, and Auntie Nae's spicy creole tetrazzini is definitely one. I finally re-created the tetrazzini for which my aunt never shared her recipe. At least I think I did? She'd make her noodles so very peppery and creamy, and here, I try to keep in that same spicy spirit with not only a generous bit of black pepper, but also Creole seasoning, hot sauce, *and* a little bit of cayenne, too. If you're scared, don't be; the cream cheese helps temper some of that heat. My favorite thing about this recipe: that I've spent years on a winding, wondrous journey trying to figure out how to recreate it from memory.

PREHEAT THE OVEN to 375°F.

BOIL THE NOODLES: Bring a large Dutch oven or heavy-bottomed pot of salted water to a boil over high heat. Add the noodles and cook them according to package instructions, then drain the noodles into a colander and return the pot to the stove.

TOAST THE SPICES: Heat the pot over medium heat. Melt the butter and, once it begins to foam and sizzle, add the spices—the Creole seasoning, paprika, garlic powder, thyme, black pepper, and cayenne pepper—and cook for about 30 seconds, stirring constantly, until fragrant. Add in the cooked noodles, tossing to coat.

MAKE THE CREAM SAUCE: Pour in the milk, then add the cream cheese, tossing until the cream cheese has melted. Add the shredded cheddar cheese, tossing until melted and a thick sauce coats the noodles. Taste and adjust seasonings as needed.

BAKE AND SERVE: Arrange the pasta evenly in the pot and sprinkle over a little more cheese and paprika for color. Cover the pot and transfer it to the oven to bake for 15 to 20 minutes, until the cheese has melted and the pasta is set. Remove the pot from the oven, sprinkle over the Parsley Dust, and allow to cool slightly before serving.

MAKE IT FANCY
Toss sliced mushrooms, cubed chicken, or jumbo shrimp with salt or extra Creole seasoning and throw them in the pot with the sizzling butter. Or, for color, fold in ½ pound halved grape or cherry tomatoes right before sending everything into the oven.

SERVES

4 TO 8

(EF, RSF)

Double Stacked Smash-Bean Burgers

with Sweet Corn Crema

SWEET CORN CREMA

sweet corn kernels 1 cup (frozen or freshly cut from 1 cob)

sour cream *or Greek yogurt* ¼ cup

lime ½ small, zested and juiced

garlic clove 1

sweet paprika *or chile powder* 1 teaspoon

kosher salt ½ teaspoon

SMASHED BLACK BEAN BURGERS

canned black beans 2 (15-ounce) cans, drained and rinsed

scallions 6 large, both green and white parts, halved and cut into medium strips

tortillas chips *or breadcrumbs* ¼ cup finely ground

canned chipotle peppers in adobo 2 peppers, finely chopped

avocado oil *or butter*, for frying

unsalted butter, for toasting

hamburger buns 4 (or 8)

hamburger pickles, shredded iceberg lettuce, and beefsteak tomatoes, for topping

Everything is smashable in this recipe, so if you really want to release some pent-up tension on a bowl of beans, this is a good one. Add the tortilla chips to a zip-top bag and go at it with a rolling pin or mallet. They should be as fine as breadcrumbs. And remember, you're really pressing down on those patties when you're cooking them—you want as much surface area getting charred as possible so you don't end up with an abominable mushy veggie burger. The mix makes enough to double stack your burgers, although they're just as delicious one patty high.

MAKE THE CREMA (SEE TIP): In the bowl of a mini food processor fitted with a steel blade, put the corn, sour cream, lime zest, lime juice, garlic, paprika, and salt and pulse on high until combined. The sauce will be chunky from the bits of corn. Set aside until ready to serve.

MAKE THE BEAN BURGERS: In a large mixing bowl, mash the black beans with a fork until you have a paste with some chunks of black beans. Add the scallions, tortillas chips, and chipotles and continue mixing everything thoroughly. Mold the balls into 8 equal-size balls and set them aside on a tray.

FRY THE BURGERS: Have a 4- or 5-inch square of parchment or wax paper nearby. Heat a large griddle pan or cast-iron skillet over medium-high heat. Brush the griddle pan with oil. Add the balls to the pan, leaving at least 2 inches of space around each ball. Depending on the size of your pan, you will need to cook them in batches. Place the piece of parchment over a ball—this will prevent your spatula from sticking—and with a wide spatula, smash the ball down into a flat patty, about ¼ inch thick. Lift the parchment and repeat with the remaining balls in the pan. Cook the patties for 2 to 4 minutes per side. You'll know they're ready to flip when you can get your spatula underneath without them tearing. Transfer the patties to a plate and set aside.

TOAST THE BUNS: To make the softest burger joint–style, pillowy buns ever, butter the cut side of the buns and, after cooking the patties, place the buns on the pan for 1 to 2 minutes, until toasted. Meanwhile, add a small splash of water to the pan to create steam, then hold a sheet pan or large lid over the buns to help trap in the steam.

BUILD THE BURGERS: Coat the bottom of each bun with a smear of the corn crema. Top with pickles, shredded lettuce, then 1 to 2 bean patties, and then add a couple slices of tomatoes. Dollop on more corn crema. Place the top of the bun on the tomatoes, smashing it down slightly. (They are called smash burgers after all.)

MAKE IT FANCY

Add **2 ounces crumbled goat cheese, cotija, or feta cheese** to the top of the burgers for extra creaminess and tang.

TIP The leftover sweet corn crema can be spooned over a cobb salad or over a warm potato salad by tossing a couple large spoonfuls with a ½ pound small roasted red potatoes, a splash of vinegar, scallions, and crumbled bacon or Shiitake Lardons (page 82).

SERVES

3 TO 4

(RSF)

raw beets (preferably golden) (see Headnote) 1¼ pounds (from about 3 medium beets), peeled and shredded (about 3 packed cups) (see Tip)

raw walnut halves or pieces 1 cup, finely ground

coconut aminos *or Worcestershire sauce* 1 teaspoon

onion powder 1 teaspoon

ground allspice 1 teaspoon

kosher salt 1½ teaspoons, divided

crushed red pepper flakes ¼ teaspoon, plus more as needed

egg 1 large

olive oil, for frying

unsalted butter 2 tablespoons

garlic cloves 2, chopped

whole milk 1½ to 2 cups

all-purpose flour *or gluten-free all-purpose flour* 1 tablespoon

ground nutmeg ⅛ teaspoon

crumbled Gorgonzola cheese *or blue cheese* ½ cup (4 ounces)

beet tops *or Swiss chard, kale, or spinach* ½ pound, cleaned and chopped (2 packed cups)

Gorgonzola Beetballs

with Creamed Beet Greens

These are inspired by Ikea meatballs (the ones we all stumble on while re-upping on more kitchen towels) and creamed spinach. These balls are made from glorious golden beets, which are sweeter, milder, and more nutty than earthy red beets, and they also don't bleed. Golden beets make for a more attractive cream sauce, which I make with the green beet tops. Serve this dish over rice or mashed potatoes.

PREHEAT THE OVEN to 375°F with the rack positioned in the middle of the oven.

SHAPE THE BEETBALLS: In a large mixing bowl, add the beets, walnuts, coconut aminos, onion powder, allspice, 1 teaspoon of the salt, the red pepper flakes, and egg. Using clean hands, mix everything together to combine. Roughly divide the mixture into 12 equal mounds and shape the mounds into balls, tossing back and forth between your hands to compact them. They will be delicate and moist but should still hold their shape.

BROWN THE BEETBALLS: Heat a large cast-iron skillet over medium-high heat. Once it's hot, coat the bottom of the pan with olive oil, then place the beetballs in the pan. This will give them a nice bottom crust. Place the skillet in the oven and bake for 30 to 35 minutes, until the balls are firm and deep golden brown.

MEANWHILE, MAKE THE CREAM SAUCE: In a medium saucepan over medium-high heat, melt the butter. Add the garlic and sauté for 1 to 2 minutes, until the garlic and butter are fragrant and the garlic is lightly toasted. Add the milk, flour, nutmeg, Gorgonzola cheese, and the remaining ½ teaspoon of salt and bring to a low simmer, being careful to never let it boil. Stir in the beet tops and cook for 1 to 2 minutes, until slightly wilted, then turn off the heat.

(recipe continues)

SMOTHER THE BEETBALLS: Once the beetballs have finished cooking, remove the skillet from the oven, increase the oven temperature to 450°, and pour the cream sauce evenly over the beetballs.

RETURN TO THE OVEN: Place the skillet back into the oven and bake for another 15 to 20 minutes, until the sauce has thickened and is lightly golden brown on top. Remove the skillet from the oven, and carefully turn the meatballs over in the sauce to coat.

SERVE: Spoon a few beetballs into bowls over rice, mashed potatoes, or alone, spooning extra cream sauce over top before serving.

TIP

You can shred your peeled beets on a box grater, but you can also use your food processor with the shredder attachment for a cleaner and breezier experience.

Sweet 'n' Sourdough Coconut Cauliflower Skewers

MAKES ABOUT
8
SKEWERS
(DF, EF, NF)

medium wooden skewers 8 to 10

jarred apricot preserves 1/2 cup

Sriracha 1 tablespoon, plus more as needed

kosher salt 1/4 teaspoon, plus more as needed

neutral oil (such as avocado, canola, or grapeseed), for frying

small cauliflower florets 1 pound (about 4 heaping cups)

active sourdough starter 1 cup (240 grams), plus more as needed (see Tip page 148 for substitute)

sweetened or unsweetened coconut flakes (keep in mind, sweetened will darken faster in the oil) 1 1/2 cups

MAKE IT FANCY

Add **a thinly sliced red Fresno chile** to the sauce as it cooks for sharper heat.

These cauliflower skewers satisfy my sweet 'n' sour takeout cravings while also proving we can feel fancy with nothing fresh in the house except that same head of cauliflower that's been living in the back of the fridge and our bubbling sourdough starter we call "Champ." Serve this over steamed rice with broccoli florets or Carrot & Miso Wedge Salad (page 184).

SOAK THE SKEWERS: Add the skewers to a shallow bowl, and cover with water, and allow to soak for at least 30 minutes. Set aside.

MEANWHILE, MAKE THE SAUCE: In a small saucepan, combine the apricot preserves (see Tip), Sriracha, **1/4 CUP WATER**, and the salt. Cook for about 5 minutes over medium heat, stirring occasionally, or until the sauce bubbles and the preserves break down. Keep warm until time to serve.

HEAT THE OIL: Fill a wok, Dutch oven, or heavy-bottomed pot with 1 to 2 inches of oil and heat the oil to 350°F. Have a sheet pan lined with paper towels and fitted with a wire rack nearby.

BUILD THE SKEWERS: Thread 3 to 4 cauliflower florets through their stems onto each skewer, packing the florets together snuggly. If you're lucky, you may be able to get a couple more skewers depending on your head of cauliflower.

BATTER THE SKEWERS: In a wide, shallow bowl, add the starter (or 2x the starter sub) and a generous pinch of salt. Slowly drizzle in some water, a couple tablespoons at a time, whisking until you have a thin pancake-like batter. Place the coconut flakes in a small bowl, and also have an empty plate nearby for catching the drips of batter.

(recipe continues)

Put a skewer into the bowl of starter to coat, spooning over more starter to fill any holes, and twirling the skewer to allow the excess batter to drip away. Next, hover it over the empty plate while sprinkling the coconut flakes over top, rotating the skewer until it's well-coated.

FRY THE CAULIFLOWER: Fry the cauliflower skewers in batches, for 5 to 7 minutes, rotating occasionally, until their shells are crispy, their centers are cooked through, and the coconut flakes are dark golden brown. Using tongs, remove the skewers from the oil, allowing the excess oil to drip away, and place them on the rack. Sprinkle them with more salt, then transfer the drained skewers to a small serving platter and set aside.

SERVE: Spoon the warm sauce over the skewers (or use a pastry brush to glaze them) and pour the remaining sauce into a small bowl to serve alongside.

TIP If you don't have a sourdough starter, for a quick replacement, combine **½ cup all-purpose flour, ¼ cup cornstarch** (for extra crispiness), **½ teaspoon baking powder**, and **¼ cup of water** (or vodka for supreme crispiness), adding more liquid to turn it into the right consistency.

Melt jams and preserves to make complex sauces and glazes for meats or even sweets like my Shiny Almond & Peach Cornbread (see page 175). To balance the sweetness, add chile paste or other forms of spice.

Working with Your Sourdough Starter

Growing your own starter has the same emotional rewards as tending a garden—watching nature take its course while slowly nurturing it along. It's both a humbling and deeply gratifying experience and a reminder of the patience and care a rewarding life requires.

In our house, we keep the family sourdough starter (which we've fittingly named "Champ" so we can cheer it on by saying *c'mon, Champ, you can do it, Champ, and rise to the occasion, Champ*) and his discard on hand because, besides making crusty, warm, buttery loaves of homemade sourdough bread, tangy breakfast pancakes, and bakery-quality pastries, we've found many other fun ways to play with him. Specifically we enjoy battering things like Sweet 'n' Sourdough Coconut Cauliflower Skewers (page 147) and fried Mahi Sliders (page 150).

MAKES
8
SLIDERS

(OR 4 REGULAR SANDWICHES)

(DF)

ISLAND ACHIOTE DRESSING

achiote paste 1 tablespoon (15 grams)

hot water 1 teaspoon

mayo ½ cup

Venusian Ketchup (page 276) *or regular ketchup* ¼ cup

light brown sugar 2 teaspoons packed

dill pickles 2 tablespoons minced plus 2 teaspoons of the brine

prepared horseradish 2 teaspoons

onion powder 1 teaspoon

ground paprika ½ teaspoon

garlic clove 1, grated

dried dill ¼ teaspoon

ground cayenne pepper ¼ teaspoon

kosher salt ½ teaspoon

MAHI SLIDERS

neutral oil (such as avocado, grapeseed, or canola), for frying

active sourdough starter 1 cup, plus more as needed (see Tip for substitute)

Old Bay Seasoning 2 teaspoons

cayenne pepper ¼ teaspoon

Mahi Sliders

with Island Achiote Dressing

Being born and raised in South Florida, I've had my taste of great fried fish sandwiches. This is my current homemade version to satisfy those flashbacks. The crust is superlight and crispy because of the batter's balance between sourdough (aka gluten structure) and vodka (which breaks down gluten and evaporates quickly when fried). The dressing it's smothered in has achiote paste added for a fun twist that gives the sauce that characteristic Floridian bronze tan and nuttiness.

MAKE THE DRESSING (SEE TIP): In a mixing bowl, using the back of a fork, mash the achiote paste with the water until smooth. Add the mayo, ketchup, brown sugar, pickles and their brine, horseradish, onion powder, garlic, dill, cayenne, and salt, and whisk until smooth. Set aside.

FILL A HEAVY-BOTTOMED POT or wok with 1 to 2 inches oil, and heat the oil to 350°F—use a thermometer to gauge the temperature.

MAKE THE SOURDOUGH BATTER: In a wide shallow bowl, whisk together the sourdough starter, Old Bay Seasoning, cayenne pepper, and vodka to make a smooth pancake-like batter, adding more vodka or starter to find the right consistency.

FRY THE FISH: Have a paper towel–lined sheet pan near the stove. Place the mahi mahi on a plate and pat dry with a paper towel. Season generously with salt and dust them all over with the cornstarch to coat, shaking off any excess. Dip the fish, one at a time, into the batter, turning it over to coat well and allowing any excess batter to drip off back into the bowl. Carefully lay the battered piece of fish in the hot oil away from your body to keep any oil from splattering toward you. Continue with 1 or 2 two more pieces of fish, taking care not to crowd the pot. Fry the fish in batches for 5 to 7 minutes, using tongs to turn them over, until their sourdough shells are evenly golden brown all over and the fish is just firm.

(recipe continues)

MAKE IT FANCY
Skewer the sliders with toothpicks, piercing cute little pickles, to keep it all elegantly held together.

vodka 1/4 cup, plus more as needed

mahi mahi *or other white flaky fish* 1 1/2 pounds (8 [3-ounce] pieces or 4 [6-ounce] pieces for full sandwiches)

kosher salt

cornstarch *or flour*, for dusting

brioche dinner rolls 8 *or 4 hamburger buns*, toasted

shredded iceberg lettuce *or coleslaw*, for topping

Pickled Pink Onions (page 287) *or thinly sliced onion*, for topping

BUILD THE SLIDERS: Spread the bottom of the rolls with the achiote dressing, top with shredded lettuce, pickled onion, a fried piece of mahi mahi, and then spread more dressing on the top roll, close the sandwich, and then devour.

TIP

If you can't make the dressing, use a store-bought Thousand Island Dressing or **Very Green Ranch (page 277)** to substitute.

Wine-Poached Salmon Cakes

with Cheesy Cauliflower "Grits"

SERVES
4 TO 6
(GF, RSF)

dry white wine (such as Pinot Grigio) 1 (750-milliliter) bottle

Old Bay Seasoning 3 tablespoons

vegetable bouillon paste 1 tablespoon

salmon 1 pound boneless, skin-on

almond meal, *panko, or freshly ground breadcrumbs* 1 cup

scallions ½ cup chopped, both green and white parts, plus more for serving

egg 1 large

lemon juice 2 tablespoons (from ½ a lemon), plus lemon wedges for serving

paprika ½ teaspoon

kosher salt 1 teaspoon

unsalted butter 1 tablespoon, plus more as needed

olive oil 1 tablespoon, plus more as needed

Cheesy Cauliflower "Grits" (recipe follows) *or hot, buttered rice*, for serving

As a kid, I always looked forward to the nights when my mom would let me make salmon croquettes for dinner. I would open a couple tins of salmon and mash everything together with my hands. They were so easy to make and delicious. It wasn't until recently in my own kitchen that I upgraded from canned salmon to fresh salmon and started poaching the salmon in wine. The juiciness and extra flavor is worlds apart from what I knew, but still has those warm feelings of nostalgia. Serve these with hot, buttered rice and sautéed spinach, or, if you really want to feel fancy, make a pot of Cheesy Cauliflower "Grits" to pair with it instead.

POACH THE SALMON: In a large pot (with a lid), combine the wine, Old Bay Seasoning, and bouillon paste. Bring the liquid to a boil, then remove the pan from the heat. Add the salmon, skin side down, making sure it's fully submerged, and cover. Allow the salmon to poach for 10 to 12 minutes, until the salmon is opaque and just barely cooked through. Using a spatula, remove the salmon from the poaching liquid and set aside to cool slightly and then discard the skin. It should still be slightly undercooked, but it will continue cooking once made into a croquette and seared.

MAKE THE CROQUETTE MIXTURE: Place the salmon into a large mixing bowl and, using two forks, shred it into chunks. Add the almond meal, scallions, egg, lemon juice, paprika, and salt and toss gently until well combined.

FORM THE PATTIES: Have a plate nearby. Using clean hands, divide the mixture into eight equal portions and shape the portions into 3-inch-wide patties. Place them on the plate and set aside. (You can also cover and refrigerate the patties overnight to allow the flavors to meld.)

(recipe continues)

PAN-FRY THE PATTIES: Heat a large skillet (preferably cast-iron) over medium-high heat. Place the butter and the olive oil into the skillet. Once the butter has melted, add the patties in batches and fry until they turn dark golden brown and begin to crisp, 2 to 3 minutes per side, adding more butter and oil as needed if the pan seems dry.

SERVE: Serve over Cauliflower Grits or rice and garnish with more scallions.

MAKE IT FANCY

Whisk together **¼ cup mayo** and **1 tablespoon red curry paste** to make an easy Red Curry Aïoli to dollop on top of the patties.

Cheesy Cauliflower "Grits"

MAKES 3 CUPS
(NF, RSF, ≤30)

dried bay leaves 1 to 2

kosher salt
½ teaspoon, plus more as needed

cauliflower
2 to 2½ pounds (1 small head), broken into medium florets

whole milk
or reduced-fat sour cream ½ to ¾ cup

freshly ground black pepper ¼ teaspoon

shredded Parmesan cheese ½ cup

shredded sharp cheddar cheese *or other melty cheese* ½ cup

COOK THE CAULIFLOWER: Place a colander in the sink. Fill a large pot with a lid with **2 QUARTS WATER**, then add the bay leaves and a large pinch of salt. Bring the water to a boil over high heat, then add the cauliflower and cook until it's al dente, about 5 minutes. Reserve ½ cup of the cooking water, then drain the cauliflower in the colander. Keep the pot nearby.

PULSE THE CAULIFLOWER: In a food processor fitted with a steel blade, pulse the cauliflower in batches until finely ground, like the texture of coarsely ground grits (not too long or it will become cauliflower mash). Return the cauliflower to the pot and add the milk, the ½ teaspoon salt, the pepper, Parmesan, and cheddar cheese and cook, covered, over low heat until the cheese has melted, about 5 more minutes, stirring halfway through. Add the reserved water as needed for thinning. Keep warm until ready to serve.

SERVES
8
(EF, NF, RSF)

Simple Whole Wheat Banana Bread

unsalted butter ¼ cup, melted, plus more for the pan (dairy-free, if desired) (56 grams)

very ripe bananas 1 cup pureed (from about 3 large) (240 grams)

coconut sugar *or light brown sugar* 1 cup (218 grams), plus more for sprinkling

virgin coconut oil ¼ cup, melted (48 grams)

oat milk *or milk of choice* 1 cup (200 ml)

pure vanilla extract 1 tablespoon

whole wheat flour 2 cups (285 grams)

baking powder 2 teaspoons

baking soda ½ teaspoon

kosher salt ½ teaspoon

Chocolate Pecan Pie in a Jar (recipe follows) *or Nutella*, for serving

MAKE IT FANCY

Replace the whole wheat flour with equal parts **buckwheat flour** and add **1 large egg** to the wet batter to make a nutty, earthy gluten-free version of this recipe.

Every kitchen needs a go-to banana bread, one that makes the space feel cozy and nourished. This is my ultimate "house" banana bread. When the bananas have ripened to the perfect stage, it's time to get out my blender and puree them. Pureeing the bananas instead of mashing them gives an even moisture to the bread making them ideal for toasting later. *My* favorite part.

GET STARTED: Preheat the oven to 375°F and have an 8 x 5-inch loaf pan buttered and lined with parchment paper nearby.

COMBINE THE WET INGREDIENTS: In a large mixing bowl, whisk together the bananas, sugar, coconut oil, the ¼ cup butter, the oat milk, and vanilla until smooth.

SIFT IN THE DRY INGREDIENTS: Place a sifter over the bowl and add in the flour, baking powder, baking soda, and salt and sift into the bowl. Using a rubber spatula, fold the dry ingredients into the wet mixture just until combined, being careful not to overmix to keep the bread tender.

BAKE THE BREAD: Pour the batter into the prepared loaf pan, smoothing the top with a spatula. Sprinkle the top with a thin layer of more coconut sugar, then take the tip of a butter knife and run it lengthwise down the center of the loaf to make that iconic bakery split top. Bake for 45 to 50 minutes, until a toothpick inserted in the center comes out clean.

COOL THE BREAD: Let the bread cool in the pan for 10 minutes, then transfer to a wire rack to cool completely before slicing and smearing with Chocolate Pecan Pie in a Jar.

MAKE IT FANCY

Make Banana Bread French Toast: Slice three or four **¾- to 1-inch-thick slices of day-old banana bread**. In a shallow dish, whisk together **2 eggs**, **½ cup whole milk** (or half-and-half for extra decadence), **a splash of pure vanilla extract**, **a pinch of cinnamon, and 1 teaspoon maple syrup**. Heat a skillet or griddle over medium heat and melt a generous **pat of butter**. Quickly dip each banana bread slice into the custard, letting it soak for just a few seconds on each side—enough to absorb flavor without becoming too soft. Cook for 2 to 3 minutes per side in the sizzling butter, until golden brown and slightly crisp on both sides. Serve warm, dusted with **powdered sugar**, topped with **fresh banana slices**, **a dollop of fresh whipped cream** (see Tip, page 254 for recipe), and drizzled with maple syrup.

Chocolate Pecan Pie in a Jar

MAKES ABOUT 1 CUP
(DF, ≤30)

Here is an emergency stash of nut spread that mimics the flavor of my favorite pie, except it's made without any rolling, layering, baking, or chilling, and is ready to be spooned like Christmas from a jar at a moment's notice. It's, of course, wonderful on a slice of toasted banana bread, or use it as a moreish dip for fresh strawberries.

unsalted raw pecan halves or pieces 1 cup (4.5 ounces)

soft medjool dates 4 to 5 (3 ounces), pitted

unsulfured molasses 2 teaspoons

pure vanilla extract ½ teaspoon

ground cinnamon ½ teaspoon, plus more as needed

ground nutmeg ⅛ teaspoon

kosher salt ½ teaspoon, plus more as needed

cocoa powder *or cacao powder* 2 tablespoons

warm water ½ cup

TOAST THE PECANS: In a large skillet, spread out the pecans in a single layer and heat the pan over medium heat. Toast the pecans for 4 to 6 minutes, tossing the pan occasionally, until they begin to smell nutty and turn a couple shades darker. Remove the pan from the heat.

BLEND THE PECANS: In a high-powered blender or food processor, blend the warm pecans, dates, molasses, vanilla, cinnamon, nutmeg, salt, cocoa powder, and water on high until the mixture is completely smooth, like peanut butter, stopping to scrape down the sides of the bowl as needed. This may take some patience. Taste and add more cinnamon and/or salt as desired.

STORE: Transfer the spread to a lidded container and refrigerate for up to 2 months.

CHAPTER 5

JAZZY RICE

The Tried and True Weeknight Staple

I GREW UP EATING INSANE amounts of rice as a kid. (My mom would buy those 50-pound bags.) Yet, I've never grown tired of it. Rice is a dinnertime savior, my #1 eleventh-hour clutch, and it's our most agreed upon answer to end the cloud of dinner confusion. But that also means needing to exercise our brains to come up with more interesting ways to eat it. "Jazzy rice" enters stage left.

Follow these basic tips to ensure you'll never suffer from boring, bad or bland rice:

BEFORE YOU COOK:

CHOOSE GOOD RICE Select a quality brand and a flavorful, fragrant variety like jasmine, basmati, or black rice.

RINSE YOUR RICE Rinse your rice under cold water to remove impurities and extra starches that could make it too sticky.

TOAST YOUR RICE Toast your rice in a tasty fat like olive oil, butter, or an infused oil for a few minutes before you boil it. (For every cup of rice add 1 tablespoon fat and ½ teaspoon salt.)

USE BROTH Replace all or part of the water called for with broth or add a bouillon cube.

COOK LOW AND SLOW Bring the rice to a boil, then reduce the heat to a simmer and cook over low, steady heat.

AFTER THE RICE IS DONE COOKING:

FLUFF IT Use a fork to fluff to allow air circulation for even cooling and to prevent smashing the kernels.

ADD MORE FAT Stir in a spoonful of compound butter (see Flavor Bombs, page 289) per 1½ to 2 cups of cooked rice.

ADD SOMETHING ACIDIC Stir in an acid like lemon or lime juice or a splash of rice vinegar at the end to enhance the flavors.

GARNISH Fold in a handful of fresh chopped herbs or scallions or top with fun things like Garlic Chips (see page 285) for even more flavor.

And, if you forgot to do all of the above:

MAKE RICE CROUTONS! For an ideal salad topper, toss day-old, plain rice with a couple teaspoons of sesame oil and soy sauce, spread it across a sheet pan, and bake in a 350°F oven until super crunchy. Try it sprinkled over these Mango Miso Salmon Grain Bowls (page 224) or this Crunchy Peanut Chicken Salad (page 99).

SERVES
8
(GF, NF, RSF)

raspberries (fresh or frozen) ½ pint (about 6 ounces)

chipotle peppers in adobo sauce 2 peppers plus 1 tablespoon adobo sauce (remove the seeds if you don't want it too spicy)

tomato paste 2 tablespoons

vegetable broth 3½ cups ← 4 cups if you want to skip the wine

unsalted butter 4 tablespoons

yellow *or white onion* 1 large, quartered and thinly sliced

garlic cloves 2, chopped

ground cumin 2 teaspoons

dried thyme 1 teaspoon

kosher salt 1 tablespoon, plus more as needed

long-grain parboiled white rice 2 cups, rinsed (it holds up to the longer cooking time)

dry white wine ½ cup

ground allspice 1 teaspoon

bay leaves 2, dried or fresh

dark red kidney beans 1 (15-ounce can), drained and rinsed

Raspberry-Chipotle Red Rice

Every culture has its own version of red rice, and every household has their take. This one is tailored to some of the things I usually have around the house like frozen berries and canned chipotles in adobo sauce. The result is a comforting Jamaican-style Peas 'n' Rice with Tex-Mex vibes. Like any other red rice, this counts as a main meal, but you can serve it with Gochujang Cabbage and Carrots (page 178) and a side of sweet plantains, pan-seared fish filets, or seasoned chicken breasts. Start this rice on the stovetop so you can sauté the onion and toast the rice. Then transfer it to the oven for even and steady cooking.

PREHEAT THE OVEN to 375°F and position a rack in the lower middle oven.

PUREE THE RASPBERRIES: In a blender, place the raspberries, chipotles and sauce, tomato paste, and vegetable broth and blend on high until smooth. Set aside.

SAUTÉ THE ONION: Heat a large Dutch oven over medium-high heat and melt the butter. When the butter has melted and begins to foam, add the onion and cook for 3 to 5 minutes to soften. Add the garlic, cumin, thyme, and a third of the salt and cook, tossing constantly, for another minute until fragrant.

TOAST THE RICE: Add the rice and another third of the salt and cook for 2 to 3 minutes, tossing occasionally to lightly toast the rice.

STRAIN THE SAUCE: Place a fine-mesh sieve over the pot with the rice and pour the raspberry sauce through to remove any seeds. Add the wine, allspice, bay leaves, kidney beans, and the remaining salt, stirring to combine and submerging any rice clinging to the sides of the pan into the broth.

BAKE: Bring the pot to a boil, cover, and carefully transfer the pot to the oven to bake for about 45 minutes, or until the rice has absorbed all the liquid. Remove from the oven, then fluff with a fork and discard the bay leaves before serving.

SERVES
4 TO 6

(DF, EF, GF, NF, RSF, ≤5, ≤30)

shredded sweetened *or unsweetened coconut* 1 cup

virgin coconut oil 2 tablespoons

uncooked short-grain white rice *or long-grain white rice* 2 cups, rinsed

coconut water *or regular water* 3 cups (see Tip)

kosher salt 1 teaspoon

MAKE IT FANCY

Replace **1 cup** of the **coconut water** with **canned coconut milk** for a creamier, richer, and slightly sweeter rice.

Sticky Stovetop Coconut Rice

In this recipe, I infuse rice with coconut in all its forms—I swap the butter with coconut oil, the water with coconut water, and even add shredded, toasted coconut. This is the perfect rice dish for salty stir-frys like Shiitake & Broccoli Stir-Fry (page 70) that need a slightly sweeter flavor in the grain base to offset the savoriness. It's also a delish rice to pair with cumin-y black beans and fajita-style chicken or veggies when you add loads of cilantro, lime juice, and a grated garlic clove. I love that this rice can even swing into the dessert territory when topped with sliced mangos or mandarin oranges and a drizzle of sweetened condensed coconut milk.

COOK THE RICE: Heat a medium Dutch oven or heavy-bottomed pot over medium-high heat. Cook the shredded coconut, for 3 to 4 minutes, tossing frequently, until the flakes are lightly toasted and fragrant. Stir in the coconut oil, and once it's melted add the rice, coconut water, and the salt and stir to combine. Bring the pot to a boil. Reduce the heat to medium-low or a simmer and cover. Cook the rice for 20 to 25 minutes, until the liquid is absorbed and the rice is tender.

SERVE: Once the rice is done, fluff it with a fork before serving.

SERVES
4 TO 6
(GF, NF, RSF)

uncooked long-grain rice (such as jasmine or basmati) 2 cups, rinsed

unsalted butter *or olive oil* 2 tablespoons

kosher salt 1 teaspoon

saffron threads *or ground turmeric* ½ teaspoon

vegetable bouillon paste 4 teaspoons

ground cumin ¼ teaspoon

dried cherries *or raisins* ¼ cup

cinnamon stick 1 small

lemon juice 1 tablespoon, plus more as needed

flat-leaf parsley 2 tablespoons chopped

fresh cilantro 2 tablespoons chopped

Baked & Bejeweled Yellow Rice

Oven-baked rice is a hands-off approach to evenly cooked grains. Cover the raw grains with boiling liquid and pop it in the oven. With consistent, evenly distributed heat, the rice will simmer and fluff into perfection, allowing you to focus on something else. Everything just does its thing in the oven. Of all the rice cooking methods, it's my go-to when I want to add a bunch of different ingredients like dried fruit, veggies, and spices to the pot and want everything to cook gently and evenly. Pair this with Lion's Mane Rosemary Kebabs (page 68) or other seared protein.

PREHEAT THE OVEN to 375°F. Into a Dutch oven or heavy-bottomed pot (or a 4-quart lidded casserole dish), put the rice, butter, salt, saffron, bouillon paste, cumin, cherries, and cinnamon stick and set it aside. (No need to stir.)

BOIL THE WATER: In a teapot or a medium saucepan on the stove, bring **3 CUPS WATER** to a boil. Once it's boiling, pour the water directly over the contents in the Dutch oven, stir, and cover.

BAKE THE RICE: Bake in the oven for 25 to 30 minutes, until the rice is cooked through. Remove the pot from the oven, remove the lid, and add the lemon juice, parsley, and cilantro. Cover and allow to sit for 10 minutes undisturbed. Uncover, remove the cinnamon stick, and fluff everything together with a fork to combine. Serve.

MAKE IT FANCY

Before serving, top the rice with **sliced toasted almonds** or **Garlic Chips (page 285)** for extra crunch.

TIP Make sheet pan rice dishes using this baking method—add uncooked rice to a sheet pan, pour over boiling water, and cover with aluminum foil. Or make a simple Warm Coconut Rice Pudding: In a medium saucepan, bring **2 (13.5-ounce) cans full-fat coconut milk**, **½ cup coconut sugar** (or other sweetener of choice) **2 teaspoons pure vanilla extract**, **1 teaspoon ground cinnamon**, and **½ teaspoon salt** to a simmer. Add **½ cup jasmine rice** to a casserole dish, and pour the coconut mixture over the rice. Stir, cover, and bake in a 350° oven for 1 hour to 1 hour 15 minutes, until creamy and the rice kernels are cooked through.

CHAPTER 6

ELEGANT SIDES

To Pick & Pair

WHETHER IT'S CREAMY GREEN BEANS with lemon and toasted almonds, tangy roasted sweet potatoes broiled with a crunchy ginger sugar, or a rainbow carrot salad brightened with herbs and dried fruit, a thoughtful side dish has the power to turn even the most basic proteins, like a boring breast of seared chicken, into something worthwhile after all, so be sure to pair with care.

Dill Pickle Pasta Salad *with Toasted Nashville Hot Chickpeas*

SERVES
6 TO 8
(DF, NF, ≤30)

kosher salt 1½ teaspoons, plus more for the pasta water

uncooked short-cut pasta (macaroni noodles, rotini, fussili, etc.) ½ pound

egg yolk 1 large

pickle juice (from the jar) 5 tablespoons, plus more as needed

garlic 2 cloves

Dijon mustard 1 tablespoon

dried dill 1 tablespoon

granulated sugar ½ teaspoon

neutral oil (avocado oil, canola oil, light olive oil) 1 cup

dill pickles ½ cup chopped

red onion ½ medium, halved and thinly sliced

parsley 2 tablespoons chopped

Nashville Hot Chickpeas (recipe follows), for topping (optional)

Here's a full-flavored pasta salad for the pickle obsessed. It also happens to be a testament to how easy it is to get creative with aïoli flavors at home. With all the creaminess from the aïoli, the salad is begging for something crispy and spicy, so topping it with pan-crisped chickpeas for contrast is the perfect plot twist.

BOIL THE NOODLES: Bring a large pot of salted water to a boil. Add the noodles and cook them according to the package's instructions. Strain, add to a large bowl, and set aside to cool.

BLEND THE AÏOLI: In the bowl of a blender add the egg yolk, pickle juice, garlic, Dijon, dill, sugar, and 1½ teaspoons of salt. Blend on high to combine, then remove the top and drizzle in the oil. Continue to blend on high until very thick.

TOSS THE SALAD: Transfer the aïoli to the bowl with the cooked noodles to combine. Add the pickles, red onion, parsley, and Nashville Hot Chickpeas, tossing to combine. Cover and chill for at least 2 hours for the flavors to come together before serving.

Nashville Hot Chickpeas

(DF, NF, GF, EF, RSF, ≤30)

chickpeas
1 (15-ounce) can, drained and rinsed

chipotle chili powder
½ teaspoon

smoked paprika
½ teaspoon

creole seasoning
½ teaspoon

cayenne pepper
½ teaspoon

garlic powder
¼ teaspoon

kosher salt ¼ teaspoon

unsalted butter
2 tablespoons

honey 1 tablespoon

DRY THE CHICKPEAS: Pat the chickpeas dry with a couple sheets of paper towel, or give them a spin in the salad spinner.

SEASON THE CHICKPEAS: Add the chickpeas to a bowl with the chipotle chili powder. smoked paprika, creole seasoning, cayenne pepper, garlic powder, and salt, and toss to coat.

TOAST THE CHICKPEAS: In a skillet over medium heat, melt the butter and add the chickpeas. Cook for 10 to 12 minutes, tossing frequently, until toasted. Remove from the heat, add the honey, and toss a final time to coat. Allow to cool.

SERVES

4 TO 6

(EF, RSF, ≤30)

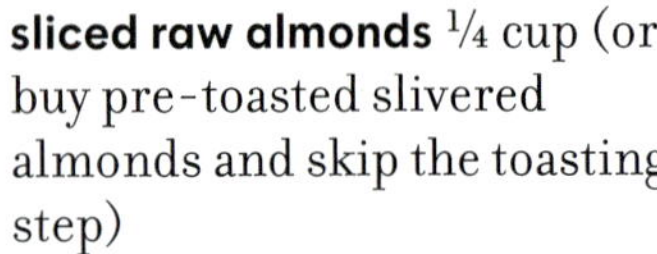

sliced raw almonds ¼ cup (or buy pre-toasted slivered almonds and skip the toasting step)

olive oil 2 tablespoons

yellow onions 2 large, peeled, halved, and thinly sliced

kosher salt

French green beans 1 pound, ends snapped

garlic cloves 3 to 4, minced or grated

cayenne pepper ¼ teaspoon

onion powder ½ teaspoon

sour cream (full-fat, not light) *or Greek yogurt or pureed cottage cheese* ¼ cup, plus more as needed

lemon juice, for drizzling

Caramelized Onion Green Beans

Eating plain, boiled green beans feels like torture and reminds me of the canned greens I felt forced to eat in childhood. But during the holidays, those same canned beans were dressed up with creamy and crunchy things, and suddenly felt like a delicacy. Ever since I witnessed that transformation, I've been a believer that the world shouldn't have to wait until November to experience decadent green beans.

TOAST THE ALMONDS: Heat a large skillet over medium heat. Toast the almonds, tossing the pan frequently, for 5 to 7 minutes, until golden brown. Transfer to a plate and set aside.

CARAMELIZE THE ONIONS: Heat the olive oil in the same skillet set over medium heat, then add the onions and a pinch of salt and let them cook down, stirring occasionally, for about 20 minutes, or until creamy and caramel brown in color.

MEANWHILE, BLANCH THE GREEN BEANS: Have a large bowl of ice water nearby. Bring a large pot of salted water to a boil and add the green beans. Cook for 5 to 7 minutes, stirring occasionally, just until the beans are bright green and firm, not limp. Then using a pair of tongs, transfer the beans to the ice water to stop their cooking.

COMBINE EVERYTHING: Using the tongs, transfer the cooled beans to the pan with the onions and sauté for 5 to 7 minutes. Add the garlic, cayenne, and onion powder and cook for 1 minute, stirring occasionally.

MAKE IT CREAMY: Reduce the heat to low and add the sour cream, folding everything together until all the green beans are coated. Fold in the almonds, saving some for topping, and drizzle with fresh lemon juice to cut through the richness. Taste and adjust seasoning as needed. Transfer to a plate and top with the reserved almonds.

Roasted Rainbow Carrots

SERVES 4

(EF, GF, NF, RSF, ≤5)

I'm always looking for new ways to eat a bundle of roasted carrots. Here they are delish over Whipped Chipotle Feta, a staple, and then I just shower them with whatever else I have around—currants, chopped apricots, a bunch of herbs, and then something crunchy, like chopped hazelnuts or Crispy Spiced Rice (recipe follows).

olive oil, for oiling the pan and drizzling

rainbow carrots (or same-colored) 1 to 1¼ pounds, tops trimmed

kosher salt and **freshly ground black pepper**

honey, for drizzling

Whipped Chipotle Feta (page 124)

PREHEAT THE OVEN to 400°F and have an oiled sheet pan nearby.

ROAST THE CARROTS: Using the back of a butter knife or citrus zester, scrape the carrots to peel off the outer skin and give them a rough texture that will allow the sauce to cling better to the surface. Using a sharp knife, cut the carrots in half lengthwise and place them, face down, on the sheet pan. Drizzle with olive oil, season with salt and pepper to taste, and roast them for 20 to 30 minutes, until a fork pierces the flesh easily. Remove from the oven and drizzle them with honey.

SERVE: Smear the base of a serving platter with the whipped feta and arrange the roasted carrots on top.

Crispy Spiced Rice

MAKES 1 CUP
(DF, EF, GF, NF, RSF, ≤30)

plain or brown rice crisps cereal (the kind used for making Rice Krispies treats) *or puffed rice* 1 cup

ground cumin ½ teaspoon

onion powder ½ teaspoon

ground allspice ¼ teaspoon

ground cinnamon ¼ teaspoon

ground cardamom ⅛ teaspoon

freshly ground black pepper ¼ teaspoon

coconut sugar *or light brown sugar* 1 teaspoon

kosher salt

olive oil *or melted unsalted butter* 1 tablespoon

PREHEAT THE OVEN to 350°F.

BAKE THE RICE: On a sheet pan lined with parchment paper, toss together the rice cereal, cumin, onion powder, allspice, cinnamon, cardamom, black pepper, coconut sugar, and salt to taste. Drizzle the olive oil over the mixture and toss again to coat. Spread the mixture out in a single layer and bake for 4 to 6 minutes, until the rice is golden and extra crispy, and the kitchen is fragrant.

STORE in an airtight container in a cabinet, and it will stay crispy for 3 to 4 weeks.

SERVES

4

(DF, EF, NF, RSF, ≤5, ≤30)

romaine lettuce 1 pound (about 2 large heads), halved through the stem

olive oil

Hippy Hemp Dressing (recipe follows) *or your favorite salad dressing*

Falafel Crumbles (page 283) *or Pesto Sprinkles (page 286) or crushed store-bought garlic croutons*, for topping

MAKE IT FANCY

if you're feeling extra experimental, top your salads with **balsamic-soaked cherries** (see Tip) for a surprising pop of tangy sweetness.

Charred Romaine

with Creamy Hemp Dressing & Falafel Crumbles

When I was younger and living in California with my aunt and uncle, I was always inspired by my aunt's discipline for eating a salad at every meal. However inspiring the dedication, I also wondered how that wouldn't become repetitive. Little did I know the wonderful world of salads still had much to teach me. Charring my romaine is one way I've learned to transform a boring head of one-note lettuce into a treasure of layered flavor.

CHAR THE ROMAINE LETTUCE: Heat a large cast-iron skillet or grill pan over medium-high heat, or if you're feeling unconventional, heat your panini press instead, keeping the lid open. Once hot, brush the surface with olive oil and lay the lettuce halves cut side down. Grill for 3 to 5 minutes until charred in spots and slightly wilted.

SERVE: Place the romaine halves onto plates and drizzle with the hemp dressing. Top with the falafel crumbles. Enjoy.

TIP To make **Black Pepper Balsamic Cherries:** Simmer **¼ cup balsamic vinegar** with **1 tablespoon of honey** and **¼ teaspoon of salt and cracked black pepper** in a small saucepan over medium heat until thick enough to coat the back of a spoon. Stir in **1 tablespoon of butter** and **½ cup dried cherries**, and cook for another minute just to plump the cherries. Spoon the cherries over this romaine salad, roasted chicken or pork chops, or, even better, **vanilla ice cream with a drizzle of olive oil.**

Hippy Hemp Dressing

MAKES ABOUT 1 CUP
(DF, EF, NF, RSF, ≤5, ≤30)

Hemp hearts are full of protein (more than chia seeds and on par with eggs), and they make a luxuriously creamy salad dressing without any added eggs or dairy. I also love that when blended into a paste, hemp hearts are much milder in flavor than tahini, my other favorite dressing base. Use this as your everyday house salad dressing when you get tired of the same ol' lemon and oil lettuce rub down.

hemp hearts *or sub untoasted sesame seeds in a pinch* ½ cup

avocado oil *or olive oil* ¼ cup

balsamic vinegar ¼ cup

garlic cloves 2 small

pure maple syrup 1 teaspoon

kosher salt 1 teaspoon

BLEND THE DRESSING: In a high-powered blender, combine the hemp hearts, **½ CUP WATER**, the avocado oil, garlic, maple syrup, and salt and blend on high for 1 to 2 minutes, until completely smooth and thick. The longer you blend it the thicker it will get. Add more water to thin if needed.

STORE: Transfer to a lidded container and keep in the fridge for up to 4 days.

MAKE IT FANCY
TURN IT INTO A BROCCOLI WALDORF

In a large bowl toss together: **2 cups chopped broccoli florets; 1 cup seedless red grapes**, halved; **½ cup sliced celery; 1 cup chopped apples; ½ cup of some toasted nut or seed (walnuts, pecans, sliced almonds, sunflower seeds, pine nuts); ¼ cup dried cranberries or dried cherries; & ½ cup of this Hippy Hemp Dressing** and serve.

TIP
Add an extra 2 tablespoons avocado oil and 2 tablespoons balsamic for an extra-thick dressing.

MAKES
1
9-INCH CORNBREAD

(GF, NF, RSF, ≤30)

ripe peach chunks *or frozen peaches, thawed* ½ pound (from about 1½ peaches)

whole milk *or milk of choice* ½ cup

large eggs 3

apricot preserves ¼ cup, plus more for brushing

medium-ground cornmeal 1½ cups (8 ounces)

almond meal *or almond flour* 1½ cups (170 grams/6 ounces)

baking powder 1 tablespoon

baking soda ¼ teaspoon

kosher salt 1 teaspoon

melted butter 5 tablespoons, divided

Ancho Honey Butter (recipe follows) optional

MAKE IT FANCY

Turn this cornbread into cake by replacing half (or all) of the milk with **heavy cream** and sprinkling **⅓ cup sliced almonds or fresh sliced fruit like peaches or strawberries** over the top before baking. Then, of course, brush the top with apricot preserves once it's out of the oven.

Shiny Almond & Peach Cornbread

I love sneaking pureed fruit and jams into my cornbread for their natural sweetness. And if there is a jar of jam I make sure to keep around, it's apricot preserves. It is the most amazing, most undetectable, edible shellac. A thin varnish over warm food using a pastry brush will make anything from fancy fruit tarts to rustic cornbreads like this shimmer and shine without overpowering the other flavors. This lightly sweetened cornbread is the perfect vehicle for ancho compound butter, which adds a complimentary smokiness. Use your leftover cornbread in Collard Green & Cornbread Ribollita (page 219).

PREHEAT THE OVEN to 400°F and place a 9-inch cast-iron skillet on the center rack.

MEANWHILE, BLEND THE BATTER: In a blender, combine the peaches, milk, eggs, and apricot preserves and blend on high into a smooth puree. To the puree add the cornmeal, almond meal, baking powder, baking soda, salt, and 4 tablespoons of the butter and blend again on medium speed just to combine.

BAKE: Using mittens, carefully remove the hot skillet from the oven and add the remaining tablespoon of butter. Swirl the pan to coat with the butter. Pour the batter into the skillet, smoothing it to the edges. Bake for 25 to 28 minutes, until deep golden brown at least an inch from the edges of the pan, is firm to the touch on top, and a toothpick inserted into the center comes out cleanly. Remove from the oven and transfer the skillet to a cooling rack.

GLAZE THE TOP: While the top is still warm, use a pastry brush to brush a thin layer of apricot preserves over the surface so it shines. Allow the cornbread to rest for at least 10 minutes in the skillet before cutting into wedges and serve with the honey butter (if using).

Ancho Honey Butter

MAKES ½ POUND
(NF, RSF, ≤5)

Here's some honey butter with the warmth and fruitiness of mild Mexican chiles plus the aroma of oranges. It's perfect for cornbread (see page 175) and cornbread waffles (see page 230). Slather it on corn cobs, dollop it in the creases of a baked sweet potato, swirl it into a pot of refried beans, or baste it over roasted Brussels sprouts. It's even stellar as the butter base in your favorite peanut brittle or chocolate ganache.

dried ancho chiles 2 whole (about 1 to 1.5 ounces)

unsalted butter 2 sticks, at room temperature

honey 3 tablespoons

orange zest from 1 orange

kosher salt ¼ teaspoon

TOAST THE CHILES: Preheat oven to 375°F. Place the chiles on a small sheet pan and bake for 3 to 4 minutes, until fragrant. Remove from the oven and let them cool slightly before removing the stems and discarding the seeds.

SOAK THE CHILES: In a medium bowl, cover the chiles with enough water to submerge. Allow the chiles to soak for 15 to 20 minutes, until softened and cooled slightly. Drain the water.

BLEND THE BUTTER: In the bowl of a mini food processor, blend the butter, drained chiles, honey, orange zest, and salt on high into a smooth puree.

STORE: In the center of a sheet of parchment paper, place the butter and roll it into a tight log, twisting the ends closed. Refrigerate for up to 1 month until you're ready to use, or freeze for up to 6 months.

MAKE IT FANCY

Add **a splash of pure vanilla extract** to the butter before blending, which surprisingly enhances the smokiness of the ancho chiles because it also has warm, smokey undertones.

TIP

Ancho chiles don't pack nearly as much heat as chipotle pepper or chiles de arbol, so it's a good neutral chile, and the one you'd usually find in the commercial ground chili powders at the store.

SERVES
4
(NF, ≤30)

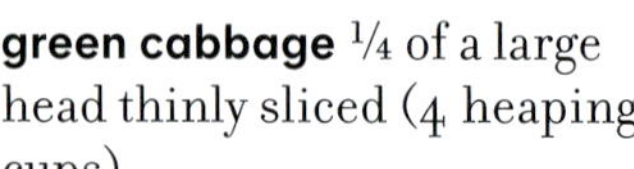

green cabbage ¼ of a large head thinly sliced (4 heaping cups)

red onion ½ large, thinly sliced

carrot 1 medium, peeled and shaved into long, thin ribbons

garlic cloves 3, chopped

fresh ginger 1 tablespoon, peeled and chopped

soy sauce *or tamari* 1 tablespoon

sherry vinegar *or red wine vinegar* 2 tablespoons

veggie bouillon paste ½ teaspoon

gochujang sauce or paste 1 tablespoon

avocado oil *or olive oil* 2 tablespoons

kosher salt and **freshly ground black pepper**

Gochujang Cabbage and Carrots

One sad day when I ran out of kimchi, I desperately scoured the fridge looking for ways to make something that could replace it. I created this spicy cabbage with the only cabbage I had on hand, and it's inspired by the Jamaican cabbage and carrots (jumbled on the side of stewed oxtail) I ate when I was a child, and all the piles of kimchi I eat today.

MAKE THE CABBAGE MIXTURE: In a large bowl, toss together the cabbage, onion, carrot, garlic, and ginger and set aside.

MAKE THE SAUCE: In a small bowl, whisk together the soy sauce, vinegar, bouillon paste, and gochujang and set aside.

SAUTÉ THE CABBAGE: Heat a large skillet over medium-high heat. Once it's hot, drizzle in the oil and add the cabbage mixture and a pinch each of salt and pepper. Cook for 7 to 10 minutes, tossing frequently, until wilted and charred in spots. Add the sauce and toss together to coat the cabbage. Taste and add more salt and pepper as desired.

Cucumber Salad

(2 Ways About It)

Creamy Cucumber Ranch Salad

SERVES 4

(EF, GF, NF, RSF, ≤5, ≤30)

Here's a crispy and refreshing side for burgers and other grilled and BBQ meats; it's great for anything heavy that needs an extra bright punch to lighten things up.

English cucumber 1 large (1 pound), thinly sliced

kosher salt

Very Green Ranch (page 277) *or favorite ranch dressing* ⅓ cup, plus more as needed

Pickled Pink Onions (page 287), for topping

freshly torn dill a handful, for topping

DRAIN THE CUCUMBER (SEE TIP) (SOME NIGHTS I SKIP THIS PART): In a salad spinner, sprinkle the cucumber with a generous pinch of salt. Allow the cucumber to rest for about 10 minutes to draw out its moisture, then twirl it in the spinner to drain the excess water.

SERVE: On a serving platter, toss the drained cucumber and Very Green Ranch to coat. Taste and add salt or more Very Green Ranch as desired. Using a clean kitchen cloth, wipe the edges of the platter of any splatters, and finish with a topping of pickled onion and dill.

MAKE IT FANCY

Crush **a handful of pita chips** into large chunks and sprinkle them over the finished salad.

Shaken Pickled Cucumber Ribbon Salad

SERVES 4

(DF, EF, NF, RSF, ≤30)

My mother makes a version of this with onions to pile onto everything: stir-fried Korean beef, hot rice, poke bowls; or use the leftovers in my Mango & Miso Salmon Grain Bowls (page 224) and anywhere else you need crunchy, slurpable soy slaw.

English cucumber 2 large (2 pounds)

kosher salt

soy sauce *or tamari* ⅓ cup

coconut aminos 1 tablespoon (optional)

toasted sesame oil 1 tablespoon

rice wine vinegar *or apple cider vinegar* 3 tablespoons

honey 1 teaspoon

garlic powder ¼ teaspoon

onion powder ¼ teaspoon

sesame seeds 2 tablespoons

gochujang sauce *or chili garlic sauce or Sriracha* 1 tablespoon

PEEL THE CUCUMBER: Using a vegetable peeler, peel the cucumber into thin, long strips. Any remaining pieces of the cucumber that are difficult to peel, cut into thin strips with a knife.

DRAIN THE CUCUMBER (SEE TIP) (SOME NIGHTS I SKIP THIS PART): In a salad spinner, sprinkle the cucumber with a generous pinch of salt. Toss and allow the cucumber to rest for about

(recipe continues)

10 minutes to draw out some moisture, then twirl it in the spinner to drain away the excess water.

SHAKE: To a lidded Tupperware container, combine the drained cucumber, soy sauce, coconut aminos, sesame oil, vinegar, honey, garlic powder, onion powder, sesame seeds, and red pepper flakes. Cover and shake to distribute the dressing well. Allow the cucumber to sit and marinate for 10 minutes for a crunchier salad (or up to a week to allow the cucumber to soak up the marinade), then plate and enjoy.

MAKE IT FANCY

Add **1 tablespoon mayo** to the rest of the ingredients before shaking for an extra-creamy dressing.

TIP Use a salad spinner for purposes outside of drying salad leaves or tumble-washing berries: Use it to extract the bitter water from large eggplants with ease after sprinkling them with salt, and for removing the excess liquid from vegetables such as cucumbers that contain lots of water, to prevent them from watering down dressings and marinades.

Crispy Buffalo Brussels Sprouts

SERVES
4
(EF, GF, RSF)

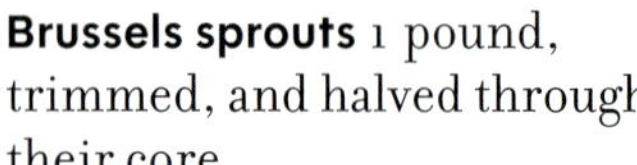

Brussels sprouts 1 pound, trimmed, and halved through their core

Bomba Buffalo Sauce (page 278) *or favorite Buffalo sauce*, 2 tablespoons, plus more for topping

honey 1 tablespoon, plus more for drizzling

kosher salt

olive oil, for drizzling

blue cheese *or Gorgonzola* 1 ounce, crumbled

toasted walnuts halves a handful

Shiitake Lardons (page 82) *or fried bacon bits*, for topping

This is hands down one of my favorite ways to eat Brussels sprouts, when they're roasted on a hot pan in the oven until they crisp and curl and get extra charred in spots. And is it just me, or are Brussels sprouts and Buffalo sauce couples goals? They have so much chemistry: The robust flavors of the bitter sprouts mellow out with the spicy creamy hot sauce, and once you add all the other toppings—walnuts, blue cheese, honey, bacon—they suddenly transform from a simple side to an irresistible salad because everything just sings.

PLACE A LARGE SHEET PAN IN THE OVEN, then preheat the oven to 450°F for about 15 minutes, so the pan gets hot.

ROAST THE BRUSSELS SPROUTS: To a large bowl, add the Brussels sprouts, Buffalo sauce, honey, and a pinch of salt and toss to coat. Carefully remove the hot pan from the oven, drizzle it lightly with olive oil, and place the Brussels sprouts cut side down on the hot pan. Return the pan to the oven and cook the Brussels sprouts for 20 to 25 minutes, until extra crispy and dark brown, rotating the pan halfway through. Remove the pan from the oven and allow the Brussels sprouts to cool slightly before serving.

SERVE: Transfer the Brussels sprouts to a serving platter and toss with more Buffalo sauce and honey. Garnish with the blue cheese, walnuts, and lardons and finish with an extra drizzle of honey.

MAKE IT FANCY

Garnish the roasted Brussels sprouts with **celery leaves** (see Tip).

TIP Reserve the top leafy greens of veggies to throw on your finished dish when you are plating. It is a resourceful garnishing hack. This is my favorite thing to do with celery stalks and those soft top leaves hidden within the center's bunch. I also love to do it with the bushy tops of carrots that look as attractive as curly parsley.

SERVES
4
(DF, EF, NF, RSF, ≤30)

carrot 1 large, peeled and chopped into chunks

fresh ginger 1 (1½-inch) piece, peeled

unsweetened applesauce ½ cup *or 1 small pear, halved and cored*

rice wine vinegar 2 tablespoons

white miso paste 2 teaspoons

lime juice 1 tablespoon (from 1 lime)

toasted sesame oil ¼ teaspoon

kosher salt ½ teaspoon

white pepper *or freshly ground black pepper* ⅛ teaspoon

sake 1 tablespoon (optional)

avocado oil *or olive oil* 2 tablespoons

iceberg lettuce 1 head, quartered through the core trimmed

Frazzled Onions (page 284), for topping

MAKE IT FANCY

Add a **confetti of Thai basil** to the wedges for a poppy anise-like depth or mint for a cooling bite.

Carrot & Miso Wedge Salad

This is one of my all-time favorite salads because it's so hydrating. The dressing is addicting and versatile, and while the sake isn't totally necessary, it punches up the flavor. If you have dressing leftover, extend its life by adding a couple cups of vegetable broth to it and simmering it on the stove for a soothing winter soup, or blend in a can of full-fat coconut milk to transform it into a chilled carrot gazpacho for the summer, topping it with the same crispy onions and herbs.

MAKE THE DRESSING: In a high-powered blender, combine the carrot, ginger, applesauce, vinegar, miso paste, lime juice, sesame oil, salt, white pepper, sake, if using, **2 TABLESPOONS WATER**, and the oil and blend on high until the sauce is a completely smooth and a creamy golden orange hue.

BUILD THE SALADS: Place each iceberg quarter on serving plates and generously spoon the dressing over. Top with Frazzled Onions and serve.

Bunny Bread

MAKES 8 SLICES
(NF, RSF, ≤5, ≤30)

Bunny ear–shaped garlic bread has all the attributes of regular garlic bread, with the added benefit of taking on the shape of a tortilla chip, making it better for dipping, scooping, or spooning sauces onto. I like to cover our bread with a thick spackle of Pizza Butter before baking, or at least, on lazier days, scrub the toasted, craggy top with a fresh garlic clove and a drizzle of good olive oil, once it's out of the oven.

demi baguette *or any kind of crusty bread you have on hand*
1 (10 to 12 ounces)

Pizza Butter (page 291), at room temperature

PREHEAT THE OVEN to 375°F and have a sheet pan nearby.

CUT THE BREAD: Using a serrated knife, cut the baguette in half across the center, then in half lengthwise through the center. Cut each piece from end to end on a heavy diagonal to make bunny ears. Or just cut the bread you're using so they're triangular shaped.

BAKE: Place the pieces on the sheet pan and smear their faces with the Pizza Butter. Bake for 10 to 12 minutes, until lightly golden brown or to desired toastiness.

Sticky Tamarind Yams *with Crunchy Ginger Sugar*

SERVES
4
(EF, GF, NF, ≤30)

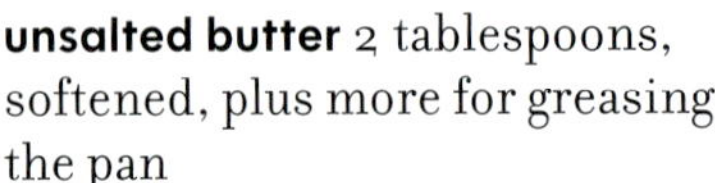

unsalted butter 2 tablespoons, softened, plus more for greasing the pan

garnet yams *or sweet potatoes* 1½ pounds (about 3 small), scrubbed and halved lengthwise

olive oil *or avocado oil*, for coating the yams

tamarind concentrate *or balsamic glaze* 1 teaspoon

light brown sugar 3 tablespoons packed

kosher salt ¼ teaspoon, plus more as needed

GINGER SUGAR

turbinado sugar 2 tablespoons

fresh ginger ½ teaspoon grated

lime zest from 1 small lime

MAKE IT FANCY

Before baking, score the sweet potato across the cut surface to make a tight grid pattern for extra adornment and better absorption of the tamarind syrup.

Instead of the traditional holiday candied yams you'd smother in a great deal of brown sugar and butter and leaves to slowly simmer on the stove, these are a lighter any-time-of-year, weekday twist. The yams simply get split in half lengthwise, roasted in the oven, and lacquered with a thin coat of sweetened tamarind paste, ginger, and lime. Try this same technique over ripe plantains, delicata squash rings, or acorn squash boats.

BAKE THE POTATOES: Preheat the oven to 450°F, and on a greased sheet pan place the halved yams face side down. Using a fork, poke their skins all over to create steam holes. Drizzle their tops with olive oil and bake in the oven for 18 to 30 minutes, until tender (the timing will depend on their size).

MEANWHILE, MAKE THE TAMARIND SYRUP: In a small bowl, mix together the 2 tablespoons butter, the tamarind concentrate, brown sugar, and salt and set aside.

MAKE THE GINGER SUGAR (SEE TIP): In another small mixing bowl, combine the turbinado sugar, ginger, and lime zest and rub everything together between your fingers to release some of the oils from the zest. Set it aside.

BROIL THE POTATOES: Remove the potatoes from the oven and set the oven to broil. Flip the potatoes cut side up and, using a pastry brush, brush their tops generously with the tamarind syrup. Sprinkle over the ginger sugar. Place the potatoes back into the oven to broil for about 90 seconds or so, watching closely, until their tops are bubbling and darker brown in color. Remove from the oven, sprinkle with more ginger sugar, and drizzle over more tamarind syrup before serving.

TIP

This ginger sugar has many uses: as a rim for holiday cocktail glasses, a sprinkle for muffin tops or pumpkin cakes, or anywhere else you can imagine it. Wherever it goes it gives a wonderful textural bite.

CHAPTER 7

MY HUNGRY INNER CHILD

Throwbacks Reimagined

SO MUCH OF WHAT PREVENTS us from truly understanding ourselves can be traced back to the wounds we endured as children, which are so formative. But if we can meet that little person and learn to love them in the ways that they thought they couldn't be loved, we can truly experience deep emotional healing in our bodies.

My little child was told in so many ways that her hunger was a burden. I met her not too long ago during a moment of deep meditation. It was a joy to pull away all the layers of what I had piled on top of her buoyant spirit to experience her pure curiosity, wonder, and restlessness. She was so insanely pure-hearted! How could I ever think she didn't deserve to do the things that lit her up and eat the things that made her smile? Instead of being a judgmental adult, I'd rather take on the role of loving mother, and respond with more nurturing and trust . . . then allow that hungry girl in me to consciously and happily down a pint of ice cream, because care is found in balance.

Rice Krispie Tofu Nuggets

with Maple Mustard

SERVES
4
(DF, EF, GF, NF, RSF, ≤30)

TOFU NUGGETS

avocado oil, for drizzling

extra-firm tofu 1 (14-ounce) block, frozen overnight and thawed (see Tip, page 24)

cornstarch *or arrowroot powder* 1/4 cup

onion powder 1 teaspoon

garlic powder 1 teaspoon

kosher salt 1 teaspoon, plus more for sprinkling

freshly ground black pepper 1/4 teaspoon

Rice Krispies cereal 1 1/2 to 2 cups (see Tip)

MAPLE MUSTARD

pure maple syrup 2 tablespoons

Dijon mustard 2 tablespoons

kosher salt 1/4 teaspoon

lemon juice 1 teaspoon

avocado oil *or grapeseed oil* 2 tablespoons

favorite BBQ sauce, for serving

Whenever my parents would pull, unannounced, into a McDonald's drive-through for dinner, my face and heart would beam and my eyes would settle on those golden arches. I would request the biggest box of chicken nuggets available plus a slew of honey mustard and BBQ sauce packets, because it was important that I dip them into both at the same time. Thanks to a combination of freezing this tofu in advance and soaking the pieces in a cornstarch slurry, these nuggets remind me of the iconic ones of my childhood, with their bouncy, chewy center.

PREHEAT THE OVEN to 450°F and arrange a rack in the upper middle part of the oven. Have a large sheet pan nearby and drizzle it liberally with avocado oil. Set aside.

PRESS AND CUT THE TOFU: Drain the block of tofu by holding it over the sink and gently press it between your palms to expel the extra water. It should be a bit like a sponge. (Alternatively, wrap it in paper towels and place a heavy pan over top for at least 15 minutes. See Make It Fancy.) With the long side of the tofu facing you, cut the block in half, then each half into 4 strips, then turn the block 90 degrees counterclockwise and cut it in half again so you have 8 flat squares. Press each cut piece again, gently without tearing, to remove any excess water.

BREAD THE TOFU: In a small bowl, whisk together the cornstarch, onion powder, garlic powder, salt, pepper, and **½ CUP WATER** to make a slurry. Place the tofu in a small tray and drizzle over the mixture, flipping the tofu so it soaks up all the slurry, allowing it a full 10 minutes to fully absorb. Flip it over in the mixture a final time before breading.

MAKE IT FANCY

Pivot: Make **tofu cutlets** instead of nuggets. Cut the block of tofu into 4 steaks, follow the steps for breading, and then pan-fry them in a ¼ inch of hot oil for 2 to 3 minutes per side until golden brown and crispy. Top with a **ruffled slaw or chopped romaine** dressed **in Caesar dressing** and sprinkled with **Parm** for an upside-down Caesar salad.

CRUSH THE RICE: Put the cereal in a large bowl and, using your hands, crush the cereal so you have an even mix of flour-like pieces and pieces of roughly crushed rice kernels. Roll the tofu pieces in the crushed cereal to coat well, then place the pieces on the prepared sheet pan.

BAKE: Drizzle their tops with more avocado oil and bake them in the oven for 18 to 20 minutes, until golden and crispy.

MEANWHILE, MAKE THE MAPLE MUSTARD: In a small mason jar with a lid, combine the maple syrup, mustard, salt, lemon juice, and avocado oil. Top with the lid and shake vigorously until combined. (Alternatively just whisk them together in a bowl.)

SERVE: Remove the tofu nuggets from the oven and sprinkle them with more salt if desired. Serve with the maple mustard and BBQ sauce on the side.

TIP

When breading foods, consider experimenting with crushed things from the cabinet (rice cereal, tortilla chips, potato chips, puffed quinoa, Takis). They all make a fun alternative to regular breadcrumbs when you're trying to make a crisp breading.

SERVES
6
(DF, EF)

Walnut Chili Cheese Dawgs

WALNUT CHILI

raw walnuts 2 cups ← or sub ½ pound of ground beef or turkey

dark red kidney beans 2 (15-ounce) cans, drained and rinsed, divided

avocado oil *or olive oil* 2 tablespoons

white onion 1 large, diced

garlic cloves 4, minced

chili powder 1 tablespoon

ground cumin 1 tablespoon

paprika 2 teaspoons

dried oregano ½ teaspoon

kosher salt ½ teaspoon, plus more as needed

cayenne pepper ¼ teaspoon

soy sauce *or tamari* 2 tablespoons

apple cider vinegar *or distilled white vinegar* 2 tablespoons

light brown sugar *or maple syrup* 1 tablespoon

dried bay leaf 1

veggie bouillon paste 1 teaspoon

CHILI CHEESE DAWGS

toasted hot dog buns 6

veggie dogs *or hot dog brand of choice* 8 (see Tip)

Smoked Almond Queso (recipe follows)

My husband's inner child was heavy into chili dogs, so as per his request, this one is on repeat. This is the ultimate vegan chili dog that really comes together when I take the time to prepare our favorite "important toppings." Luckily the chili dawg base is a cinch. Use the leftover chili (or double it) to serve over tortilla chips or curly fries to make killer nachos, top a loaded baked potato, spoon some into hard taco shells, serve over rice, or nestle a little over or inside a cheese burrito.

MAKE THE CHILI: In a food processor fitted with a steel blade, pulse the walnuts on high until the crumbs resemble ground beef. Transfer to a bowl and set aside.

PUREE THE BEANS: Back in the food processor, blend 1 can of the beans with **1 CUP WATER** until smooth. Set aside.

TOAST THE NUTS: Heat a medium pot over medium-high heat and drizzle in the oil. When it's hot, add the onion and sauté for 5 to 7 minutes, until translucent, tossing occasionally. Add the garlic and cook for about 30 seconds, or until fragrant. Add the ground walnuts (or ground meat, if using), chili powder, cumin, paprika, oregano, salt, and cayenne pepper. Reduce the heat to medium and cook for 5 minutes, or until the nuts begin to toast, tossing frequently.

SIMMER THE CHILI: Add the soy sauce and vinegar to deglaze the pot, then add the pureed beans, the remaining can of whole beans, the light brown sugar, bay leaf, and bouillon paste and cook covered for 30 minutes on medium-low heat. Stir occasionally throughout until the flavors come together. Taste and add more salt if desired.

(recipe continues)

MAKE IT FANCY

Add all your favorite chili dog toppings: **Frazzled Onions (page 284)** or other crispy onions such as French's, **your mustard of choice**, **Relly's Relish (page 288)**, **jalapeños**, **diced white onion**, **Venusian Ketchup (page 276)** or store-bought ketchup, or sauerkraut.

COOK AND ASSEMBLE THE DOGS: Place the toasted buns on a platter. Heat a grill pan or a large cast-iron skillet over medium-high heat and cook the veggie dogs in the dry skillet for 3 to 5 minutes, until lightly charred on all sides, tossing occasionally. Place the grilled hot dogs in the center of the buns and top with chili, Smoked Almond Queso, and other favorite toppings and serve.

TIP

Nothing's worse than a hot dog link that gets swallowed by its bun. Buy a couple extra hot dogs, cut them in half, and add them as extensions to each of your dawgs. Your buns will hold more toppings, and you'll suddenly have a gourmet-looking dawg.

Smoked Almond Queso

MAKES 2 GENEROUS CUPS
(DF, GF, RSF, ≤30)

This recipe is the reason I keep an obscene stock of smoked nuts in the cabinet. It's also evidence of the wonders even just a handful can do. This is a dairy-free queso I make for its simplicity. Serve as a dip for pretzel sticks, veggies, or tortillas chips.

hickory-smoked almonds (such as Smokehouse Almonds) ½ cup (3 ounces) (see Tip)

lemon juice ¼ cup (from about 2 large lemons), plus more as needed

onion powder 1 tablespoon

garlic cloves 4

nutritional yeast ¼ cup

tomato paste 2 teaspoons

kosher salt ½ teaspoon, plus more as needed depending on the saltiness of your almonds

BLEND THE QUESO: In a high-powered blender, combine the smoked almonds, **1 CUP WATER**, lemon juice, onion powder, garlic, nutritional yeast, and tomato paste, and salt, blending on high for about 5 minutes, or until completely smooth and the sauce is ultra thick and hot. Thin with more water, if needed, and taste and season with more salt and more lemon juice as desired.

STORE: Transfer to a small lidded container and keep in the fridge for up to 1 week.

MAKE IT FANCY

Once the queso has been blended, stir in **2 (4-ounce) cans diced green chiles** or **1 (10-ounce) can fire roasted diced tomatoes** for extra flavor and heat.

TIP

If you have almonds that aren't smokey or smokey *enough*, add a teaspoon or so of smoked paprika to wake them up.

Beans & Hasselback Sausages

with Peppers and Onions

SERVES
4 to 6
(DF, EF, GF, NF)

sausages 4 (¾ pound) Italian-style sweet and spicy sausages (we choose the vegetarian brand Field Roast)

olive oil, for frying

red onion ½ medium, thinly sliced

green bell pepper *or yellow* ½ medium, seeds and ribs removed, thinly sliced (see Tip)

red bell pepper ½ medium, seeds and ribs removed, thinly sliced

kosher salt

garlic cloves 4, minced

pinto beans 3 (15-ounce) cans

vegetable bouillon paste 1 tablespoon

light brown sugar 4 to 5 tablespoons, plus more as needed

Venusian Ketchup (page 276) *or store-bought ketchup* 3 tablespoons

Dijon mustard *or yellow mustard* 1 tablespoon, plus more as needed

unsulphured molasses 1 tablespoon

smoked paprika ½ teaspoon, plus more as needed

cayenne pepper a pinch

This is really just beans and weenies, a classic latchkey kids grew up eating, except I'm swapping hot dogs for juicy, sweet sausages and adding caramelized peppers and onions to the mix. They remind me of those insanely fragrant Fenway Park sausages grilled outside our window every game day when we lived in Boston. I leave the sausages whole, instead of in little coins, but Hasselback them—which simply means that I cut them in thin slices along their surface, but not all the way through. This makes them feel more like dinner, and it's a proper move that allows more control over the bean-to-weenie ratio, something any official adult deserves.

BROWN THE SAUSAGES: Using a sharp knife, score the sausages Hasselback style (see Headnote) along one side in parallel slits, about ¼ inch apart, without cutting through to the other side. Heat a large cast-iron skillet over medium-high heat. Swirl a couple tablespoons of olive oil into the skillet to coat. Add the sausages and cook, turning them over occasionally, for 5 to 7 minutes, until the sausages are golden brown and charred in spots. Remove the sausages from the pan and set them aside on a cutting board.

SAUTÉ THE VEGETABLES: In the same skillet, add a little more oil, if needed, then add the onion, green and red bell peppers, and a generous pinch of salt and sauté for 5 to 7 minutes, until the onion begins to soften and the peppers char slightly. Add the garlic and sauté for about 30 seconds, or until fragrant, stirring constantly.

SIMMER: Add the beans and their juices to the skillet, scraping up any bits of onion and peppers from the pan. Then add the bouillon paste, brown sugar, Venusian Ketchup, mustard, molasses, paprika, and cayenne pepper and stir. Reduce the heat to a simmer, nestle the sausages into the beans, and cook for 15 to 20 minutes, stirring occasionally, making sure nothing sticks to the bottom of the pan, until the beans are tender and the sausages impart some flavor to the beans.

SERVE: Taste, adjusting the salt, paprika, mustard, and brown sugar as desired before serving.

MAKE IT FANCY

For a Jamaican-style twist, add **1 tablespoon freshly grated ginger** (from one 2-inch peeled knob) as you sauté the garlic, and once it's time to add the canned beans add **one 12-ounce bottle of ginger beer** (such as Reed's) to simmer.

TIP

It's always fancy not to cut yourself, but the waxy skin of a bell pepper can make this a tricky job. To make thin slices, first cut the top and bottom off the pepper, then cut it in half, then cut away the core and membrane. Place the skin side down on the cutting board, so your knife can grip the inside instead of slipping on the waxy skin.

CHAPTER 8

FANCY BY MYSELF

Big Bowls & Teetering Toast

COOKING AND EATING ALONE CAN be one of the sweetest gifts you give yourself. It's a simple way of saying, *I'm worthy of my own care*—a conviction that feels powerfully self-affirming, especially when no one is around to witness it. There's something impactful about slowing down and creating an intentional dinner just for yourself, even if it's alone in bed furnished with a cushioned lap desk. Those solo dinners don't have to be extravagant. Usually they can take the shape of toast, arranged in a considered way, topped with a little of this and that, or bowls filled with comforting, layered flavors. They're not fancy for anyone else's approval—but they're thoughtful in a way that matters to you.

Solo Toasts

SERVES 1

Depending on how much energy you have to give in the moment, throw together eye-catching toast. On a slice of your favorite toasted bread, tower any in season, roasted, or fresh-cut fruit over a spread of creamy dairy or other luscious ingredient, like pureed cannellini beans. It never gets old because the variations are endless. It can be as minimal or as elaborate as you like.

IDEAS	THE TOAST	SOMETHING CREAMY (A PUREE, NUT BUTTER, COMPOUND BUTTER, ETC.)
STRAWBERRY FETA BRUSCHETTA	Grilled sourdough bread	Crumbled feta smashed with Greek yogurt
SMASHED BEAN TOAST WITH TOMATOES	Toasted whole-grain or rye bread	Canned white beans or chickpeas smashed with olive oil
UPSIDE-DOWN TAHINI TUNA MELTS	Whole grain or rye bread toasted with cheese	Canned tuna + tahini paste + lemon juice + S + P
RED PIZZA TOAST	Grilled sourdough bread or other crusty bread	Pizza Butter (page 291)
SWEET AND TANGY TOAST	Grilled sourdough bread	Goat cheese, cream cheese, or Swiss Ricotta Lemon Cream (page 108)
BASIL AND LIME AVOCADO TOAST	Toasted whole-grain bread or sourdough	Smashed avocado + lime juice + garlic salt
FALAFEL TOAST	Toasted whole-grain bread	Hummus
SUNDAE TOAST (DESSERT)	Grilled sourdough bread or toasted brioche	Smear of nut butter + 1 scoop vanilla ice cream

FRUIT OR VEG	SOMETHING CRUNCHY	SOMETHING GREEN	SPRINKLES OR DRIZZLES TO FINISH
Diced strawberries + honey + lemon	Pistachios or chopped roasted almonds	Basil or mint confetti	Olive oil + freshly ground black pepper
Chopped tomatoes + olives + garlic	Sliced red onion	Chopped parsley or Charred Scallion Sauce (page 275)	Smoked salt; za'atar; BBQ rub; Aleppo pepper flakes
Pickled jalapenos or Relly's Relish (page 288)	Crushed salt & vinegar chips (or other salty chip)	Minced dill or chives	More lemon juice; Everything Bagel seasoning
Tomato paste	—	Dried oregano	Olive oil, Arrabbiata Flakes (page 286), grated Parm
Blueberry preserves, mango chutney, roasted figs, squash, or peaches	Candied chopped nuts or seeds	Microgreens	Lemon, lime, or orange zest
Sliced radish	Crispy fried eggs (see page 239)	Basil confetti	Arrabbiata Flakes (page 286); chili crisp
Sliced roasted beets, radish, and/or sliced cucumber	Falafel Crumbles (page 283)	Arugula	Olive oil, Basil Oil (page 294), balsamic glaze
—	Crushed pistachios	—	Black Pepper Balsamic Cherries (page 172)

Creamy Coconut Ramen

SERVES
1
(DF, NF, ≤30)

coconut milk 1 (13.5-ounce) can (if you like it extra creamy, go with full-fat)

white miso paste 1 tablespoon

tamari *or soy sauce* 1 tablespoon

vegetable bouillon paste 1 tablespoon

toasted sesame oil 2 teaspoons

chili powder 2 teaspoons

paprika ½ teaspoon

garlic powder ½ teaspoon

onion powder ½ teaspoon

cayenne pepper ¼ teaspoon

coconut sugar *or sweetener of choice* ½ teaspoon

ramen noodles 1 (3.5- to 4-ounce packet), flavor packet discarded or added in, whatever you think is best

chile crisp

One day when I was all alone, after staring down the hole of my kitchen cabinets to the very back where I stash my emergency supply of ramen noodles, I eventually learned that a single can of coconut milk can make a packet of instant ramen feel suddenly luxurious. Here I use a quick homemade (slightly Tex-Mex–inspired) spicy vegetarian broth to replace those sus flavor packets. This recipe makes a lot of broth because I only like to sip my soup as if it were a behemoth bowl of pho, but, of course, you can freeze the extra broth if you like.

MAKE THE BROTH: In a medium pot, whisk together the coconut milk, miso paste, tamari, bouillon paste, sesame oil, chili powder, paprika, garlic powder, onion powder, cayenne pepper, sugar, and **1 CUP WATER**. Bring the mixture to a boil, then reduce it to a simmer until ready to serve.

BOIL THE NOODLES: Bring a large pot of water to a boil and cook the noodles according to their package instructions. Drain the noodles and transfer to a serving bowl. Pour over the coconut broth, top with chile crisp, and serve.

MAKE IT FANCY

Thankfully ramen is entirely customizable and garnish-friendly. Simmer **a handful of mushrooms** like shiitake or kikurage (wood ear) in the pot of broth or add an egg directly in the broth to poach: Crack **a large egg** into a small bowl, gently slide it into the simmering broth, and let it cook undisturbed for 3 to 4 minutes, until the white is set and the yolk is still soft.

SERVES
1, 4 x
(DF, NF, ≤30)

Watermelon Sushi Bowls *with Wasabi Mayo*

WATERMELON SASHIMI

avocado oil, for oiling and drizzling

store-bought watermelon spears (see Tip) *or sushi-grade tuna* 1 pound

soy sauce 2 tablespoons

toasted sesame oil ½ teaspoon

sesame seeds 1 teaspoon

scallions 2 tablespoons sliced, green part only

SUSHI RICE

uncooked sushi rice, *arborio rice, or short-grain white or brown rice* 1 cup

rice wine vinegar *or apple cider vinegar* 1 tablespoon

honey *or granulated sugar* ½ teaspoon (optional)

kosher salt ¼ teaspoon

WASABI MAYO

mayo ¼ cup

wasabi paste 1½ to 2 teaspoons

sesame oil ¼ teaspoon

fresh ginger ½ teaspoon grated

turbinado sugar ¼ teaspoon, plus more as needed

Making anything sushi-inspired feels innately special, which is why I think you won't insist on perfecting the technique for rolling sushi to feel like you're treating yourself. You could simply pile those same colorful ingredients into a bowl and still be comfortably ambitious. If you want to break this recipe into parts to make some of it ahead, marinate the watermelon for up to 3 days in advance. Any longer and the watermelon's texture will begin to break down. It will still taste delicious, it just won't be as firm. And because this makes extra servings, keep the leftovers for a desk lunch or a few more solo dinners later in the week.

PREHEAT THE OVEN to 350°F.

ROAST THE WATERMELON: Oil a sheet pan with the avocado oil and place the watermelon on the pan. Drizzle with more avocado oil, rubbing the spears to coat all over. Place into the oven to roast for 1 hour, gently flipping the spears over about every 20 minutes, or until the flesh of the watermelon has tightened and darkened and released about 20 percent of its liquid.

MARINATE THE WATERMELON: Remove the watermelon from the oven, let it cool completely, then cut the watermelon into ½-inch cubes. In a medium mixing bowl, combine the cubed watermelon, soy sauce, sesame oil, sesame seeds, and scallions and toss to coat. Transfer the cubes to a lidded container and store in the fridge while you cook the rice.

MAKE THE RICE: In a rice cooker or in a saucepan on the stovetop, cook the sushi rice according to the package instructions. Once cooked, add the vinegar, honey (if using), and salt. Using a fork, fluff the rice to mix everything together.

(recipe continues)

MAKE THE WASABI MAYO: In a small bowl, whisk together the mayo, wasabi (depending on the mayo you will need to adjust the amount for the best balance), sesame oil, ginger, and sugar to combine.

BUILD AND TOP A BOWL: Fill the bottom of your favorite serving bowl with rice and top with a scoop of the marinated watermelon and some of its juices. Dollop some of the mayo over top and garnish with your toppings of choice.

MAKE IT FANCY

Top your bowl with **sliced avocado** (see Tip), **pickled sushi ginger**, **crunchy wasabi peas**, **2 to 3 nori sheets**, **microgreens**, **steamed edamame**, **julienned cucumbers**, or **Shaken Pickled Cucumber Ribbon Salad (page 179)**.

TIP

If you can't find precut watermelon, just buy a small watermelon, cut it in half, place each half flat side down, slice it into 1-inch-wide strips vertically, followed by horizontal cuts, then trim away the rind to create easy-to-eat spears.

There is an entire corner of the internet devoted to the art of avocado design, and I see why. It's a malleable material, and it takes barely any time to shape into patterns. Take half of a peeled and pitted avocado and thinly slice it lengthwise. Press it gently on the sides to flatten and fan the pieces into a thin line, then roll the line into a spiral.

SERVES

1

(GF, NF, ≤30)

BYO Burger Bowl

A deconstructed burger in a bowl without the bread is a brilliant and satisfying dinner, especially when you have unlimited toppings and sauces to choose from. This is my go-to burger bowl, a semi-Asian fusion–style burger loaded with briny and spicy things and, of course, silky caramelized onions. But, as with any byob, to each their own. You can even top your bowl with croutons made from brioche bread or sesame hamburger buns if you find yourself missing those bready carbs (see Tip). My only advice when making this, or any burger for that matter: For the most flavor, fry the ground meat on high heat long enough so it gets extra crispy all over.

shredded iceberg lettuce *or mixed salad greens, or olive-oil massaged kale*

tomatoes (Roma or plum), sliced or diced

Adobo Onions (recipe follows) *or Pickled Pink Onions (page 287)*

dill pickles *or cornichons*, sliced

avocado oil *or olive oil*, for frying

lean ground beef *or meatless crumbles* ¼ to ½ pound

seasoned salt *or salt and freshly ground black pepper*

cheese (whatever you have on hand), finely shredded or crumbled

Spicy Sesame Aïoli (page 292) *or Island Achiote Dressing (page 150) or burger sauce(s) of choice*

FILL A BOWL with iceberg lettuce and top with tomatoes, the Adobo Onions, and pickles and set aside.

BROWN THE BEEF: Heat a large cast-iron skillet over medium-high heat. Once it's hot, drizzle in 1 tablespoon of avocado oil, add the ground beef, and season with seasoned salt to taste. Cook the beef, tossing for 5 to 7 minutes, until completely cooked through and all the liquid has evaporated. Add another 2 tablespoons of avocado oil to the pan and cook the beef for another 2 to 3 minutes, until it begins to fry and turn crispy, caramelized, and deep golden brown. Remove from the heat and allow to cool slightly.

SERVE: Spoon the beef over the bowl of lettuce and top with cheese and spicy sesame aïoli. Enjoy.

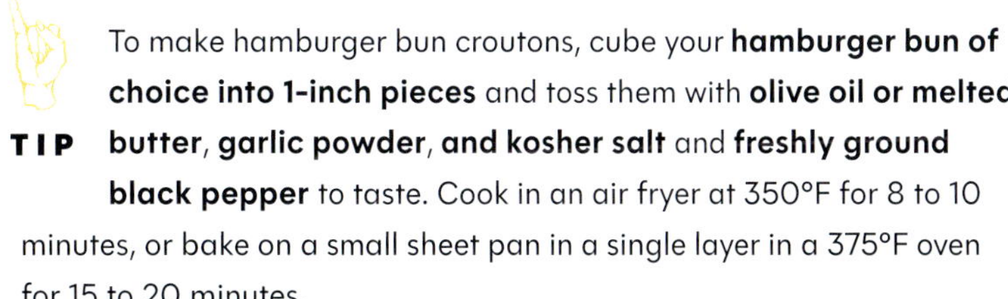

TIP To make hamburger bun croutons, cube your **hamburger bun of choice into 1-inch pieces** and toss them with **olive oil or melted butter, garlic powder, and kosher salt** and **freshly ground black pepper** to taste. Cook in an air fryer at 350°F for 8 to 10 minutes, or bake on a small sheet pan in a single layer in a 375°F oven for 15 to 20 minutes.

Adobo Onions

MAKES ABOUT 1 QUART

I could pile a tangle of these sticky, rich onions over a bowl of hot rice with roasted veggies and be immediately taken back to the '90s and my mom's sumptuous, baked, and nearly blackened chicken adobo. You can't convince me that there's anything that smells better than onions sautéing in oil or butter. There are a lot of onions in this pot, so use an extra-large pot or Dutch oven. Pile them into a Burger Bowl (page 207), over Animal-Style Hot Mess Baked Potatoes (page 210), or onto a thick slice of crusty country bread topped with a slice or two of Gruyère cheese and dried thyme, then broiled till gooey as an ode to French onion soup.

olive oil 2 tablespoons

yellow onions *or white* 2 pounds (about 3 large), halved and thinly sliced

soy sauce *or tamari* 1/3 cup ← or sub with 2 tablespoons white miso paste + 1/3 cup water

distilled white vinegar *or apple cider vinegar* 1/2 cup

honey 1 tablespoon

garlic cloves 2, chopped

red pepper flakes *or freshly ground black pepper* 1/4 teaspoon

SAUTÉ THE ONIONS (SEE TIP): In a large skillet over medium-high heat (or large Dutch oven), heat the olive oil and, once it's hot, spread out the onions in the skillet. Sauté them for about 5 minutes, or until the onions begin to sweat and soften, tossing occasionally.

MAKE THE SAUCE: Meanwhile, in a small bowl, whisk together the soy sauce, vinegar, honey, garlic, and red pepper flakes to combine. Add the mixture to the onions and toss to coat. Continue cooking for another 15 to 22 minutes, depending on how much water the onions release, until the onions have completely collapsed and all the liquid has turned into a dark molasses-like syrup and coats the onions.

STORE: Allow to cool completely, then transfer to a lidded container and refrigerate for 1 to 2 weeks until ready to use.

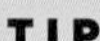

TIP

Turn on your vent hood to help prevent your eyes from burning too badly.

Hot Mess Baked Potatoes 4 Ways

SERVES
1

avocado oil *or olive oil*, for oiling and drizzling

Russet potatoes *or sweet potatoes*, scrubbed well

kosher salt and **freshly ground black pepper** *or other spice mix or seasonings* (ideas follow), for coating

favorite potato toppings (ideas follow)

A baked potato is a lonely man's meal, but it doesn't have to feel like a sad one. When you cut your potatoes in a grid pattern and then leave them in the oven to bake, they will flower and their tops will crisp, producing a literal visual explosion of potato wonder. You'll be left with a cross between a basket of French fries and a creamy baked potato—and a true blank canvas for imaginative topping ideas. I bake a bunch at a time, and then reheat them (in a hot oven or air fryer) when I'm alone. Some house favorites include Curry Bomb potatoes with lime juice, cilantro, scallions, and Sambal Butter; Greek fries: potatoes rubbed with herbs de Provence and topped with Iceberg Tzatziki, cheeses, more herbs, and olive oil; "Animal Style" inspired by In-N-Out's smothered fries; and finally a migas potato—my absolute favorite: a sweet potato topped with a scrambled egg, shredded cheese, salsa verde, crispy tortilla strips, and uncontrollable dashes of Cholula hot sauce. Tuck into one of these and hell is nowhere to be found.

PREHEAT THE OVEN to 450°F and have a well-oiled sheet pan nearby.

CUT THE POTATOES: I usually bake 4 potatoes at a time because they reheat well in the air fryer. With a sharp chef's knife, trim a small piece off the bottom of the potatoes so they lay flat (choose the side that the potatoes naturally roll onto). Cut the potatoes in a tight grid pattern without cutting all the way through. You can rest the potato on a large wooden spoon to make a knife guard so your knife doesn't cut too far.

ROAST THE POTATOES: Drizzle with avocado oil, sprinkle with salt and pepper to taste, and bake for about 1 hour and 20 minutes, or until the potatoes are soft to their cores and extra crispy along their edges and tips. Timing will depend on their size and how tight a grid pattern you make.

Dressing Up Your Potato

CURRY BOMB Rub a gridded potato with olive oil and Curry-Spice Mix (recipe follows), and bake. When ready to serve, dollop with Sambal Butter (recipe follows), and top with lime juice, cilantro leaves, and scallions.

CURRY-SPICE MIX Stir together 1/4 teaspoon ground turmeric, 1 teaspoon mild curry powder, 1 teaspoon ground chili powder, and 1/4 teaspoon ground cumin.

SAMBAL BUTTER Stir together 2 tablespoons softened unsalted butter or ghee, a pinch of kosher salt, and 1/2 to 1 tablespoon sambal oelek or other hot chili paste.

GREEK FRIES Rub a gridded potato with olive oil and Herbes de Provence Mix (recipe follows), and bake. When ready to serve dollop with Iceberg Tzatziki (recipe follows), grated Parmesan cheese or crumbled feta, store-bought or homemade tabbouleh, sauteed spinach, or Falafel Crumbles (page 283).

HERBES DE PROVENCE MIX: Stir together 1/2 teaspoon of granulated garlic, 1/4 teaspoon cracked black pepper, 1 teaspoon herbes de Provence (crushed in hand), and 1/4 teaspoon dried mint.

ICEBERG TZATZIKI: Mix together 1/4 cup finely shredded iceberg lettuce, 1/4 cup shredded cucumber, 1/4 cup Greek yogurt, 1/4 cup roughly chopped fresh herbs (like parsley and dill), 2 teaspoons olive oil, and salt and pepper to taste.

ANIMAL STYLE Rub a gridded potato with olive oil, kosher salt, and freshly ground black pepper to taste and bake. When done, top with shredded cheddar cheese and bake for another 5 minutes, or until the cheese has melted. Serve with Adobo Onions (page 208), Spicy Sesame Aïoli (page 292) and/or Venusian Ketchup (page 276) or regular ketchup.

MIGAS Rub a gridded sweet potato with oil and kosher salt and freshly ground black pepper to taste, and bake. When ready to serve, top with a scrambled egg, Monterey Jack cheese or cheddar, Carrot Top Salsa Verde (page 119) or other salsa, fried tortilla strips, and a few dashes of hot sauce (like Cholula).

SERVES

1

Gigantic Guava & Cream Cheese–Swirled Danish Cookie

guava paste 2 ounces, cut into small pieces ← or sub apricot, blueberry, or raspberry preserves

plain cream cheese 4 ounces, divided

egg 1 large, separated

unsalted butter 2 tablespoons, softened

light brown sugar 2 tablespoons

pure maple syrup 1 tablespoon

lemon zest ½ teaspoon (from 1 lemon), divided

almond extract ¼ teaspoon

baking soda ⅛ teaspoon

kosher salt ½ teaspoon

all-purpose flour *or gluten-free flour blend* ½ cup (60 grams)

pure vanilla extract ¼ teaspoon

raw sliced almonds 2 to 3 tablespoons

This cookie fulfills all my wildest dessert desires, as it's sort of a cookie, but also a cake and Danish all in one (plus it's huge!). It requires just enough care that I feel like I am creating something thoughtful and special for myself, yet it's doable because it's on such a small scale that no one even has to know it is being made; no one except me and my tiny little air fryer (see Tip).

THIN THE GUAVA PASTE: In a small saucepan over medium heat, combine the guava paste and **2 TABLESPOONS WATER** (1 tablespoon if using preserves) and cook, breaking it up with a whisk until no more lumps remain and it is the consistency of jam. Add more water, if needed. Set aside.

COMBINE THE COOKIE BASE INGREDIENTS: In the bowl of a mini food processor, blend together until completely combined 1 ounce (2 tablespoons) of the cream cheese, the egg yolk, butter, brown sugar, maple syrup, half of the lemon zest, the almond extract, baking soda, and salt. Add the flour and blend just until it is completely incorporated, stopping to scrape down the sides of the bowl as needed.

SHAPE THE COOKIE BASE: Have a piece of parchment nearby just large enough to fit the bottom of an air fryer. Using a rubber spatula, scrape all the batter from the bowl and blade and pile it onto the center of the parchment paper. Using damp hands, shape the dough into a 6-inch-wide disc and create a wide well in the center of the disc (still maintaining a thin layer of dough at the bottom and about ½ inch of dough around the edges) to hold the filling. Set aside.

(recipe continues)

MAKE THE FILLING: In the same food processor bowl, combine the remaining cream cheese, the egg white, the remaining lemon zest, and the vanilla and blend on high until completely smooth and runny. Pour the filling into the center of the cookie. Using a spoon, drop small dollops of the guava paste over top of the cream cheese mixture, and using the tip of the spoon (or a toothpick), slowly drag the guava through the cream cheese to make swirls. Sprinkle the edges of the cookie with the almonds.

AIR FRY: Transfer the cookie on the piece of parchment to the bottom of the basket of an air fryer or onto the tray of a toaster oven with an air-fryer setting and air fry at 290°F for 12 to 14 minutes, until the center is set and the cookie is puffed, cooked through, and golden around the edges. Remove from the fryer and allow to cool and set slightly for 15 to 20 minutes before eating, otherwise you'll risk burning the roof of your mouth with hot guava.

OR BAKE: Transfer the parchment paper with the cookie onto a sheet pan and into an oven preheated to 375°F to bake for 15 to 18 minutes, until puffed and wonderfully golden brown. Remove from the oven and allow at least 15 to 20 minutes to cool.

MAKE IT FANCY

Dust a little **confectioners' sugar** around the edges of the cookie to hide any imperfections.

CHAPTER 9

LAVISH LEFTOVERS

The Pleasure in Repurposing

I WANT TO CELEBRATE THE MAGIC of making things out of what feels like nothing by sharing methods and tricks for turning leftovers into meals that are anything but lackluster. Here's a starting point for beginning to reimagine your dinner using last night's "paints." Once you start playing, you'll start stretching your imagination, which will only mean better dinners in the future.

SERVES
4
(NF)

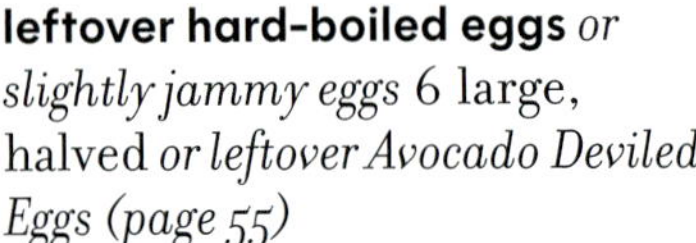

leftover hard-boiled eggs *or slightly jammy eggs* 6 large, halved *or leftover Avocado Deviled Eggs (page 55)*

mayo 1/4 cup

Dijon mustard *or spicy brown mustard* 2 teaspoons

diced scallions *or minced chives* 1/4 cup

dill pickles, 1/4 cup diced *or 1 tablespoon sweet pickle relish*

yellow curry powder 1 teaspoon, plus more as needed

kosher salt and **freshly ground black pepper**

vegetables *or herbs* (such as radishes, cucumbers, or asparagus, ends trimmed; or fresh cilantro leaves)

unsalted butter, for spreading

favorite soft sandwich bread 8 slices

hot sauce, for serving (optional)

Smashed Curry Egg Salad Tea Sandwiches

If you made a bunch of hard-boiled or jammy eggs and don't know what to do with them, turn them into these fancy finger sandwiches. You can even use leftover straggling Sky-High Avocado Deviled Eggs (page 55) for this, and hold back on some of the mayo and mustard.

MAKE THE EGG SALAD: In a large mixing bowl, mash together the egg yolks along with the mayo, Dijon mustard, scallions, pickles, curry powder, and salt and pepper to taste just until smooth. Then add the egg whites and roughly mash them, keeping some of the whites in larger chunks.

PREP THE VEGGIES/HERBS: Using a vegetable peeler, thinly slice the vegetables: Slice the radishes into thin rounds, cut the cucumber and/or asparagus into thin strips, and pluck full leaves of cilantro. Set the vegetables aside.

MAKE THE SANDWICHES: On a sheet of plastic large enough to wrap the sandwich, overlap some of the thinly sliced vegetables in the center, making sure to extend them at least 1/2 inch longer than the surface of the bread you're using on all sides. Butter one side of a piece of bread all the way to the edges, and place it buttered side down over the vegetables, pressing slightly to adhere. Spoon 1/4 of the egg salad over the bread, then top with another slice of bread. Repeat with the remaining vegetables, egg salad, and bread.

WRAP AND CHILL: Using a serrated knife, trim the edges off the sides of the bread. (Eat those!) Then pull the ends of the plastic up around each sandwich tightly to secure the veggies. Refrigerate the sandwiches for at least 30 minutes or up to 2 days to firm.

SERVE: Remove the sandwiches from the fridge. Unwrap them, and using a serrated knife, carefully cut the sandwiches in half, being sure not to disturb the vegetable pattern. Plate and serve with hot sauce, if you want.

Collard Green & Cornbread Ribollita

SERVES
6
(NF)

leftover Shiny Almond & Peach Cornbread (page 175) *or other cornbread* 1 pound, cubed into 1-inch pieces (about 4 cups)

olive oil *or avocado oil*

onion 1 large, chopped

carrots 2 large, chopped

celery stalks 2, chopped

jalapeño 1 small, diced (with or without the seeds)

garlic cloves 8, chopped

kosher salt and **freshly ground black pepper**

collard greens *or a mix of mustard and turnip greens*, 2 bundles, cleaned, ribs removed, and thinly sliced

fire roasted tomatoes 1 (14.5-ounce) can

vegetable broth 5 cups, plus more as needed

apple cider vinegar *or distilled vinegar* 2 tablespoons

light brown sugar *or coconut sugar* 2 teaspoons

soy sauce *or tamari* 2 teaspoons

black-eyed peas 1 (14-ounce) can, drained and rinsed

hot sauce, for serving (optional)

This soup is inspired by Ribollita, a rustic Italian soup that uses day-old crusty bread as a thickener. This is everything I'd put on my plate during the holidays all jumbled in a bowl. I love cutting and slurping ribbons of greens, and since you'd usually use cornbread to help sop up the juices from the greens, I'm happy to give it a solid head start by adding it directly to the pot. Greens can take a while to get tender, and if you're in a rush, try cooking this in an Instant Pot or multi-cooker before stirring in the beans and cornbread only at the end.

PREHEAT THE OVEN to 350°F, and have a large sheet pan nearby.

TOAST THE CORNBREAD: Spread the cornbread on the sheet pan, drizzle with olive oil, and bake for 25 to 28 minutes, until very deep brown on the edges and fairly crispy. Remove from the oven and set aside. The cornbread will continue to dry out while it sits.

SAUTÉ THE VEGGIES: Heat a large pot or Dutch oven over medium-high heat. Once it's hot, drizzle in 2 to 3 tablespoons of olive oil, then add the onion, carrots, celery, jalapeño, garlic, and a pinch of salt and pepper and cook, stirring occasionally, for about 10 minutes, or until the veggies are tender.

SIMMER THE COLLARDS: Add the sliced collard greens to the pot with the vegetables along with the tomatoes, broth, vinegar, brown sugar, and soy sauce. Cover with the lid slightly ajar and cook for at least 25 to 30 minutes, until the collard greens are a muted green and very soft and tender, but longer if you like extra tender greens. Taste and season with more salt and pepper as needed. Stir in half of the toasted cornbread along with the black-eyed peas and cook for another 5 to 10 minutes. Since the cornbread isn't glutenous like regular bread, it will begin to disintegrate in the soup after a while, thickening the soup and giving it more flavor.

SERVE: Spoon the soup into bowls, top with the remaining cornbread and a few dashes of hot sauce (if using), and enjoy.

Black Garlic Suppli

MAKES ABOUT
18 TO 20
SUPPLI

(NF, RSF, ≤30)

olive oil, for oiling the sheet pan and drizzling

leftover Nearly Instantaneous Black Garlic Risotto (page 72) 2 cups

tomato paste 6 tablespoons

dried oregano 2 teaspoons

Parmesan cheese ½ cup shredded

eggs 2 large

Italian-style panko breadcrumbs 2 cups

Rosemary Truffle Aïoli (page 293), for serving

MAKE IT FANCY

Decorate your plate with a drizzle of **Basil Oil (page 294)** if you really want to impress, or simply sprinkle the suppli with **Pesto Sprinkles (page 286)** or a little **Parsley Dust (page 27)**.

The art of making croquettes—turning leftover starchy grains like polenta, grits, sticky rice, mac 'n' cheese, mashed potatoes, and in this case, risotto into crispy bites—is more intuition than recipe prescription. It depends on the grain. How starchy is it? Do you need to add extra starch? Is there cheese? Should you add an egg? Flour? Whatever you're starting with will determine what will need to be tweaked to make sure your croquettes hold their shape when cooked. It's a golden ratio between grains and just enough binding to hold it together without making your croquettes stiff and dry.

PREHEAT THE OVEN to 450°F and have a well-oiled sheet pan nearby.

MIX THE FILLING: In a large mixing bowl, place the risotto, tomato paste, oregano, and Parmesan cheese. Using clean hands or a wooden spoon, mix all the ingredients together thoroughly. Using a 1.5-ounce ice cream scoop or by just eyeballing it, scoop the warm mixture and roll in your palms into golf ball–size balls. Transfer them to a plate and set aside.

MAKE THE BREADING STATION: In a small mixing bowl, combine the eggs and **2 TABLESPOONS WATER**. In a large bowl, place the breadcrumbs and 1 tablespoon of the beaten egg mixture (see Tip) and toss together with your hands to make a slightly damp, crumbly mixture.

BAKE: Roll the balls through the egg wash to coat, shaking off any excess egg, then through the egg/breadcrumb mixture to coat. Place the balls on the prepared sheet pan and drizzle their tops with more olive oil. Bake them in the oven for 15 to 20 minutes, until crunchy and golden brown.

SERVE warm and top with a dollop of the truffle aïoli on each.

TIP

For an extra-crispy coating without needing to double-bread your croquettes, add a little wet mixture to the dry mixture to make a slightly damp, crumbly mixture. This will help the batter fry or bake with extra surface texture.

SERVES
4
(DF, EF, RSF, ≤30)

olive oil, *butter, or ghee* 2 tablespoons

garlic 1 tablespoon chopped

fresh ginger 1 tablespoon chopped

mild curry powder 2 teaspoons, plus more as needed

chili powder 1 teaspoon

leftover Sun-Dried Tomato Soup **(page 66)** *or other store-bought creamy tomato soup (such as Pacific)* 2 cups

coconut milk 1 (13.5-ounce) can

chickpeas 2 (15-ounce) cans ← or sub 1 cup vegetable broth + 1 cup dried brown or green lentils

kosher salt

cilantro, a handful, chopped

lemon juice, for serving

warm naan *or pita bread* 4 pieces, for serving

Tomato & Ginger Curry

Use almost any creamy tomato soup as a base for a simple, creamy curry. If you don't have a couple cups of Sun-Dried Tomato Soup leftover, try one from the store like Rao's, Pacific, or Imagine's Creamy Tomato Soup. After you get the base simmering, you can add any protein you have around such as canned chickpeas, dried lentils, chopped cauliflower, leftover lamb, cubed chicken breast, etc.

BLOOM THE SPICES: Heat a large skillet over medium-high heat. Once hot, drizzle in the olive oil and add the garlic and ginger and sauté for 1 to 2 minutes, until fragrant. Add the curry powder and chili powder and cook, stirring constantly, for another 30 seconds.

SIMMER THE CURRY: Stir in the tomato soup, coconut milk, chickpeas (or vegetable broth and lentils, if using), and a pinch of salt to taste. Bring to a simmer. Allow it to cook for 10 to 15 minutes, until the chickpeas have softened slightly and the flavors have married (or, if cooking dried lentils, 25 to 35 minutes until they are tender).

SERVE: Stir the cilantro into the pot and season with more salt and lemon juice to taste. Spoon the curry into bowls or on plates and serve with warm naan for scooping.

MAKE IT FANCY

Add **2 packed cups fresh baby spinach** or **1 cup chopped fenugreek leaves**; if using frozen spinach, thaw and drain before adding to the pot to wilt before serving; or for nutty depth, stir in **1 to 2 tablespoons unsweetened creamy peanut butter**.

SERVES
4
(EF)

Mango & Miso Salmon Grain Bowls

Make one of my favorite summer grain bowls that helps me use up the last bits of Shaken Pickled Cucumber Ribbon Salad still marinating in the fridge.

MISO SALMON

salmon 4 (4-ounce) skinless filets ← or sub 1 pound chicken tenderloins

kosher salt and **freshly ground black pepper**

white miso paste 1 tablespoon

rice wine vinegar *or apple cider vinegar* 2 tablespoons

maple syrup *or honey* 1 tablespoon

garlic powder ½ teaspoon

olive oil *or avocado oil*, for frying

GRAIN BOWL

mixed greens (such as baby spinach, chopped kale, or arugula), 6 cups

warm cooked grains (such as brown rice, white rice, or quinoa) 2 cups

shredded carrots 1 cup

mango 1 cup diced, divided ← choose slightly underripe for more crunch

leftover Shaken Pickled Cucumber Ribbon Salad (page 179) 1 cup, drained and roughly chopped

cilantro ¼ cup chopped

roasted salted almonds ¼ cup, roughly chopped

Tahini Teriyaki Dressing (recipe follows)

SEASON THE SALMON: Pat the salmon dry and season with salt and pepper to taste. In a large bowl, whisk together the miso paste, vinegar, maple syrup, and garlic powder, then add the salmon and toss gently to coat.

SEAR THE SALMON: Heat a large cast-iron skillet over medium-high heat. Once hot, drizzle in enough olive oil to coat the pan. Add the salmon and cook for about 4 minutes, then using a spatula, flip the filets, reduce the heat to medium, and continue cooking for another 2 to 3 minutes, until just cooked through. (If searing chicken, cook for 3 to 4 minutes per side, until cooked through and has reached an internal temperature of 165°F.) Remove from the skillet and set aside.

SERVE: Divide the greens, grains, carrots, mango, cucumber salad, cilantro, and almonds among four bowls. Top with the cooked salmon (or the chicken, roughly chopped). Drizzle some of the dressing over the bowls and toss everything together, adding more dressing as desired. Serve.

Tahini Teriyaki Dressing

MAKES 1 CUPS
(GF, ≤30)

This is a favorite dairy-free dressing, and it doubles as a tofu marinade. The sake, which is found in traditional teriyaki sauces, is optional, but, man, does it add punch, the same way vodka does in the One-Pot Penne alla Fennel-y Vodka Sauce (page 84). It also helps prolong the dressing's shelf life. Drizzle this over salad greens, roasted cabbage wedges or other roasted veggies, and of course grain bowls to transform them into meals that go from blah to ZING!

tahini paste 1/4 cup (65 grams), stirred in the jar before measuring

fresh ginger 1 (2½-inch/15 grams) knob, peeled

garlic clove 1

toasted sesame oil 1 teaspoon

sake 1 to 2 tablespoons (optional)

coconut aminos 1 tablespoon

pure maple syrup 1 tablespoon

rice wine vinegar *or white wine vinegar* 2 tablespoons

kosher salt 1/2 teaspoon, plus more as needed

MAKE THE DRESSING: In a high-powered blender, combine the tahini paste, **¼ CUP WATER**, the ginger, garlic, sesame oil, sake (if using), coconut aminos, maple syrup, vinegar, and salt and blend on high for at least 1 minute. The longer you blend the thicker it gets, so add a little more water to thin if it gets too thick. Taste and add more salt as desired.

STORE: Transfer to a lidded container and keep in the fridge for up to 10 days.

Shakshuka Bolognese

SERVES
2
(RSF, ≤5, ≤30)

leftover Wednesday Sauce (page 113) *or other tomato-y sauce* 2 cups

eggs 2 to 4 large

ground sumac, for sprinkling ← or sub crumbled feta for tang

Parsley Dust (page 27) *or freshly chopped parsley*, for sprinkling

lemon wedges, for serving (optional)

Bunny Bread (recipe see page 186), for serving ← or sub other crusty bread

I eat shakshuka so often for dinner it doesn't register as a breakfast anymore. I lean on it because, really, any leftover tomato-based sauce will work for it—Bolognese, ragu, pizza sauce, spicy Arrabiata—they all answer to the duty of being a wonderful coddle nest for simmering eggs.

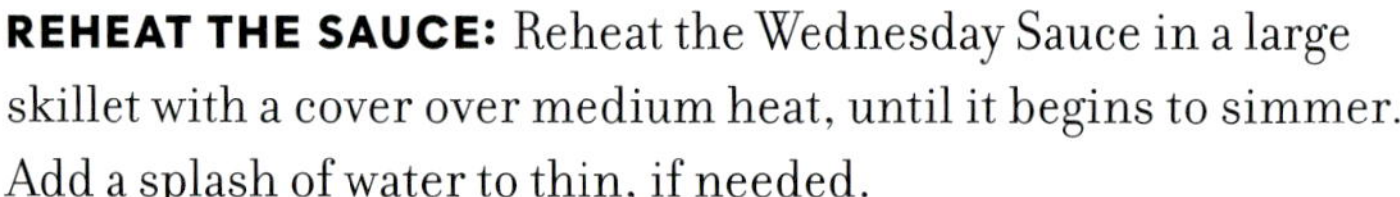

REHEAT THE SAUCE: Reheat the Wednesday Sauce in a large skillet with a cover over medium heat, until it begins to simmer. Add a splash of water to thin, if needed.

COOK THE EGGS: Using a spoon or spatula, make divots in the sauce so you have room to drop in the eggs. Crack the eggs, one at a time, into each hole. Place the lid on the skillet and cook until the eggs are opaque and the yolks are to your desired doneness, for 8 to 10 minutes (for me because I like a hard yolk), but about 6 minutes for a jammy one. Adjust the heat if the sauce begins to evaporate too quickly and gently shake the pan to keep the sauce from sticking to the bottom.

SERVE: Remove the lid and sprinkle the eggs generously with sumac and Parsley Dust. Serve with lemon wedges (if using) and Bunny Bread for dipping and soaking up the sauce and yolky egg.

MAKE IT FANCY

For even more flavor, cook **2 to 3 ounces chorizo or nduja sausage** or **veggie chorizo crumbles, such as Pumfu**, in the skillet with a couple tablespoons of oil before adding in the Wednesday Sauce to simmer.

CHAPTER 10

BREAKFAST FOR DINNER

When Two Worlds Collide

YOU MAKE THE RULES OF YOUR LIFE, so you can achieve the same joyous freedom and satisfaction usually reserved for a weekend brunch any night of the week. Cooking your favorite breakfast foods can transport you to that same leisurely state of mind when you're losing steam midweek. Make all your favorites, mixing and matching to create a small feast, or just add unconventional toppings to your pancakes, devise an innovative omelet (Open-Faced Hatch Green Chile & Pimento Cheese–Stuffed Egg Sandwiches, page 236), add pizza toppings to a frittatta, make your oats savory (Green Crackly-Edged Eggs with Savory Oats, page 239) instead of sweet, add breakfast sausage to your fried rice, or stuff your hashbrowns (Frico Kimchi Hash, page 240); you can do just about anything your heart desires. I think it holds true: Breakfast foods after breakfast opens a world of possibilities.

SERVES

4

(NF)

HOT HONEY MUSHROOMS
cooking spray

all-purpose flour 1 cup, divided

kosher salt 1 teaspoon, divided, plus more for sprinkling

cayenne pepper ½ teaspoon, divided

milk (dairy or nondairy) 1 cup

lemon juice *or apple cider vinegar* 1 teaspoon

panko breadcrumbs ½ cup, plus more as needed

granulated garlic 1 teaspoon

chili powder *or paprika* 1 teaspoon

freshly ground black pepper ¼ teaspoon

lion's mane mushrooms ½ pound *or oyster mushrooms* ¼ pound, cleaned

WAFFLES (MAKES 10 MINI WAFFLES, AND 5 REGULAR-SIZE; SEE TIP)
Medium-ground yellow cornmeal 1 cup

all-purpose flour 1 cup

baking powder 2 teaspoons

pearl sugar ⅓ to ½ cup ← or sub ¼ cup turbinado sugar

kosher salt ½ teaspoon

milk (dairy or nondairy) 1 cup

Pearl Sugar Cornbread Waffles

with Crispy Hot Honey Mushrooms

If you've never had a Belgian waffle from a real Belgian guy who handed it to you straight off the back of his food truck, you might not understand the hype of a Belgian waffle, but I promise you it's justified. I bought myself a bag of pearl sugar thinking I would try to remake those very waffles, where the crystals of sugar melt into chewy pockets of sweetness like mini sugar bombs in the batter, but the bag sat around in the back of my cabinet for years. I finally decided to do something with it and added it to the batter for these cornbread waffles. It's not what I originally planned, but the final verdict: It was worth the wait.

PREHEAT THE OVEN to 450°F and have a large sheet pan fitted with a wire rack nearby. (The wire rack will create airflow under the mushrooms for a crisper crust.) Spray the wire rack generously with cooking spray and set aside.

MAKE THE WET BATTER: In a medium bowl, whisk together ½ cup of the flour, ¼ teaspoon of the salt, ¼ teaspoon of the cayenne pepper, the milk, and lemon juice until smooth. Set aside.

MAKE THE DRY BATTER: In a separate bowl, combine the remaining flour, remaining salt, remaining cayenne pepper, the panko, garlic, chili powder, and black pepper. Set aside.

BATTER THE MUSHROOMS: Using a damp kitchen towel, clean any dirt on the mushrooms. With your hands, pull any large mushrooms apart to create nugget-size strips (2 to 3 inches). Dip them in the wet batter to coat well. Lift the mushrooms from the liquid, shaking away any excess, then drop them into the dry batter, gently tossing to coat and pressing the crumbs into the mushrooms to help adhere.

lemon juice *or apple cider vinegar* 1 teaspoon

unsalted butter 4 tablespoons, melted and cooled slightly

egg 1 large ← or sub ¼ cup unsweetened applesauce

cooking spray

hot honey (such as Red Clay) *or pure maple syrup and hot sauce*, for serving

pickled veg *and/or fresh thyme*, for garnish (optional)

MAKE IT FANCY

Serve dinner with **"Midnight Modelinis"**: Fill champagne flutes or wineglasses halfway with **pineapple juice** and top with Mexican beer, ideally **Modelo**.

TIP

In a hurry? Use boxed cornbread mix for your cornbread waffles, adding the pearl sugar to elevate it with pops of chewy caramel.

AIR FRY THE MUSHROOMS: For the crispiest mushrooms, air fry them at 400°F for 8 to 10 minutes, stopping halfway through to toss and spray again with cooking spray, until the mushrooms are golden brown and crispy. Keep the mushrooms warm in the air fryer until ready to plate.

OR BAKE THE MUSHROOMS: If you don't have an air fryer, transfer the breaded mushrooms to the sheet pan and spray the tenders generously with cooking spray, being sure there are no dry patches of flour remaining. Bake in the oven for 25 to 30 minutes, until the mushrooms are golden brown and crispy, stopping halfway through to turn the mushrooms over and spray again with cooking spray. Remove from the oven and sprinkle with more salt.

MEANWHILE, MAKE THE WAFFLES: In a large bowl, whisk together the cornmeal, flour, baking powder, pearl sugar, and salt until just combined. Add the milk, lemon juice, butter, and egg.

COOK THE WAFFLES: In a waffle maker sprayed generously with cooking spray, add the waffle batter in batches and cook according to the waffle maker instructions.

SERVE: Transfer the waffles to plates and top with the crispy mushrooms. Drizzle over the hot honey and enjoy.

SERVES
2
(GF, NF, ≤30)

Brûléed Lemon Yogurt

with Berry & Thyme Pico

BERRY PICO

berries (fresh or frozen blueberries and strawberries) ½ cup, diced

fresh thyme leaves 1 teaspoon

lemon juice 1 teaspoon

olive oil 2 teaspoons

kosher salt

YOGURT CRÈME BRÛLÉE

Greek yogurt (full-fat) *or labneh* 1 cup

turbinado sugar *or granulated sugar*, for sprinkling

MAKE IT FANCY

Mix the yogurt with **2 to 3 tablespoons lemon curd** and **½ teaspoon pure vanilla extract** before transferring to the ramekins to add a pleasant tang to the sugar coating.

Yogurt with fruit is probably my favorite anytime meal. As is, with a little drizzle of honey, it's simple and heavenly. But it's also true that coating anything with a layer of sugar and taking a torch to it until the sugar beads into hard candy is alchemy, so I also love brûléeing the most simple things—French toast, lattes, warm oatmeal, fresh bananas, grapefruit halves, the peanut butter on my peanut butter sandwiches. And whenever I brûlée my yogurt, it becomes decadent. I think of it as a no-bake, healthier version of crème brûlée, and a loophole to having dessert as a main course. The berry pico (aka fruit salsa) in this recipe bursts with color—saturated red and blue berries meet pops of green from the thyme—and complements the sweetness of the caramelized sugar.

MAKE THE PICO: In a small bowl, combine the berries, thyme, lemon juice, olive oil, and a pinch of salt and set aside to allow the berries some time to release their juices.

MIX THE YOGURT: Divide the yogurt among four 4-ounce ramekins (or two 8-ounce ramekins) or small heat-proof bowls and spread in a smooth, even layer. Wipe any splattered edges of the ramekins with a clean kitchen cloth. (You can cover the yogurt and refrigerate overnight to firm, or for up to 3 days, or until ready to eat.)

BRÛLÉE THE YOGURT: Sprinkle turbinado sugar over the tops of the yogurt in a thin, even layer under a broiler or holding a blow torch and moving in circular motions, burn the sugar until it beads, then caramelizes and melts into puddles. Allow the sugar to harden.

SERVE: Top with the pico and serve.

SERVES

4 TO 8

(DEPENDING ON WHO YOU ARE)

(NF)

Hawaiian dinner rolls *or an uncut loaf of brioche bread* 1 pound ← or if you have leftover brioche hot dog rolls, use those!

unsalted butter 2 tablespoons, melted

milk of choice 1½ cups

large eggs 2

coconut sugar *or light brown sugar* ½ cup

dark *or white rum* 2 tablespoons

pure vanilla extract 2 teaspoons

kosher salt 1 teaspoon

confectioners' sugar, for dusting

warm pure maple syrup *or Miso Coconut Caramel (page 281) or warmed preserves*, for drizzling

Sheet Pan Rummy French Toast Bites

A splash of rum in French toast custard is no longer optional for me, it's what gives it its signature nostalgic taste. You could probably pile these bites on a spoon and inhale them as if they were dainty little Cheerios. I know I could. I use Hawaiian sweet rolls here out of family tradition, depending on the enriched bread you use, you'll need to adjust the sweetness, adding less or more sugar to your taste.

PREHEAT THE OVEN to 350°F. Place an oven rack in the center of the oven and have a sheet pan lined with parchment paper nearby.

TOAST THE BREAD: Using a serrated knife, cut the bread into 1-inch cubes and add them in a single layer to the prepared sheet pan. Bake them in the oven for 10 to 12 minutes, until dry and toasted.

MAKE THE CUSTARD: In a large mixing bowl, whisk together the butter, milk, eggs, coconut sugar, rum, vanilla, and salt until combined. One at a time, using a fork, dip the cubes of bread briefly in the custard, just until softened, and transfer back to the same lined sheet pan.

BAKE AGAIN for 25 to 30 minutes, until the bread cubes are deep, deep golden brown and crispy on the edges. Remove from the oven.

SERVE: Pile the French toast cubes into serving bowls, dust their tops with confectioners' sugar, then drizzle over maple syrup and enjoy.

SERVES

2

(NF, ≤30)

whole-grain English muffins 2, toasted

wild arugula a handful, for topping

olive oil *or butter*, for frying

large eggs 4

Hatch Green Chile & Pimento Cheese Spread (recipe follows) *or storebought pimento cheese* 6 to 8 tablespoons

hot sauce, for serving

Open-Faced Hatch Green Chile & Pimento Cheese–Stuffed Egg Sandwiches

There's something relaxing about building these stuffed egg toppers, filling them with pimento cheese and carefully tucking the egg under itself to seal all the gooeyness inside. They take focus and a little finesse, but they're so beautiful and fancy in the end; they are perfect for impressing someone special.

ON A LARGE PLATE, arrange the English muffins and top each one with a small handful of arugula. Set aside.

FRY THE EGGS: Heat a small, 8-inch skillet over medium heat. Once hot, drizzle enough olive oil to coat the pan. Working one at a time, into a small bowl, break an egg. Add **1 TABLESPOON WATER** and whisk to combine. Pour the beaten egg into the hot skillet, tilting the pan to coat the bottom in a single even layer without any holes. Allow the egg to cook, watching carefully, for 2 to 3 minutes, until the bottom is cooked and the top is only slightly underdone. Using a small spoon, scoop about 1½ to 2 tablespoons of the cheese spread into the center of the egg. Using a rubber spatula, fold the sides of the egg over the cheese spread to cover and form a little pouch. Carefully flip the egg over and allow it to finish cooking through.

TOP THE MUFFINS: Doing your best to keep the egg intact, deposit it over one of the English muffin halves and repeat with the remaining eggs (see Tip).

SERVE: Add a few dashes of hot sauce to each open-faced sandwich before serving and enjoy.

TIP

Heat the oven to 225°F and keep the sandwiches on a sheet pan in the oven while you finish the meal.

Hatch Green Chile & Pimento Cheese Spread

MAKES ABOUT 1¼ CUPS
(NF, ≤30)

Add this to macaroni and cheese, put it in omelets, melt it on burgers, or just spread it on toast.

plain cream cheese 4 ounces, softened

mayo ¼ cup

chopped hatch green chiles 1 (4-ounce) can, drained

diced pimentos 1 (4-ounce) can, drained

smoked Gouda *or smoked cheddar* 4 to 5 ounces shredded

freshly ground black pepper 1 teaspoon

kosher salt ¼ teaspoon, plus more as needed

garlic powder ½ teaspoon

onion powder ¼ teaspoon

hot sauce

fresh lemon juice 1 teaspoon, plus more as needed

MIX THE SPREAD: In a large mixing bowl, using a spatula or spoon, stir together the cream cheese, mayo, hatch chiles, pimentos, Gouda, pepper, salt, garlic powder, onion powder, a few dashes of hot sauce, and the lemon juice until evenly distributed. Taste and add more salt and lemon juice as desired.

STORE: Transfer to a lidded container and keep in the fridge for at least 2 weeks.

Green Crackly-Edged Eggs *with Savory Oats*

SERVES
2
(NF, ≤5, ≤30)

white miso paste 2 tablespoons

uncooked quick-cooking steel-cut oats 1 cup

Chunky Charred Scallion Sauce (page 275) 4 to 5 tablespoons, plus more for serving

CRISPY FRIED EGGS
avocado oil *or olive oil*
2 tablespoons, plus more as needed

large eggs 2 cracked into a small bowl

kosher salt and **freshly ground black pepper**

MAKE IT FANCY

Add **a handful of thinly shredded cabbage** under each egg while frying for *extra* crispiness. Finish with a splash of **soy sauce or tamari, slices of avocado**, and **Diamond Scallions (page 27)**.

I've been into savory oats since I was a weirdo in high school, adding soy sauce to my oatmeal and treating them like savory, Asian-style grits. I was copying my mom who would add soy sauce to her grits and bacon at breakfast because it reminded her of a version of rice and salty fried spam. She put soy sauce on everything actually. In this recipe, I use Charred Scallion Sauce to coat the oats and turn them brilliantly green, and because dark soy sauce could muddle that vibrant color, I use miso instead.

COOK THE OATS: In a medium saucepan bring **3 CUPS WATER** to a boil. Whisk in the miso paste to dissolve, then add the oats, reduce the heat to low, and simmer, uncovered, for about 7 minutes, or longer for a thicker texture, stirring continuously. Once the oats are cooked, stir in 4 tablespoons of the scallion sauce, or more to taste. Cover to keep warm while you fry the eggs.

FRY THE EGGS (SEE TIP): Heat a small or medium skillet (just wide enough to fit the eggs snuggly) over high heat. Once hot, drizzle in enough avocado oil to coat the pan and, as it begins to smoke, carefully add the eggs. Sprinkle with salt and pepper to taste and allow the eggs to fry, undisturbed, until their edges turn dark, crispy, and lacy and the yolk is cooked to your desired doneness. Baste the edges and whites of the eggs with some of the scallion sauce toward the end. Remove from the heat.

SERVE: Divide the warm oats between two serving bowls and top each bowl with a crackly-edged egg.

TIP

A hot puddle of oil in a very hot pan will give your fried eggs very crisp and crackly burnt edges.

Frico Kimchi Hash

SERVES
4
(GF, NF, ≤30)

frozen hash browns 4 heaping cups ← or sub 4 medium russet potatoes, shredded and drained (see Tip)

lemon juice 1 tablespoon

onion powder ½ teaspoon

garlic powder ½ teaspoon

kosher salt 1 teaspoon

freshly ground black pepper ½ teaspoon

unsalted butter 2 tablespoons, melted, plus more for brushing the pan

kimchi 1 cup, lightly drained and roughly chopped ← or sub other fillings

cheddar cheese *(or a blend)* 1 cup finely shredded

Venusian Ketchup (page 276) *or other ketchup*, for serving

You can add anything to these hash browns—chopped cooked breakfast meats, sautéed peppers and onions, veggies, tomatoes, black olives, absolutely anything goes when it comes to breakfast hash, but I am clearly obsessed with my kimchi.

SEASON THE POTATOES: In a large mixing bowl, toss together the hash browns (or shredded and drained potatoes), lemon juice, onion powder, garlic powder, salt, and pepper. Add the butter and toss to coat, followed by the kimchi, tossing to coat.

CRISP THE HASH: Heat a panini press and brush it with butter. Mound the potatoes on the griddle in sections. You can also do this in a waffle maker. In either case you may need to do this in batches depending on the size. Cook for 3 to 5 minutes, until the potatoes are soft and beginning to crisp on the outside, then lift the cover of the panini press and sprinkle the top of the potatoes evenly with the cheese. Put the top of the press back down and continue cooking for another 2 to 4 minutes, or until the cheese is very deeply golden brown and extra crispy.

SERVE: Transfer the hash to a cutting board and cut into four sections. Drizzle with ketchup and serve.

MAKE IT FANCY

Top it with **crispy fried eggs (see page 239)** to make it a full meal.

TIP If using freshly shredded potatoes, drain and season the potatoes: Wrap the shredded potatoes tightly in a clean kitchen towel, hold the ball over the sink, and squeeze the potatoes to remove the excess water.

ORIGINAL
LOW SODIUM

CHAPTER 11

WEEKNIGHT DESSERTS

(Everything Chocolate, à la Mode or Pudding-y)

A night feels incomplete without something sweet. Personally, I think the best desserts are both sweet and savory. With ingredients like herbs, complex sugars, and liqueurs, the desserts here weave in bitter, savory, or floral notes that cut through excess sweetness. They're not afraid of earthy olive oils or the heat of chiles.

And while now would be the perfect time to get decorative, I prefer desserts that feel approachable, not overly fussy. I want them to look like an extension of dinner—slightly messy and organic. I have a weak spot for desserts that melt on the tongue—puddings, mousses, custards. Dishes you can eat straight from the pan with a spoon. I love the ingenuity of bread, the resourcefulness of packaged cookies passing as crusts, and desserts that welcome ice cream as a supporting character. On that note, grab a pint of vanilla ice cream before moving into this chapter. Besides being cake's best friend, you'll see why it's one of the greatest, most reliable weeknight tools to keep around.

"Fried" Banana Split

SERVES
2
(EF, ≤30)

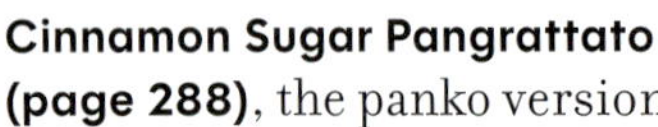

Cinnamon Sugar Pangrattato (page 288), the panko version

ripe, firm bananas 2

vanilla ice cream 2 to 3 scoops, for serving

Salted Black Sesame Fudge Sauce (page 280) *or favorite chocolate sauce*, warmed, for serving

roasted peanuts *or roasted almonds* 2 tablespoons roughly chopped

whipped cream, for topping (see Tip page 254 for homemade whipped cream)

Maraschino cherry, for topping

Bread and breadcrumbs are underrated dessert ingredients. You can do so much more with them than bind a bowl of meatballs or bread a tray of mozzarella sticks. Think of all the other ingredients that can use some crispy texture, like a whole banana! A banana with this toasted cinnamon sugar pangrattato–crusted shell and a salted sesame fudge sauce takes a basic banana split to another level.

MAKE THE PANGRATTATO: Spread the Cinammon Sugar Pangrattato out on a small tray.

COAT THE BANANAS: Roll the bananas through the pangrattato, turning them and pressing the crumbs gently into the flesh to help adhere. Get as much onto the surface without harming the fruit.

SERVE: Transfer the bananas to a plate and top with 2 to 3 scoops of ice cream, a generous drizzle of warmed Salted Black Sesame Fudge Sauce, the peanuts, whipped cream, a glistening Maraschino cherry with some of its juices, and any leftover Pangrattato.

SERVES

4

(EF, ≤5, ≤30)

Cinnamon Sugar Pangrattato (see page 288) and (see Tip), *or crushed cookies from the cabinet*

apples 2 medium (any variety)

light brown sugar *or coconut sugar* 1/4 cup packed

lemon juice *or apple cider vinegar* 1 tablespoon

kosher salt 1 teaspoon, plus more as needed

vanilla ice cream 1 tablespoon, plus 4 large scoops for serving

Biscoff, vanilla wafers, amaretti cookies, gingersnaps, etc., for topping

MAKE IT FANCY

Add **2 leaves fresh sage or thyme** to the pot while the apples are cooking for earthy, savory notes to complement the sweet caramel sauce. If you don't have herbs, **1 teaspoon Calvados or brandy** would work nicely, too.

Apple Caramel

(à la Mode)

I've never been satisfied with anything that isn't a full-blown apple pie, with an official top and bottom flaky crust, but this one makes me rethink my attitude. It's so fast I'd be a fool to pass it up over nothing at all. This recipe (and maybe most of this chapter) is proof why it's smart to always keep vanilla ice cream around. Adding a little ice cream *directly* to the syrup makes for an easy, all-in-one vanilla-plus-the-cream caramel hack that is great for spooning over more ice cream, late-night waffles, or hot sopapillas.

MAKE THE APPLE SYRUP: Peel and core the apples and cut them into 1/4-inch slices, or chop them into 1/2-inch chunks. In a small pot, toss the apples, brown sugar, lemon juice, and salt to coat. Heat the pot over medium-high heat and allow the mixture to come to a boil for 6 to 8 minutes, depending on how you've cut the apples, stirring occasionally, until the syrup has reduced and thickened and the apples are tender. Stir in the 1 tablespoon ice cream and cook for another minute, or until you have a thick caramel sauce.

SERVE: Spoon 1 scoop of cold ice cream into four serving bowls. Divide the apples and their caramel-ly syrup among the bowls. I like to tuck them around the ice cream, instead of spooning them directly over top, to slow the melting, and top liberally with the Cinnamon Sugar Pangrattato. Enjoy.

TIP For this recipe in particular, when making the Cinnamon Sugar Pangrattato, you can experiment with different breads and flavors like leftover brioche, sesame seed, pumpernickel, pretzel buns, etc. I leave some larger pea- and chickpea-size pieces of bread intact when crumbling because I like the variety of textures—some crispy, some chewy. You could also just roughly crush up some cookies from the cabinet in place of the Cinnamon Sugar Pangrattato.

Sticky Date Cakes

SERVES

2

(DF, GF, RSF, ≤30)

Miso Coconut Caramel (page 281) *or other salted caramel or toffee sauce* 60 grams (1/4 cup), plus more for serving

pitted medjool dates 135 grams (7 to 9) ← choose the squishy ones

unsalted creamy almond butter 60 grams (1/4 cup), stirred before measuring

jumbo or large eggs 2

baking powder 2 teaspoons

kosher salt 1/4 teaspoon

oat milk *or milk of choice* 2 tablespoons (30 milliliters)

MAKE IT FANCY

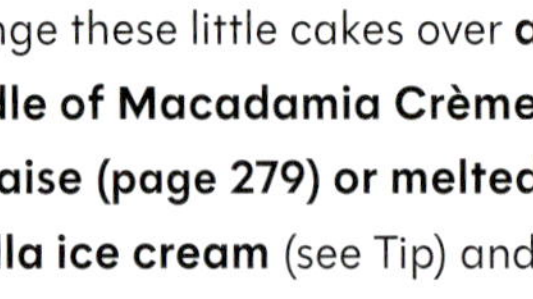

Arrange these little cakes over **a puddle of Macadamia Crème Anglaise (page 279) or melted vanilla ice cream** (see Tip) and top each cake with **crushed spiced or candied pecans** for crunch.

I take great pleasure in squishing dates between my fingers to find the juiciest ones. Dates are extra sweet and do heavy lifting in desserts to add structure replace the refined sugars. They are like little jewels! This is my much healthier, flourless version of sticky toffee pudding that feels effortless to pull together because I weigh many of the ingredients directly on a scale.

INTO THE BOTTOM OF two 8-ounce ramekins, divide the caramel sauce and set aside.

BLEND THE BATTER: Pull the dates apart and discard the inedible top stems. Place the bowl of a high-powered blender on a scale and add the dates, almond butter, eggs, baking powder, salt, and milk. Attach the bowl back to the motor and blend on high until completely smooth, stopping to scrape down the sides of the bowl as needed. Divide the batter between the two ramekins, smoothing the top.

STEAM THE CAKES: Tent the ramekins loosely with foil, leaving at least an inch of clearance above for the cake to rise. Fill your Instant Pot with about an inch of water, and add the rack to the pot. Place the ramekins on the rack, close the lid, and pressure cook on HIGH for 20 minutes, allowing for a natural release.

OR, BAKE THE CAKES: Preheat the oven to 350°F, place the ramekins on a sheet pan and bake for 20 to 22 minutes, until puffed and golden brown and a toothpick inserted inside is just slightly sticky.

SERVE: Remove the ramekins from the Instant Pot (or oven), slide a butter knife carefully around the inside edges of the ramekins to help release the cakes, then, using mittens, carefully flip the cakes out into the center of the two serving plates. While the cakes are still warm, drizzle their tops with more caramel sauce and serve.

TIP

For a fun, last-minute version of crème anglaise, add some vanilla ice cream to a small bowl; melt it in the microwave or small saucepan, spoon a puddle on your plate and top with your cake. It makes for a pretty presentation and a slight changeup from the everyday dessert à la mode.

SERVES

4 TO 6

(GF, ≤30)

Olive Oil Brownie Pudding

I've shared versions of this brownie recipe (they're around, hidden like Easter eggs in corners of the internet) for the true dark chocolate lovers out there like me, those of us who feel a predictable longing for rich, bitter chocolate to close a satisfying dinner.

olive oil ¼ cup, plus more for greasing the pan

bittersweet chocolate 4 ounces (115 grams), chopped

kosher salt 1 teaspoon

eggs 2 large

light brown sugar ½ cup (105 grams)

cocoa powder *or cacao powder* ¼ cup (25 grams)

almond flour *or hazelnut flour* ½ cup (50 grams)

vanilla ice cream, for serving

MAKE IT FANCY

Right before baking, top the batter with ¼ **cup chopped hazelnuts or almonds** for crunch and/or **ribbons of orange zest** to help bring out the notes in the olive oil and dark chocolate.

PREHEAT THE OVEN to 325°F and oil an 8-inch cake pan. Alternatively, you can cook these in the air fyer. In that case have two 16-ounce gratin dishes oiled.

MELT THE CHOCOLATE: In a small saucepan over low heat, gently warm the olive oil, chocolate, and salt, stirring the entire time so the chocolate doesn't burn, until it is mostly melted, then turn off the heat and allow any residual heat to melt the rest.

WHIP THE EGGS AND SUGAR: In the bowl of a stand mixer fitted with a whisk attachment, beat the eggs and sugar on high speed for a full 3 to 4 minutes until thick and silky—it will resemble cappuccino cream. With the beater on medium, drizzle in the melted chocolate and beat until combined. Continue mixing for another minute to thoroughly incorporate the chocolate.

FOLD IN THE DRY INGREDIENTS: Remove the bowl from the stand and place a sieve on top. Sift in the cocoa powder and almond flour to remove any clumps. Using a rubber spatula, fold the dry ingredients into the wet.

IF BAKING: Transfer the batter to the prepared cake pan and using the spatula spread evenly to the edges. Bake for 18 to 20 minutes, until the top has completely set but the center is still slightly gooey.

IF AIR FRYING: divide the batter between the prepared gratin dishes, spreading to the edges and cook in batches in the air fryer at 300 degrees for 14 to 16 minutes, until the top has set but the center is still a little gooey.

SERVE warm with a scoop of ice cream.

SERVES
4

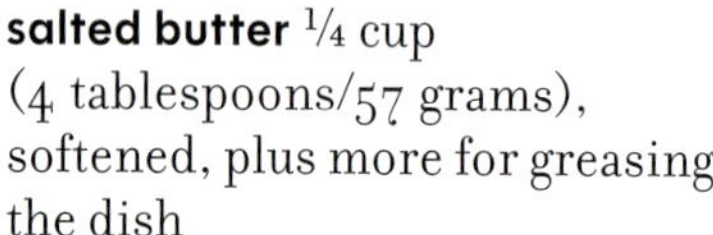

salted butter 1/4 cup (4 tablespoons/57 grams), softened, plus more for greasing the dish

challah bread *or brioche* 1 (1-pound) loaf, preferably unsliced and day-old

light brown sugar *or coconut sugar* 1/2 cup (100 grams), divided

ground cinnamon 1 1/2 teaspoons

ground nutmeg 1/4 teaspoon

low-fat buttermilk *or makeshift buttermilk (see Tip)* 1 cup (240 milliliters)

pure maple syrup 3 tablespoons

baking soda 1 teaspoon

canned sweet potato puree *or canned pumpkin puree* 1/4 cup (60 grams)

pure vanilla extract 1 teaspoon

kosher salt 1/4 teaspoon

VANILLA BEAN MASCARPONE

mascarpone cheese *or plain cream cheese* 1/4 cup (57 grams)

salted butter 2 tablespoons (28 grams)

vanilla bean paste *or pure vanilla extract* 1/2 teaspoon

pure maple syrup 1 teaspoon, plus more as needed

Sweet Potato Challah Bread Rolls

with Melted Vanilla Bean Mascarpone

Here's another weeknight shortcut for when you crave cinnamon rolls but don't want to deal with any kneading of dough, or wait for yeast to activate, or have messy floured countertops. Although I can't promise you won't get breadcrumbs in some wild places, I can promise you will have the satisfying pleasure of flattening squishy bread with no repercussions. It's crazy that these are just slices of challah filled with butter and cinnamon and baked like little bread puddings, and, in the end I actually struggle to tell that these aren't the insides of a cinnamon roll (the best part).

PREHEAT THE OVEN to 325°F and have a greased 8-inch-square casserole dish nearby.

CUT THE BREAD: Using a serrated knife, cut the bread into eight 1-inch-thick slices.

ROLL OUT THE BREAD: On a clean work surface, using a rolling pin, roll out the slices to flatten them. With a sharp knife, cut each slice of bread in half lengthwise to create 16 long strips. Connect 4 strips together, overlapping them at the ends, to create 4 long strips total (see Tip).

MIX THE FILLING: In a small mixing bowl, combine the butter, 1/4 cup of the brown sugar, the cinnamon, and nutmeg. Spread the butter/sugar/nutmeg mixture in an even layer over the strips of bread. Starting from one end, roll the strips into a tight roll, tucking them next to each other in the prepared baking dish as you go. Set aside.

(recipe continues)

MIX THE SWEET POTATO TOPPING: In a liquid measuring cup, whisk the buttermilk, remaining ¼ cup of brown sugar, the maple syrup, baking soda, sweet potato puree, vanilla, and salt together to combine. Pour the mixture evenly over the rolls, making sure there are no dry spots.

BAKE: Cover the baking dish loosely with foil and transfer it to the oven to bake for 30 minutes. Remove the foil and allow it to bake, uncovered, for an additional 30 minutes (a total of 60 minutes), until all the liquid has absorbed and the top of the rolls are deeply golden brown. Remove from the oven and set aside while you make the icing.

MAKE THE MASCARPONE ICING: In a small saucepan over low heat, heat the mascarpone, butter, vanilla bean paste, and maple syrup, whisking together, and cook until it is a smooth, silky sauce. Drizzle the sauce over the rolls and serve.

TIP

For **Makeshift Buttermilk:** Add 1 tablespoon lemon juice or vinegar to every 1 cup of milk of choice. Fill a measuring cup with the acid, then add milk until you reach the 1 cup mark. Allow the milk to sit and curdle before using.

When cutting and rolling your bread, try to arrange your rolls so the golden edges of the challah are all facing up. It'll make the best-looking buns that resemble real, golden cinnamon rolls.

MAKES ONE

9-INCH CAKE

(SERVES 10 TO 12)

(EF)

plain cream cheese 1 pound, at room temperature

chocolate liqueur 1/2 cup (120 milliliters) ← I use Borgata Classic

finely ground sugar (see Tip) *or confectioners' sugar* 1 cup (120 grams)

instant espresso powder *or instant coffee powder* 2 tablespoons ← such as Medaglia d'Oro

pure vanilla extract 1 tablespoon

cold heavy whipping cream 3 cups (48 ounces)

graham cracker sheets about 16 (240 grams)

unsweetened cocoa powder, for dusting

MAKE IT FANCY

Dollop or pipe **whipped cream** (see Tip) onto each of the slices and sprinkle over **curls of shaved dark and/or white chocolate (see Tip).**

Overnight Tiramisu Cheesecake

I think of this as a strategic cheesecake dupe with 100 percent tiramisu vibes. I am grateful for the typically American ingredients that enable effortless shortcuts so you can have this at the table easily. Sheets of graham crackers straight from the box provide a base for billowy whipped cheese that's been infused with chocolate liqueur. For the finishing touch, I snow the whole thing with sifted cocoa powder. You can refrigerate the cake, but I like to freeze it because when cut, delineated lines of crust against cream appear. Make sure to start with soft cream cheese (leave it on the counter in the sun for a few hours) and cold whipping cream so you get a smooth whip.

PREP THE PAN: Line the bottom of a 9-inch springform pan with parchment paper and set it aside.

WHIP THE CREAM FILLING: In a stand mixer fitted with a whisk attachment, beat together the cream cheese, chocolate liqueur, sugar, espresso powder, and vanilla until smooth. With the mixer on medium-low, slowly drizzle in the heavy cream and beat until fluffy.

MAKE THE CHEESECAKE: Reserve 1 cup of the cream mixture. In the prepared pan, spread the remaining filling in an even layer. Insert the graham cracker sheets vertically all the way to the base of the pan, so they're standing on their sides in lines, leaving about 3/4 inch between each row. You can break them into smaller pieces so they fit snugly against the edges of the pan. Top with the reserved filling and spread evenly to the edges, being careful not to shift the crackers.

FREEZE: Using a fine-mesh sieve, dust the top of the cake with an even layer of cocoa powder. Cover and freeze for 8 to 10 hours, or overnight, before serving.

(recipe continues)

SLICE AND SERVE: Thirty minutes before serving, remove the cake from the freezer. After 15 minutes at room temperature, when it's just soft enough to cut but still frozen, use a sharp chef's knife to cut the cake into slices. This will maintain the visibility of the layers. Then give the individual slices another 10 to 15 minutes to thaw before serving. For any slices you don't plan to eat, individually wrap them in plastic wrap while they're still hard, and place them in an airtight container or freezer-safe bag to enjoy later. You can freeze the cake for up to 3 months.

TIPS

To make long and luscious curls of chocolate, warm **a small chocolate bar** (wrapper off) on a small plate for just 2 to 3 seconds in the microwave before running a vegetable peeler along its edge.

I sometimes enjoy making homemade confectioners' sugar using turbinado sugar, which has a toastiness and mild sweetness that's a little more nuanced than blitzed granulated sugar or powdered sugar. In a high-powered blender on high, blend the sugar until ground into powder, stopping to scrape down the bottom and sides of the blender as needed for an even pulverizing. If you want you can even add a teaspoon or two of cornstarch to truly replicate powdered sugar.

To make fresh, homemade whipped cream: In a chilled bowl, whisk together **1 cup cold heavy cream** with **2 tablespoons powdered sugar** and **1 teaspoon pure vanilla extract** using a hand mixer or whisk, until soft peaks form, being careful not to overwhip or you'll end up with homemade butter.

SERVES

4

(EF)

unsalted butter ½ cup (1 stick/113 grams), plus more for greasing the pan

fresh strawberries 6 ounces (170 grams), hulled ← or use frozen and thawed

coconut sugar *or light brown sugar* ⅔ cup (134 grams), divided

low-fat buttermilk *or makeshift buttermilk (see Tip, page 252)* ½ cup (120 milliliters), at room temperature

kosher salt ¼ teaspoon

all-purpose flour 1 cup (120 grams)

poppy seeds 1½ teaspoons

baking powder 1 teaspoon

flaky sea salt, for sprinkling

vanilla ice cream, for serving

MAKE IT FANCY

Add **1 teaspoon rose water** to the macerating strawberries before spooning over the cake batter.

Strawberry & Poppy Seed Buttermilk Spooncake

I created a version of this recipe for *The New York Times* in 2019, during my deepest moment of depression, but I watched from the sidelines as the world devoured it, and so it feels only right to include it in this book. I've upgraded it over the years so the flavor really delivers in every way possible. I now brown the butter, add extra strawberries, and I've swapped the brown sugar with coconut sugar and the regular milk with tangy buttermilk. I even use a local, stone-ground Texas flour, Barton Springs Mill. These seemingly tiny upgrades have a big impact on flavor and make the cake rich and original.

PREHEAT OVEN to 350°F and grease an 8-inch round baking dish with butter. Set aside

BROWN THE BUTTER (SEE TIP): In a small saucepan, cook the butter over medium-low heat for 5 to 8 minutes, until the color turns a tawny color and begins to emit some nutty aromas. Remove the butter from the heat and set it aside.

MACERATE THE STRAWBERRIES: Using your hands or the back of a fork, mash the strawberries to release their juices. Stir in ⅓ cup of the coconut sugar and set aside.

MAKE THE BATTER: In a medium bowl, whisk together the brown butter, the remaining ⅓ cup of coconut sugar, the buttermilk, and kosher salt, then add the flour and poppy seeds and baking powder and continue whisking just until the batter is smooth.

TOP THE BATTER: Transfer the batter to the prepared baking dish and spread evenly to the corners. Spoon the strawberries and their juices over top. Bake for 20 to 25 minutes, until the edges are set and the cake is just slightly gooey in the center. Remove from the oven and sprinkle lightly with flaky sea salt. Always serve with vanilla ice cream.

SERVES
4 TO 5
(EF)

raw pine nuts, *chopped walnuts, or pecans* 1/4 cup (28 grams)

shredded sweetened coconut flakes 1/2 cup (45 grams)

raisins, dark or golden 1/4 cup (36 grams)

grated carrot 1/2 cup (55 grams) (from about 1 large)

unsweetened applesauce 1 cup(245 grams)

lemon juice 1 teaspoon

light brown sugar 3/4 cup packed (165 grams) ← or 1 cup (170 grams) coconut sugar

pure vanilla extract 2 teaspoons

ground cinnamon 1 teaspoon

ground ginger 1/2 teaspoon

grated nutmeg 1/8 teaspoon

ground cloves 1/8 teaspoon

kosher salt 1/2 teaspoon

avocado oil *or mild olive oil* 1/2 cup (120 milliliters)

all-purpose flour 1 cup (140 grams)

baking powder 1 teaspoon

baking soda 1/2 teaspoon

Warm Stovetop Carrot Cake

with Goat Cheese Icing

Stovetop cakes should be more of a thing. If you have a good heavy-bottom, nonstick pan, you should take this no-bake route more often. And while we're questioning the status quo, why aren't warm carrot cakes more popular? The cinnamon, nutmeg, and clove are vivid, aromatic, and comforting when heated. The goat cheese icing, which also has a little tahini stirred in, is a funky, tangy, nutty twist on traditional cream cheese icing that brings an edge to all the spices as it melts into the warm cake.

TOAST THE NUTS AND RAISINS: Place a heavy-bottom 9-inch skillet over medium-low heat and add the nuts, coconut, and raisins. Cook for 8 to 10 minutes, tossing occasionally, until the nuts are lightly browned and toasted and the raisins have plumped. Remove the skillet from the heat and allow a few minutes to cool slightly.

ADD THE WET INGREDIENTS: Add the carrot, applesauce, lemon juice, brown sugar, vanilla, cinnamon, ginger, nutmeg, cloves, salt, and oil and stir to combine.

ADD THE DRY INGREDIENTS: Add the flour, baking powder, and baking soda, and using a rubber spatula, fold everything together until just combined, being careful not to overmix.

"BAKE" THE CAKE: Return the skillet to the stovetop, cover with a lid or sheet of foil and cook over medium-low heat for 40 to 45 minutes, until the top is set and a toothpick inserted directly in the center comes out fairly clean.

(recipe continues)

HONEY

GOAT CHEESE ICING

goat cheese 4 ounces (113 grams), softened ← *or use plain cream cheese in a punch*

unsalted butter 2 ounces (57 grams), softened

tahini paste 1/2 tablespoon, stirred before measuring

honey 1 1/2 tablespoons (32 grams)

MAKE IT FANCY

For pops of color and flavor, garnish the top of the cake with **ribbons of rolled carrots** or **diced candied orange peels**.

MAKE THE ICING: To a small bowl add the goat cheese, butter, tahini, and honey and mix until smooth. Once the cake has cooked, dollop the icing over the top, spreading gently to the edges and allowing the heat to soften the icing.

SERVE warm, gooey, and with spoons.

TIP

You can also bake this cake the traditional way in a greased and lined 9-inch cake pan for 25 to 30 minutes at 350°F.

SERVES

4

(NF, ≤5, ≤30)

granulated sugar 6 tablespoons (75 grams)

yuzu juice *or fresh lemon juice or limoncello* 1/4 cup (60 milliliters)

kosher salt

cold heavy whipping cream *or dairy-free heavy whipping cream* 1 1/2 cups (360 milliliters)

lemon curd 3 tablespoons (60 grams) (see Tip)

thin gingersnaps (such as Nyåkers) 12 cookies (100 grams), plus more, finely crushed, for topping

MAKE IT FANCY

Complete the yin and yang theme and decorate the glasses by hovering the edge of a straight-edged piece of parchment paper (or a bench scraper) over one half of the parfait cup while generously sprinkling **crushed gingersnaps** over the top, finishing the look with **a mound of ribboned lemon zest.**

Yin and Yang Yuzu Parfaits

I felt like reinterpreting a retro British dessert: the syllabub, which, if I was forced to explain it, is essentially just a slightly frothier version of mousse. And my favorite way to eat mousse is with lots of citrusy lemon-y things that I then layer with gingersnap cookies, because the two are a charming pair. If you'd rather not fuss with the individual glasses, layer everything into a single large container instead.

DISSOLVE THE SUGAR: In a small bowl, whisk together the sugar, yuzu juice, and a pinch of salt and whisk until the sugar has dissolved. Set aside.

WHIP THE CREAM: In a large stand mixer fitted with a whisk attachment, or in a large mixing bowl armed with a handheld mixer, whip the cream on high speed until soft peaks are formed. Re-whisk the sugar/yuzu mixture and pour it into the whipping cream. Add the lemon curd and continue whipping until combined.

BUILD THE PARFAITS: Have four 8-ounce, straight-edged drink glasses or mason jars ready. Line the bottoms of each glass with a cookie and spoon over some of the whipped cream mixture. Continue layering cookies and cream to the top of each glass ending with a final layer of the cream. Cover the parfaits loosely and chill for 2 hours or overnight to allow the cookies to soften. Top with crushed cookies before serving.

TIP

Have lemon curd on hand to elevate tart desserts like cheesecake or whipped cream. You can also stir it into yogurt and elevate your Brûléed Lemon Yogurt with Berry & Thyme Pico (page 232).

GF-33 Cookies

MAKES
1
DOZEN

(GF, RSF)

The first time I had mushrooms in a dessert was over a decade ago, when I was treated to a tasting menu at FT33 in Dallas. It was considered one of the best restaurants in the country at the time. The restaurant has since closed, but that moment single-handedly influenced my appreciation for savory sweets.

finely ground almond flour 3 cups (340 grams)

kosher salt 1 teaspoon

baking soda ½ teaspoon

creamy almond butter ¼ cup (65 grams)

agave syrup ¼ cup (85 grams)

pure vanilla extract 1 teaspoon

Porcini Butter (page 290) ¾ cup (1½ sticks/170 grams), at room temperature

coconut sugar ½ cup (85 grams)

large egg 1, at room temperature

bittersweet chocolate (60 to 70%) 9 ounces (255 grams), plus extra for topping

flaky sea salt, for sprinkling

PREHEAT THE OVEN to 375°F and have two large sheet pans lined with parchment nearby.

MIX THE DRY INGREDIENTS: In a medium bowl, combine the almond flour, salt, and baking soda and set aside.

CREAM THE BUTTER AND SUGAR: In the bowl of a stand mixer fitted with a paddle attachment beat the almond butter, agave, and vanilla together until smooth. Add the porcini butter and coconut sugar and beat on medium speed for 4 to 5 minutes until light and fluffy, stopping to scrape down the bowl and beater as needed. Add the egg and mix until combined, again, scraping down the bowl as needed.

ADD THE DRY MIX: With the mixer on low speed, add the almond flour mixture. Once incorporated, add the chocolate, mixing to combine.

SCOOP: Using a standard-sized ice cream scoop, portion the dough into 12 equal mounds, placing them on the sheet pans a few inches apart. Gently press the extra chocolate into the top and sprinkle with flaky salt.

BAKE THE COOKIES for 12 to 14 minutes, rotating the pans halfway through, until golden brown and set on the outside.

SHAPE: Working quickly, remove the pans from the oven and bang them on the counter a few times to deflate the excess air in the cookies, then place a large cookie cutter or glass ½ inch or more wider than the cookies around each cookie, and swirl quickly like a hula-hoop until they are at least ¾ of an inch in height (see Tip). Allow to cool for at least 20 minutes or overnight before enjoying.

TIP

Shaping the cookies as soon as they're out of the oven, before they fully set, will not only smooth their edges, but it will give the cookies better height and a chewier and fudgier texture. If you're lucky, you might even coat the rim of your milk glass with melted chocolate in the process.`

SERVES

12

(MAKES ONE
¼ SHEET CAKE)

(NF)

SHEET CAKE

unsalted butter 6 tablespoons (85 grams), melted and cooled, plus more for greasing the pan

all-purpose flour *or gluten-free flour* 1½ cups (180 grams)

cocoa powder ¼ cup (20 grams)

light brown sugar ½ cup packed (100 grams)

ground cinnamon ½ teaspoon

ground ginger ¼ teaspoon

ground cloves ¼ teaspoon

baking soda 1 teaspoon

kosher salt ½ teaspoon

Greek yogurt *or sour cream* ½ cup (120 grams)

vanilla extract 2 teaspoons

large egg 1

boiling coffee ½ cup (120 milliliters)

ICING

unsalted butter 4 tablespoons (57 grams)

confectioners' sugar ¾ cup (90 grams) ← or see page 254 to make your own

cocoa powder 3 tablespoons (18 grams)

Diamond-Cut Chocolate Sheet Cake

We all need an easy, decadent weeknight chocolate cake that we can bake quickly and, if we really had our way, preferably in a handy sheet pan. That's when I whip up a Texas sheet cake. Except, because traditional versions of this cake are baked to feed a crowd, I've halved the cake, baking it in a ¼ sheet pan, so it's slightly more appropriate for personal snacking. It's one cake you may need to keep reminding yourself (who am I kidding? *myself*) to let it cool before cutting into it so that it slices cleanly for a good presentation. But honestly, maybe the mess is all the fun of it.

PREHEAT THE OVEN to 350°F. Butter a quarter sheet pan (9½ × 13 inches) and set it aside.

SIFT THE DRY INGREDIENTS: In a large bowl, whisk together the flour, cocoa powder, brown sugar, cinnamon, ginger, cloves, baking soda, and salt. Set aside.

MIX THE WET INGREDIENTS: In a separate mixing bowl, whisk the melted butter, yogurt, vanilla, and egg together, then pour the wet ingredients into the bowl with the dry mixture, mixing to combine. Then add the boiling coffee, whisking until just combined. The batter will be thin.

BAKE: Pour the batter into the prepared sheet pan and smooth the top with a spatula. Bang the pan a few times on the counter until it settles some of the bubbles slightly. Bake for 12 to 15 minutes, or just until a toothpick inserted in the center comes out clean. Be careful not to overbake.

(recipe continues)

vanilla extract 1 teaspoon

cold brew coffee *or cold leftover coffee* 3 tablespoons

kosher salt 1/4 teaspoon

cacao nibs *or toasted chopped pecans* 2 to 3 tablespoons, for topping

MAKE IT FANCY

Make a Boozy Sambuca Mud Cake Shake (see Tip): Add **2 cups of vanilla ice cream** to the chilled bowl of a stand mixer and mix with **2 tablespoons of Sambuca** until combined. Add in **2 slices of chilled sheet cake** and mix just until the cake is crumbled throughout.

MEANWHILE, MAKE THE ICING: In a small saucepan heat the butter, confectioners' sugar, cocoa powder, vanilla, coffee, and salt over medium-low heat, whisking until smooth. Keep warm until the cake is ready.

SERVE: Remove the cake from the oven, and, while warm, evenly pour the icing over the top, using the back of a spoon to gently push the icing to the edges so the cake is completely covered. Allow at least 10 minutes, preferably more, for the icing to set. (And I'm sure you'll be a better person than I, and wait for it to cool.) Cut the cake into diamond-shaped pieces (slice the cake into even rows diagonally from one corner to the opposite corner, then make parallel cuts in the opposite diagonal direction). Sprinkle the center of each piece with cacao nibs. Store the cake, covered, on the counter for up to 3 days.

TIP I love to use liqueurs the same way I use vanilla extract, adding them to my desserts for extra complexity or personality. They have a sharp edge that can cut through fat and sugar. Where the flavor profiles fit, try brandy, rum, or banana liqueur for cream-heavy desserts or things like anisette or espresso liqueur for chocolate-y ones.

SERVES

4

(GF, ≤30)

Panini-Pressed Peaches *with Banana Zabaglione*

peaches 2 large (ripe but firm) washed, halved and pitted

butter, for brushing

egg yolks 4 large

granulated sugar ¼ cup

banana cream liqueur ¼ cup

vanilla extract ½ teaspoon

kosher salt ¼ teaspoon

ground cinnamon, for dusting

MAKE IT FANCY

Crush whatever cookies you have hanging around in the cabinet on top to give this more of a blissed-out banana pudding vibe, except with glorious, juicy peaches and no refrigeration time.

I know the summer peach is one of nature's fruits that need no tinkering. At its peak, it's simple and perfect—already dessert. But most times I can never stop there, and here's one of those times: I char them on my handy panini press to add some bitterness, then whisk up a warm banana zabaglione, which is basically like boozy, melted marshmallow fluff to me, and puddle it over the peaches. It's exactly the kind of over-the-topness I'm into.

"GRILL" THE PEACHES: Brush the face of the peaches with butter and place the peaches face-side down on a hot panini press or waffle iron, close the lid, and cook without disturbing them for 2 to 3 minutes, gently pressing the peaches into the hot grill to make sure they have proper contact with the grates. You can also do this with a grill pan or a large cast-iron skillet over medium-high heat. Remove them to a plate and set aside, or cover and refrigerate for up to 2 days until ready to serve.

WHISK THE ZABAGLIONE: In a metal bowl, add the egg yolks and sugar and whisk until pale. Whisk in the banana liqueur, vanilla, and salt. Place the bowl over a bain-marie—a pot of boiling water that fits the bowl just enough so the water doesn't touch the bottom of the bowl—and begin whisking the egg mixture constantly and vigorously until thickened, about 5 to 6 minutes.

SERVE: Remove the zabaglione from the heat and spoon generously over the peaches. Dust the tops with cinnamon and enjoy.

SERVES

4

(NF, ≤30)

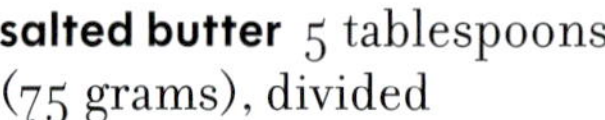

salted butter 5 tablespoons (75 grams), divided

black plums 1 pound (4 to 5 medium plums), halved, pits removed

crusty bread (such as plain focaccia, sourdough, or baguette) about 2 heaping cups (200 grams), torn into large chunks

ground cinnamon ½ tablespoon

turbinado sugar *or light brown sugar* 2 to 4 tablespoons ← depending on how tart or sweet the fruit

lemon ½ large

confectioners' sugar, for dusting

vanilla ice cream, for serving (optional)

MAKE IT FANCY

After searing the fruit and transferring them to a plate, sprinkle over **¼ teaspoon freshly ground black peppercorns** or **¼ teaspoon ground juniper berries.**

Pan-Roasted Black Plum Panzanella

I can go on and on about the wonders of leftover bread and how it's an amazing dinner resource. Use it to make fresh toasted breadcrumbs to add a crunchy top to casseroles, dips, and desserts. Or, make them into a weeknight clean-the-fridge strata, French toast, or, in this case, a marvelous dessert panzanella. For this you can use any fruit, adjusting the cooking time as some fruits may take a little longer to break down. But I haven't met a fruit (or a pair of fruits) that doesn't love this method. Here, the plum juices soak into the crusty and buttery bread, and . . . I mean, what else is there to say? It's like a much simpler version of the Marian Burros's famous plum torte that *The New York Times* prints each fall.

PREHEAT THE OVEN to 375°F.

SEAR THE FRUIT: Heat a 9-inch cast-iron pan over medium heat and melt 2 tablespoons of the butter. Add the plums cut side down and sear for 5 to 6 minutes, until they begin to caramelize and give off some of their juices and the butter begins to smell nutty. Transfer the plums to a plate and set aside.

CARAMELIZE THE BREAD: Back in the same skillet, add the remaining 3 tablespoons of butter, then add the bread in a single layer and cook for about 2 minutes per side, flipping until the bread is caramelized and crusty on both sides. They'll begin to pick up some of those plum juices. Place the plums, cut side down, and any juices back over the bread. Sprinkle the top with the cinnamon and the turbinado sugar and squeeze the lemon cut side up evenly over the plums.

ROAST (SEE TIP): Place the skillet in the oven to bake for about 15 minutes, or until the plums begin to burst and soften and release their juices into the bread. Remove from the oven, transfer to a platter, and dust with confectioners' sugar before serving warm. Serve with ice cream, if desired.

TIP

While pan *searing* uses high heat directly on the stovetop to create an exterior crust, pan *roasting* combines that technique with oven time to break down the tissues and juices within a food, whether cooking chicken thighs or fruit. It creates succulent insides, so you get the best of both worlds.

SERVES
2 TO 4
(GF, ≤5, ≤30)

Lazy Girl Chocolate Bars

70% to 85% dark chocolate 4 large (1 ounce) squares (Aldi's Moser Roth 70% dark chocolate bar is my go-to for this, but any thin snappy chocolate bar will do)

medjool dates 4 large, pitted

peanut butter *or nut or seed butter of choice* 4 to 8 tablespoons

raw walnut halves or pieces, *roasted salted peanuts or other nuts* a handful

flaky sea salt *or other salt*, for sprinkling

Sometimes I do have the patience to melt a pool of dark chocolate to swathe my stuffed dates, but sometimes I don't. These are as their name states—*lazy*! Seemingly jumbled together for emergency ease, but best believe, not without the same satisfaction.

The point is these "chocolate bars" are not fully formed, yet they still manage to get the job done in this arguably elegant, haphazard state.

PLACE THE CHOCOLATE squares on a serving platter.

STUFF THE DATES: Split each date. Using a small spoon, fill each one with the peanut butter (1 to 2 tablespoons). Top the peanut butter with the nuts, pressing the nuts into the butter so they stay in place. Place the stuffed dates on top of each piece of chocolate and sprinkle the bars with sea salt and serve (see Tip).

MAKE IT FANCY

Add **a drizzle of extra-virgin olive oil** over the chocolate bars to bring out some of its earthy notes or sprinkle each piece with **a pinch of chile powder** for smokey heat.

TIP

For easier eating, flip the stuffed dates over onto the chocolate bar. The peanut butter will act as a glue, helping to keep the peanuts in place while you chow away.

PART

HOMEMADE TOPPINGS

Sauces, Sprinkles, and Flavor Bombs

Keep these toppings around throughout the week because they add lots of flavor to recipes with little effort. If you won't use them in time, remember, **nearly everything is freezable!** (see Learn to Master Time, page 22).

Use squeeze bottles and deli containers for easy storage, and label your containers with their contents and the made-by date with a Sharpie on a strip of masking tape; or, if you're in a hurry, just write directly on the labels with a dry-erase marker. As you get a rhythm and build out a collection of sauces, sprinkles, and fat bombs you'll come to appreciate those little reminders of what's inside.

SAUCES

Savory & Sweet Drizzles, Dips, and Dollops

THE THING I LOVE ABOUT creating sauces is that you can experiment by simply stirring things together in a bowl or blending them in a food processor, tweaking and tasting as you go. It allows for intuition, common sense, and your five senses to take the lead.

MAKES ABOUT
2
CUPS

(DF, EF, GF, NF, RSF, ≤30)

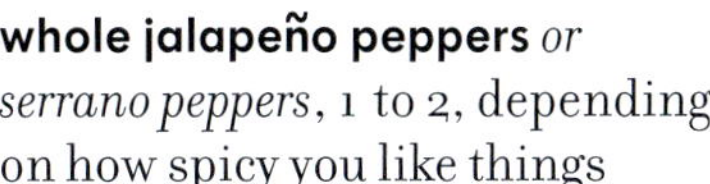

whole jalapeño peppers *or serrano peppers*, 1 to 2, depending on how spicy you like things

scallions 6 to 7, both green and white parts, roots trimmed

garlic cloves 6, skin-on

lime 1 halved, plus fresh juice as needed

lemon 1 halved, plus fresh juice as needed

fresh basil a handful, roughly chopped

fresh cilantro 2 packed cups, tender stems are fine, roughly chopped

fresh parsley 2 packed cups, tender stems are fine, roughly chopped

olive oil ¼ cup, plus more for topping

kosher salt ½ teaspoon, plus more as needed

TIP

Charring ingredients caramelizes their natural sugars and deepens their flavor. It's my favorite thing to do with alliums; and charring limes and lemons helps them release more juice, while removing some of their bitterness, too.

Chunky Charred Scallion Sauce

This chimichurri-esque green sauce will transform simple ingredients into spicy, herby wonders. Stir it into warm grains like rice pilaf or Savory Oats (page 239). Add it to scrambled eggs, marinate kebabs with it, or spoon it over a sea of roasted cherry tomatoes. Mix into softened butter to make a compound butter to baste over mushrooms or chicken thighs, use it to marinate a skirt steak, or even stir into mayo for dipping fries or smearing onto sandwiches.

CHAR THE VEGETABLES (see Tip): Heat a large cast-iron skillet over medium-high heat (or use your panini press!). Place the jalapeños in the skillet and cook for 12 to 14 minutes, or until soft and tender, turning occasionally. Add the scallions to one section of the skillet and cook for 4 to 5 minutes. Add the garlic cloves to another section of the skillet and cook for 3 to 4 minutes, flipping until charred and softened. Add the lime and lemon halves to another section of the pan, cut side down, and cook for 2 to 3 minutes, until charred.

CHOP THE VEGETABLES: Transfer each ingredient to your cutting board as it finishes cooking. Once cooled, discard the skins from the garlic and the seeds from the peppers, then roughly chop the garlic, scallions, and jalapeños.

BLEND THE SAUCE: Into the bowl of a food processor, place the garlic, scallions, jalapeños, basil, cilantro, and parsley. Squeeze over the charred citrus juice, holding back any seeds. Pulse until finely chopped. Add the olive oil and salt and blend to incorporate. Taste and season with more salt or fresh citrus as needed.

STORE: Transfer the sauce to a lidded container and cover with ¼ inch of olive oil. Keep in the fridge for up to 1 week, or freeze in ice trays for up to 6 months.

Venusian Ketchup

MAKES ABOUT 4 CUPS

(DF, EF, GF, NF, ≤30)

crushed tomatoes 1 (28-ounce) can

white wine vinegar ½ cup

dry white wine such as Pinot Grigio ¼ cup

tomato paste 1 (6-ounce) can

light brown sugar ¼ cup packed

garlic clove 1, grated

Dijon mustard 1 teaspoon

dried tarragon 4 teaspoons

kosher salt 2 tablespoons

pure maple syrup ¼ cup

I've never enjoyed homemade ketchup until I made this sultry version with white wine and tarragon. This one is worth making for the rest of time, as no other ketchup will do for me now, plus it's insanely quick with the help of an Instant Pot or other multicooker. You can make this faster than you can air fry a couple batches of French fries. It's not too sweet, has absolutely no corn syrup and, I'll be so bold to say, tastes more rounded than Heinz. Of course, if you don't have an Instant Pot, simply simmer it away on the stove like a classic Italian red sauce.

IN THE BOWL OF AN INSTANT POT, stir together the crushed tomatoes, vinegar, wine, tomato paste, brown sugar, garlic, mustard, tarragon, salt, and maple syrup. Secure the lid and pressure cook on high for 6 minutes, followed by a quick release. Alternatively, cook the ingredients in a large Dutch oven over medium-low heat for 45 to 60 minutes, stirring occasionally, until thickened.

PUREE (SEE TIP): Remove the lid, and using an immersion blender with a guard, blend the ketchup until completely smooth.

STORE: Transfer to a squeeze bottle or jar with a lid and keep in the refrigerator for up to 3 months.

TIP if you don't have an immersion blender, or if your blade doesn't have a guard and you're worried about scratching the inside of your pot, allow the ketchup to cool completely before transferring to a high-powered blender and blending until smooth.

Very Green Ranch

MAKES ALMOST
2
CUPS

(GF, NF, RSF, ≤30)

whole-milk Greek yogurt 1 cup

fresh cilantro 2 packed cups, tender stems are fine, roughly chopped

fresh flat-leaf parsley a handful, tender stems are fine, roughly chopped

fresh dill ¼ cup chopped ← or 1 teaspoon dried dill or tarragon

garlic cloves 4

lemon juice 2 tablespoons

sweet paprika ¼ teaspoon

kosher salt 1 teaspoon, plus more as needed

scallions 2 large, both the white and green parts, roots trimmed

MAKE IT FANCY

Roast **1 small jalapeño** until tender, and after removing the seeds, blend it along with the other ingredients for an addictive Jalapeño Ranch Dressing.

I have an unrestrained habit of adding herbs to sauces so they turn green—in some way the recipe feels instantly elevated and more nutritious; keep an eye out for me with this. This herby ranch is actually made with yogurt instead of buttermilk, and it's my favorite thing to put on almost everything you think it should go with—grilled corn, salads, baby carrots, Blackened Palm Stick Tacos (page 122), nachos, simple black beans and rice with a side of fried sweet plantains—and even anywhere else it probably shouldn't, yet my American mind makes it make sense, like French fries or a slice of pizza.

BLEND THE SAUCE: Into a food processor or high-powered blender, put the yogurt, cilantro, parsley, dill, garlic, lemon juice, paprika, and salt. Tear the scallions into chunks and add them as well. You may need to pack everything in to fit. Blend on high until well combined.

STORE: Transfer to a lidded container and keep in the fridge for up to 10 days.

MAKES APPROXIMATELY ¾ CUP

(EF, GF, NF, RSF, ≤30)

crushed Calabrian chiles (from a jar) ½ cup, stirred before measuring

unsalted butter 4 tablespoons, melted

fresh lemon juice 2 tablespoons, plus more as needed

dried basil ½ teaspoon

ground celery seeds ½ teaspoon

cayenne pepper ¼ teaspoon

kosher salt ¼ teaspoon, plus more as needed

Bomba Buffalo Sauce

Please put this wherever you put your Buffalo sauce (or hot sauce) and never look back. I love it tossed over roasted Crispy Buffalo Brussels Sprouts (page 182) that I eat with a fork *and* knife. But this stuff is so magical it will rescue even the most lackluster dinner; even one of those last-minute frozen veggie pizzas from the store.

MAKE THE SAUCE: In a small mixing bowl, whisk together the chiles, butter, lemon juice, basil, celery seeds, cayenne pepper, and salt. Taste and adjust the lemon juice and salt as desired.

STORE: Transfer the sauce to a lidded container to keep in the fridge for 1 week.

Macadamia Crème Anglaise

MAKES ABOUT
2
CUPS

(DF, EF, GF, RSF, ≤5, ≤30)

roasted salted macadamia nuts 1 cup (5 ounces) ← If you can find roasted and unsalted, great! Just adjust the salt as necessary.

boiling water 1 cup, plus more for soaking the nuts

pure maple syrup 1/4 cup

pure vanilla extract 1 tablespoon

kosher salt 3/4 teaspoon

MAKE IT FANCY

Add **a pinch of ground turmeric** for color and/or **¼ teaspoon kala namak** (see Tip) for more flavor.

This sauce is totally eggless, but it still has the necessary sweet velvety vibes of an authentic crème anglaise. Spoon it over Sheet Pan Rummy French Toast Bites (page 234), Sticky Date Cakes (page 246), or drizzle it over a pack of frozen or homemade cinnamon rolls before they go into the oven. And if there's any leftover, spill it over a warm, out-of-the-oven apple or peach galette, and eye it as it trickles through the nooks and crannies of the tender, roasted fruit. Really, just put it anywhere you could imagine a creamy sweet sauce . . . without getting too carried away with this advice, of course.

QUICK-SOAK THE NUTS: In a medium-size heatproof bowl, cover the macadamia nuts with boiling water. Allow them to soak for at least 20 minutes to soften, then drain them.

BLEND THE NUTS: In a high-powered blender, blend the soaked macadamia nuts and maple syrup on high. With the blade still running, slowly pour the 1 cup boiling water through the top spout, continuing to blend, increasing the speed as needed, until the sauce is completely smooth and creamy. Add the vanilla and salt and blend to combine. Taste adjusting the maple syrup or salt as needed.

STORE: Transfer to a lidded container and keep in the fridge for up to 1 week.

TIP Kala namak, a Himalayan black salt, packs a powerful punch—a little goes a long way. It serves as an excellent vegan substitute for egg flavor due to its distinctive sulfurous taste and smell. For a stronger effect, add it at the end of cooking rather than during the process.

Salted Black Sesame Fudge Sauce

MAKES ABOUT
½
CUP

(DF, EF, GF, NF, RSF, ≤5 , ≤30)

black sesame seeds *or white sesame seeds in a pinch* ½ cup

honey ¼ cup

virgin coconut oil ¼ cup, melted

soy milk *or milk of choice* ½ cup

semisweet *or bittersweet chocolate chips* 2 ounces (about ½ cup)

kosher salt 1 teaspoon, plus more as needed

This complex fudge sauce strikes the perfect balance between savory and sweet, making it less cloying than other fudge sauces made with corn syrups and heavily processed things. I can eat it by the spoonful, but when I prefer to be a little more discreet, I just put it in a squeeze bottle and drizzle it over my banana split (see page 244) or swirl it into a loaf of Simple Whole Wheat Banana Bread (page 156) before baking, because bananas are its ultimate complement.

TOAST THE SESAME SEEDS: Heat a small skillet over medium-high heat and toast the sesame seeds for 1 to 2 minutes, until fragrant, tossing occasionally for even browning.

BLEND THE SESAME SEEDS: In a blender or mini food processor, blend the toasted seeds on high until crushed and a paste begins to form, stopping to scrape down the sides of the bowl as needed. Add the honey and coconut oil and blend on high until completely smooth.

MAKE THE FUDGE: Into a small saucepan over medium heat, pour in all of the sesame seed mixture, the soy milk, chocolate chips, and salt and cook, stirring for 2 to 3 minutes, until combined and the chocolate chips have fully melted. Taste and season with more salt if needed. Remove from the heat and enjoy warm over your favorite desserts.

STORE: You can store sauce that has come to room temperature in a lidded container in the refrigerator for about 2 weeks. Reheat on the stove, adding more milk to thin the sauce, if needed.

Miso Coconut Caramel

MAKES ABOUT
2½
CUPS

(DF, EF, GF, NF, RSF, ≤5, ≤30)

coconut cream (preferably the Thai Kitchen brand) 1 (13.5-ounce) can

coconut sugar 1 cup

white miso paste *or red* 2 teaspoons

I'm obsessed with the caramelly flavor of coconut sugar, and using it to make this two-ingredient, dairy-free caramel sauce creates one of the most concentrated yet easiest versions I've made. You can taste notes of espresso and chocolate. It's a simple sauce I love to serve warm over Sundae Toast (page 202) and my Sticky Date Cakes (page 246). But it's also just good as a fruit dip for fresh strawberries and cut apples, drizzled over popcorn, ice cream, and brownies stirred into your iced latte, or turned into chocolate-coated coconut caramel candies (see Tip).

MAKE THE CARAMEL: In a small saucepan, stir together the coconut cream, coconut sugar, and miso and bring to a boil over medium-high heat, watching the mixture carefully so it never boils over. Then reduce the heat to a simmer and cook, uncovered, stirring occasionally, for about 20 minutes, or until very thick. Make sure there are active bubbles the entire time. Cook for another 8 to 10 minutes for a darker caramel with a deep, espresso/fudge flavor, or remove from the heat after 20 minutes for more subtle toasty, caramel notes.

COOL AND STORE: Allow to cool completely, and transfer to a lidded container and keep in the fridge for up to 3 weeks.

MAKE IT FANCY

Make Coconut Caramel Candies: Mix **1 cup caramel sauce** with **1 cup unsweetened coconut flakes**. Spoon into a silicone ice tray and freeze overnight or until hardened. Once frozen, melt **1 cup bittersweet chocolate chips** with **1 teaspoon coconut oil**, stirring until smooth. Using a fork, dip each frozen caramel piece into the melted chocolate, letting the excess drip off. Place the coated pieces on a parchment or wax paper-lined sheet pan. Sprinkle over **flaky salt** and allow them to sit at room temperature for a few minutes so the centers soften into a gooey caramel with the outside sets into a crunchy chocolate shell.

SPRINKLES & CRUNCHIES

SOMETIMES IT'S JUST A LITTLE SPRINKLE of something thoughtful and textural that can bring life and pizazz to an otherwise ordinary day and dish. Turn to these sprinkles, toppings, and crunchies when you want to spruce up veggies, salads, and grains with a quick flick of your wrist.

Falafel Crumbles

MAKES ABOUT
2
CUPS
(DF, EF, GF, NF, RSF)

olive oil *or avocado oil*, for drizzling

chickpeas (garbanzo beans) 2 (15-ounce) cans, drained and rinsed

cilantro leaves 1 packed cup (1 ounce), tender stems are fine, finely chopped

parsley leaves 1 packed cup (1 ounce), tender stems are fine, finely chopped

garlic cloves 4, grated

ground cumin 2 teaspoons

ground cardamom ½ teaspoon

kosher salt ½ teaspoon

We are a house of falafel lovers and now we can sprinkle falafel bits over everything we eat without the effort of rolling or frying balls (although we still love to do that, too). In general, you make falafel from raw chickpeas soaked overnight because starting with cooked and canned chickpeas would make them too mushy. But my husband and I have found that roasting canned chickpeas before grinding them actually creates a similar nubby texture and saves on soaking time. Sprinkle these over buddha bowls, spring pastas, crispy Brussels sprouts with lots of hot honey and parm, and (obviously) over all of your hummuses and salads, and in place of breadcrumbs for an extra crunchy, gluten-free topping.

PREHEAT THE OVEN to 375°F.

On a baking sheet, add the chickpeas. Drizzle with oil and roll them around to coat in the oil. Spread them out in an even layer and baking for 15 to 20 minutes, until the chickpeas are very crispy and golden brown, shaking the pan every 10 minutes or so. Remove from the oven and allow them to cool.

PULSE THE CHICKPEAS: Into a food processor fitted with a steel blade, pulse the chickpeas until the mixture resembles coarsely ground breadcrumbs. Transfer to a mixing bowl the cilantro, parsley, garlic, cumin, cardamom, and salt and, using your clean hands, toss everything to combine well.

USAGE AND STORAGE: Use or freeze for up to 3 months in a freezer bag, scooping from it as needed. It may clump when frozen, but just use a mallet to help break up the clumps.

MAKES ABOUT
2
CUPS

(DF, EF, GF, NF, RSF, ≤5, ≤30)

neutral oil (such as avocado, grapeseed, or canola), for frying

chickpea flour *or all-purpose flour* 1 cup

white onions *or yellow* 2 large, peeled, quartered, and thinly sliced

kosher salt

MAKE IT FANCY

Add **1 to 2 thinly sliced jalapeños** to the batter for extra color and a little spice—their heat will soften after frying.

Frazzled Onions

Think French's onions in the can, but better. You can make this with shallots, which is even fancier, and, in a pinch, you can also make this without the chickpea flour breading. Add the sliced alliums directly to the oil and they'll still crisp nicely; we just happen to prefer them extra audibly crunchy. Once it's time to store these, drain them completely on a paper towel and keep them in an airtight container for up to 1 week.

IN A SMALL, HEAVY-BOTTOMED POT or wok, heat 1½ to 2 inches of oil over medium heat. Prepare a sheet pan fitted with a wire rack and top it with a couple paper towels.

MAKE THE ONION BATTER: In a mixing bowl, combine the chickpea flour and **¾ CUP WATER** to make a thin batter. Add the onions, breaking them apart with your fingers, and toss to coat.

FRY THE ONIONS: Once the oil is hot (test a few onion pieces to see if they sizzle), begin adding the onions in batches, shaking off any excess batter, and fry for 5 to 6 minutes, until golden brown, watching closely toward the end so they don't burn. Remove with a slotted spoon and transfer to the prepared wire rack and sprinkle with salt, to taste. Repeat with the remaining onions.

Garlic Chips

MAKES ABOUT
¼
CUP

(EF, GF, NF, RSF, ≤5, ≤30)

milk (whole, almond, or oat) *or water* ¼ to ½ cup

garlic 1 bulb, skin removed, cloves separated and sliced thinly lengthwise

olive oil, 2 cups, for frying (see Tip)

kosher salt, for sprinkling

TIP

Reserve the residual oil for elevated cooking, as it's now infused with amazing garlic flavor. Allow to cool completely, then store it in the fridge in an airtight container and use quickly, within 1 to 2 days.

Whenever I think of garlic chips, I think of the iconic scene from *Goodfellas*, where Paul Sorvino thinly slices garlic cloves with a razor blade in prison. It's a good lesson that there's no excuse to not revere the cooking process. Don't we all? Instead of disintegrating in a pan of oil like his, this garlic crisps like sliced almonds, and when I have no social events to attend, I sometimes even munch on them as if they were. They're a wonder. If they outlast your own impatience long enough, serve them over sautéed spinach, in a warm goat cheese salad, over Baked & Bejeweled Yellow Rice (page 163), soups, dips, and anywhere else you feel like sprinkling them, besides directly into your mouth.

BLANCH THE GARLIC (SO THEY DON'T TURN BITTER AND BURN): In a small microwave-safe bowl, microwave the milk on high for 30 to 45 seconds, until steaming. Remove the bowl, add the garlic and allow it to sit for 3 to 4 minutes before draining. Blot the garlic completely dry between a couple sheets of paper towel. Make sure they have no residual liquid on them or they will splatter when they hit the hot oil.

FRY THE GARLIC: Have a paper towel–lined plate nearby. In a small saucepan, heat the oil over medium heat, until it begins to shimmer. Add the garlic and fry them gently, tilting the pan if needed to make sure the garlic chips are fully covered in the oil, until they become evenly golden brown. Watch closely so that they don't burn, which can happen quickly. Remove the garlic chips with a slotted spoon and place them on the prepared plate to absorb the excess oil. Sprinkle them with salt while they're still hot.

STORE the garlic chips wrapped in a paper towel in the fridge inside a zip-top bag or airtight container for 1 to 2 weeks. Recrisp in an air fryer, dry pan, or the oven at a low temperature for a few minutes before serving.

Pesto Sprinkles

MAKES ABOUT 1¼ CUPS

(GF, NF, RSF, ≤5, ≤30)

Here's a sprinkle-able pesto with the same essence of the paste but with more tooth and texture for sprucing up everything from grain bowls, noodles, and seared proteins, to crispy potato wedges, pizzas, avocado toasts, and salad dressings. You can swap the almonds with pistachios, toasted hazelnuts, or any other nut, and go for finely chopped peppery greens like watercress or arugula instead of basil. Maybe add some grated orange zest or freshly grated horseradish for extra flair.

Parmesan cheese *or Romano cheese* 2 ounces, cut into small chunks

unsalted roasted almonds *or pistachios, hazelnuts, pine nuts, or walnuts* ½ cup

garlic cloves 3

basil leaves *or spinach, arugula, watercress, or other tender greens* 1 large handful

lemon zest from 1 lemon

MAKE THE PESTO: In a mini food processor fitted with a steel blade, pulse the Parmesan, almonds, and garlic several times until just coarsely ground. Tear over the basil leaves, add the lemon zest, and continue to pulse just until the basil is roughly chopped.

STORE: Transfer the mixer to a small, lidded container and refrigerate until ready to use, up to 1 week or freeze for 6 months.

Arrabbiata Flakes

MAKES ABOUT ⅓ CUP

(GF, NF, DF, RSF, ≤30)

And if there's a single seasoning I sprinkle on almost everything, it's this one. It's a replica of a souvenir mix we got from the Amalfi Coast. Just a pinch takes me back to the hidden village by the sea where we dined mountainside, which is exactly why I keep it on the back of the stove at the ready.

dehydrated garlic flakes 2 tablespoons

dried parsley ¼ cup

dried basil 2 tablespoons

dried oregano 2 tablespoons

crushed red pepper flakes 1 tablespoon

dried rosemary 2 teaspoons, finely crushed

dehydrated onion flakes 1 tablespoon

freshly cracked black pepper 1 teaspoon

dehydrated lemon peel 2 teaspoons

flaky salt 1 teaspoon

MIX AND STORE: Into a lidded container add the garlic flakes, parsley, basil, oregano, red pepper flakes, rosemary, onion flakes, pepper, lemon peel, and salt. Cover and shake to distribute the spices, and store in a cool, dry place for a year.

Pickled Pink Onions

MAKES ABOUT
1
CUP
(DF, GF, NF, RSF, ≤5)

red onion 2 small or 1 large

red wine vinegar ½ cup, plus more as needed

If there's one garnish I always keep around, it's pickled onions. They're the acidic crunch and pop of pink your plate seems always to need (especially here in the southwest). Since these are a weeknight version, heating the brine and cutting the onions super thin allows them to soak up the warm liquid and tenderize quickly, although you could skip heating the ingredients and just pack them into the jar to slowly marinate for a couple hours all the way up to a couple weeks. The sweetness of the red wine vinegar balances the spicy red onion, so you won't need to add any additional sweetener.

CUT THE ONIONS: Using a sharp chef's knife, cut the onions in half through the stem, and then discard the outer skins and tough outer layer. Place the onion halves cut side down, and following the natural ribs on the onion, slice the onion very thinly into ⅛-inch-thick slices.

PACK THE ONIONS: Place the the slices into a 16-ounce heat-proof jar with a lid, packing it down so it fits snuggly, then set the jar aside.

HEAT THE BRINE: In a small saucepan over medium-high heat, bring the vinegar to a simmer. Remove from the heat and pour it directly over the onions. If needed, use a spoon to help pack down the onions to make sure they're completely submerged in the brine, or add a little more vinegar. Allow the onions to sit for about 30 minutes, or until cooled.

STORE: Cover the jar with it's lid and transfer to the fridge to chill until ready to use, or for up to 2 weeks.

MAKE IT FANCY

Add **1 small piece of a raw red beet** to the brine for richer color and sweetness, include **a bay leaf** or **a few thyme sprigs**, **1 teaspoon black or pink peppercorns** for fragrance and heat, or even add **1 or 2 smashed garlic cloves** for extra flavor.

Relly's Relish

MAKES ABOUT 1 CUP

(DF, EF, GF, NF, ≤5, ≤30)

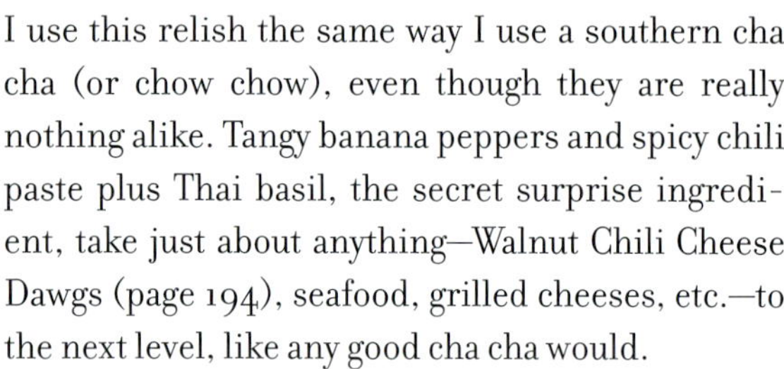

I use this relish the same way I use a southern cha cha (or chow chow), even though they are really nothing alike. Tangy banana peppers and spicy chili paste plus Thai basil, the secret surprise ingredient, take just about anything—Walnut Chili Cheese Dawgs (page 194), seafood, grilled cheeses, etc.—to the next level, like any good cha cha would.

pickled banana pepper rings 1 (16-ounce) jar, drained

sambal oelek (chili garlic paste) 2 tablespoons, plus more as needed

Thai basil or regular basil 1 tablespoon, minced

CHOP THE BANANA PEPPERS: Using a sharp knife, finely chop the banana peppers to a consistency similar to pickle relish. You should have about 1 cup chopped.

COMBINE: In a small bowl, mix together the banana peppers, sambal oelek, and Thai basil. Add more sambal if you like it spicier.

STORE: Transfer the relish to a small lidded container and keep in the fridge for up to 2 weeks.

Cinnamon Sugar Pangrattato

MAKES ABOUT 1½ CUPS

(EF, <RSF, ≤5, <30)

Pangrattato translates to "grated bread" in Italian. It's made by toasting leftover bread crumbs (and sometimes in my case, panko) in olive oil with garlic, herbs, or spices. But it doesn't have to stay savory. Swap the garlic and herbs for butter, sugar, cinnamon, or even cocoa, and you've got a rustic, crunchy, no-fuss crumble topping that's incredible sprinkled over ice cream (page 244), custards, or even yogurt.

unsalted butter 2 tablespoons

ground breadcrumbs *or plain panko breadcrumbs* 1½ cups

ground cinnamon 1 tablespoon

kosher salt ½ teaspoon

coconut sugar *or light brown sugar or granulated sugar* 1 to 2 teaspoons, to taste

MAKE THE PANGRATTATO: Heat a large skillet over medium heat and melt the butter. Once it begins to melt, add the cinnamon and salt, tossing to coat in the butter. Spread the crumbs out in a thin layer, and cook for 6 to 10 minutes, tossing the pan constantly, until they're toasted and crunchy to the touch, depending on the type of breadcrumbs you use and how toasted you prefer them. Remove the pan from the heat and toss in the sugar to taste.

FLAVOR BOMBS

Compound Butters, Aïolis, and Infused Oils

COMPOUND BUTTERS, AÏOLIS, AND INFUSED OILS are amazing color and flavor bombs, plus they offer a playground for experimentation. The fats become a sponge for flavor and vehicles for any ingredient you mix in. I can play in this section inventing new recipes forever. The ideas are limitless, because when you're working with butter (or other yummy fats) as your base, there's no such thing as failure. Here are my absolute staples, plus creations we've played with throughout this book with helpful tips.

MAKES
1
POUND

(EF, GF, NF, RSF, ≤5)

dried porcini mushrooms 1 ounce

salted butter 1 pound (4 sticks), softened

kosher salt ½ teaspoon, plus more as needed

Chill melted compound butters in fun-shaped silicone molds to make life worth living.

Make compound butters vegan-friendly by swapping in dairy-free butter.

For longer storage, freeze your butters wrapped tightly in parchment or plastic wrap and stored in freezer bags.

Porcini Butter

If there's a single compound butter I recommend keeping around for everyday use, it's this one. Dried porcini mushrooms are an umami gold mine, but they can sometimes be a pain to source. Once you get your hands on a small stash, you can stretch a small amount by preserving it in butter. This butter is a good back pocket weeknight secret for bringing subtle but noticeable flavor to a dish, similar to the way anchovies or MSG do. I especially lean on it to make tomato sauces seem like they've simmered for twice the time. We make a lot at once because it freezes well for up to 6 months, but if you want to start off committing to a smaller batch, this can easily be halved.

SOAK THE MUSHROOMS: In a medium bowl, cover the mushrooms with **1 TO 1½ CUPS WARM WATER** and soak for 20 minutes. Then squeeze the rehydrated mushrooms gently over the bowl to expel most of the excess water (see Tip). Dab them with paper towels and mince.

WHIP THE BUTTER: In the bowl of a mini food processor, combine the minced mushrooms, butter, and salt. Process on high until the mushrooms are fully incorporated with the butter and the mixture becomes beige in color, stopping to scrape the sides of the bowl as needed. Taste and add more salt as desired.

STORE: Place a large sheet of parchment paper on the counter. Using a rubber spatula, scrape the butter mixture into the center of the parchment in a line, then wrap it in a tight log. Seal in a zip-top freezer bag and refrigerate for up to 2 weeks or freeze for up to 6 months. Pull back the parchment on the butter log and slice off knobs as you need them.

TIP Reserve the water you've used to soak the mushrooms. You can freeze it or store it in the fridge for a few days to use in stews and soups like Wednesday Sauce (page 113). Just be sure to strain out any sand and debris floating at the bottom of the bowl before storing and using.

Pizza Butter

MAKES ABOUT A HEAPING CUP

(EF, GF, NF, RSF)

garlic 3 bulbs (about 5 ounces), plus 4 cloves

extra-virgin olive oil, for drizzling

kosher salt and **freshly ground black pepper**

salted butter 1 cup (2 sticks), at room temperature

lemon zest from 1 lemon, plus 1 tablespoon juice

dried oregano 2 teaspoons

flat-leaf parsley leaves a handful, roughly chopped

crushed red pepper flakes ½ teaspoon, plus more as needed

The heat and spice from the raw garlic paired with the sweet fragrant butteriness of roasted garlic makes this a no-brainer for smearing onto bread or melting over hot noodles. I like it spread over warm, charred sourdough alongside a heavy streak of tomato paste—it becomes a whole lazy pizza toast experience (see Red Pizza Toast, page 202). This butter is great on charred naan, Bunny Bread (page 186), and melted and drizzled over fresh popcorn. Applying the butter solid (not melted) keeps the ingredients evenly suspended throughout the fat. If you melt the butter, the bits will start to sink, so just give it a whisk prior to any basting or pouring.

PREPARE THE GARLIC: Preheat the oven to 400°F and have a small lidded casserole dish nearby. Using a sharp knife, cut the tops off the garlic bulbs just enough to expose the tops of each clove, leaving the papery skins. Place the garlic into the casserole dish, drizzle them generously with olive oil, and season them with salt and pepper. (Alternatively, you can wrap the bulbs in foil and roast them on a small sheet pan.)

ROAST THE GARLIC: Cover and roast the garlic for 40 to 50 minutes, until the cloves caramelize into a light golden brown color and soften. Check for doneness by poking the tops of the cloves with a fork. The fork should pierce through as if it were butter. Remove from the oven and place the garlic on a cutting board to cool completely (so it doesn't melt the butter).

MIX THE BUTTER: Into the bowl of a mini food processor, squeeze the bulbs of cooled roasted garlic from the base to force out the cloves (like toothpaste). Add the butter, lemon zest, lemon juice, oregano, parsley, and red pepper flakes to the bowl. Then using a Microplane, grate the raw garlic cloves over the bowl. Blend the mixture on high until smooth.

STORAGE AND REHEATING: Transfer the butter to a small lidded container or wrap it in parchment, and keep in the fridge for 2 to 3 weeks or freeze for up to 6 months. Spread it on bread or melt it in the microwave, whisking to redistribute the ingredients in the butter before using.

MAKES ABOUT

½

CUP

(DF, NF, ≤30)

mayo ⅓ cup (see Tip)

lime juice 1 tablespoon

Sriracha, *gochujang sauce or chili garlic sauce* 2 tablespoons, plus more as needed

granulated garlic or 2 grated cloves 2 teaspoons

pure toasted sesame oil ¼ teaspoon, plus more as needed

white miso paste *or red* ½ teaspoon

MAKE IT FANCY

Stir in **1 tablespoon tahini paste** for a thicker, nuttier spread.

Spicy Sesame Aïoli

Adding the smallest amount of sesame oil to Sriracha aïoli adds nutty depth and makes this an addictive sauce. Try playing with sesame oil in other dips or recipes for a touch of toastiness. (Remember a little goes a long way.) Use this aïoli on Frico Kimchi Hash (page 240), in the BYO Burger Bowl (page 207), for dipping crispy fried shrimp, drizzled over sushi bowls (see page 205), crunchy-bottom fried rice (see page 131), or stir into instant ramen for extra creaminess.

MAKE THE AÏOLI: In a small mixing bowl, whisk the mayo, lime juice, Sriracha, granulated garlic, sesame oil, and white miso paste together. Taste and adjust the Sriracha and sesame oil to desired level.

STORE: Transfer to a small lidded container and store in the fridge for up to 1 week.

On Store-Bought Mayo

For something quick from the store, Vegenaise wins my vote every time—the flavor is balanced and subtle, never overpowering, and still nice and creamy, but if you're looking for a bold version of mayo that's very rich and stands up to other hefty ingredients with its luxurious, nearly butter-like texture, Japanese Kewpie is the path to go. If you're from the South, Dukes is probably your tried-and-true.

Rosemary Truffle Aïoli

MAKES ABOUT ½ CUP

(GF, NF, RSF, ≤30)

dried rosemary 1½ teaspoons

dried oregano ½ teaspoon

mayo ½ cup

white truffle oil 2 teaspoons, plus more as needed

Parmesan cheese 2 tablespoons finely grated

garlic cloves 4

kosher salt and **freshly ground black pepper**

This is my now very-overused French fry and burger aïoli. It's also great with Black Garlic Suppli (page 220), but you can also brush a glop of this over a tile of scalloped potatoes or skin-on chicken thighs before they enter a 425°F oven to roast for an extra-crispy browned top with notes of rosemary and garlic.

GRIND THE HERBS: Using a mortar and pestle, grind the rosemary and oregano into a fine powder to reawaken them.

MIX: In a small mixing bowl, add the mayo, ground herbs, truffle oil, and Parmesan cheese. Using a Microplane, grate the garlic over top, then stir everything together to combine. Season with salt and pepper to taste and adjust the other ingredients as desired.

STORE: Transfer the aïoli to a small deli container and keep in the fridge for 1 to 2 weeks until ready to use.

MAKES ABOUT
1¼ TO 1½
CUPS
AFTER STRAINING

(DF, EF, NF, RSF, ≤5)

fresh basil leaves 2 large handfuls ← use Thai basil for even more fragrance

olive oil 2 cups

Basil Oil

Here is a vibrant finishing oil that will add color and summer sweetness to anything you choose. For a more concentrated basil flavor, just add more basil. Keep this oil in a squeeze bottle (with a nozzle tip) and drizzle some Pollock-y lines along the surface of your tomato soup and on anything else you deem worthy. I am obsessed with Thai basil so I use that. Basil always wilts and dies quickly, so this oil is a great way to have its flavor on hand without waste, or, if like me, you can't get basil easily all the time. It lasts weeks in the fridge; just run it under lukewarm water to help it loosen after being chilled. **Remember that this technique is not just for making fancy finishing oils—use it to preserve herbs and capture the essence of ingredients with otherwise short shelf lives.**

BLANCH THE BASIL: Have a large bowl of ice water nearby. In a large pot, bring **5 CUPS WATER** to a boil, then add the basil to the water and remove it after 10 seconds. Immediately transfer the basil to the bowl of ice water to stop the cooking. Once cooled, remove the basil leaves and squeeze them with your hands to remove most of the water, and then dry them as much as possible by blotting them between paper towels.

BLEND THE BASIL AND OIL: Put the basil into a blender, add the olive oil, and blend on high until it's smooth. Transfer it to a small lidded container and let it rest for 8 hours or overnight to allow the basil to infuse the oil.

STRAIN THE OIL: Using a fine mesh strainer with a couple sheets of cheesecloth or a single sheet of paper towel laid over it, strain the bits of basil from the oil into a medium bowl. Allow it to sit for a while so all the oil filters through. Press the basil residue with a spoon to extract any absorbed oil. Use the leftover solids in an impromptu pesto, stir it into eggs, or add it to chimichurri (see page 275) for subtle sweetness.

STORE: Transfer the oil into a lidded squeeze or oil bottle and keep for up to 2 months.

The Bookshelf

Here is a short list of many books that inspired me to write We Fancy and put words to what I've experienced in and out of the kitchen. Some of the books don't necessarily reflect all of my beliefs, but their words and wisdom brought me clarity around my own journey and encouraged me to continue leaning into my kitchen and my "fancy."

Awakened Imagination *by Neville Goddard*

The Artist's Way *by Julia Cameron*

The Art of Abundance: Ten Rules for a Prosperous Life *by Dennis Merrit Jones*

Healing Environments *by Carol Venolia*

The Power Pause: How to Plan a Career Break After Kids—and Come Back Stronger Than Ever *by Neha Ruch*

The Burnout Society *by Byung-Chul Han*

Eyes on the Road *by Michell C. Clark*

Women, Food, and God *by Geneen Roth*

Change Your Brain Change Your Life: The Breakthrough Program for Conquering Anxiety, Depression, Obsessiveness, Lack of Focus, Anger, and Memory Problems *by Daniel G. Amen, MD*

The Creative Act: A Way of Being *by Rick Rubin*

Tiny Experiments: How to Live Freely in a Goal-Obsessed World *by Anne-Laure Le Cunff*

We Need Your Art: Stop Messing Around and Make Something *by Amie McNee*

Mindfulness in Action: Making Friends with Yourself through Meditation and Everyday Awareness *by Chögyam Trungpa*

Flow: The Psychology of Optimal Experience *by Mihaly Csikszentmihalyi*

What Happened to You?: Conversations on Trauma, Resilience, and Healing *by Bruce D. Perry, MD, PhD and Oprah Winfrey*

The Courage to Be Disliked: How to Free Yourself, Change Your Life and Achieve Real Happiness *by Ichiro Kishimi and Fumitake Koga*

Happy at Last: The Thinking Person's Guide to Finding Joy *by Richard O'Connor, MSW, PhD*

The Gift of Fear: Survival Signals that Protect Us from Violence *by Gavin De Becker*

Good Stress: The Health Benefits of Doing Hard Things *by Jeff Krasno*

The Myth of Normal: Trauma, Illness & Healing in a Toxic Culture *by Gabor Maté, MD*

When the Body Says NO: Exploring the Stress-Disease Connection *by Gabor Maté, MD*

Attuned: Practicing Interdepence to Heal Our Trauma—and Our World *by Thomas Hübl*

The Emotion Code: How to Release Your Trapped Emotions for Abundant Health, Love, and Happiness *by Dr. Bradley Nelson*

My Grandmother's Hands: Racialized Trauma and the Pathway to Mending Our Hearts and Bodies *by Resmaa Menakem*

Ikigai: The Japanese Secret to a Long and Happy Life *by Héctor García and Francesc Miralles*

Inner Bonding: Becoming a Loving Adult to Your Inner Child *by Margaret Paul, PhD*

The Nervous System Workbook: Practical Exercises to Ease Anxiety, Find Safety, and Come Home to Yourself Using Polyvagal Theory *by Deb Dana, LCSW*

Your Body Is Your Brain: Leverage Your Somatic Intelligence to Find Purpose, Build Resilience, Deepen Relationships and Lead More Powerfully *by Amanda Blake*

Cognitive Behavioral Therapy: Simple Techniques to Instantly Be Happier, Find Inner Peace, and Improve Your Life *by Olivia Telford*

The Art of Living Well (book series) *by Damon Zahariades*

The Life-Changing Magic of Tidying Up: The Japanese Art of Decluttering and Organizing *by Marie Kondo*

Zen and the Art of Motorcycle Maintenance: An Inquiry into Values *by Robert M. Pirsig*

The Sedona Method: Your Key to Lasting Happiness, Success, Peace, and Emotional Well-Being *by Hale Dwoskin*

The Body Keeps the Score: Brain, Mind, and Body in the Healing of Trauma *by Bessel van der Kolk, MD*

The Power of Now *by Eckhart Tolle*

The Highly Sensitive Person: How to Thrive When the World Overwhelms You *by Elaine N. Aron, PhD*

The Boy, the Mole, the Fox and the Horse: Inspiring Conversations on Hope, Love and Personal Growth *by Charlie Mackesy*

Four Thousand Weeks: Time Management for Mortals *by Oliver Burkeman*

It's All Imagined: Reframe Your Reality to Evolve Your Existence *by Lars Vegas*

Journal Reflections/Cookbook Club Discussion Questions

Grab your journal and a pen and whichever Wind-Down Drink (page 37) suits your mood, and sip along while you consider one or two of the journal prompts below.

Chapter 2: Dinner Snacks &
Chapter 10: Breakfast for Dinner

These two chapters challenge what an "appropriate" dinner should look like. Have you ever felt restricted by meal "rules" (like, no pancakes for dinner, no snacks as a full meal)? What happens when you let go of those? What foods do you love that don't traditionally fit into dinner and how can you incorporate them more freely? Where else in your life are you following unnecessary rules that make dinner feel dull? How can you challenge them?

Chapter 3: Fast 'n' Fancy &
Chapter 4: What's the Rush?

These two chapters play with the concept of time. Do you often rush through cooking? Where does that urgency come from? What's your relationship to slowness in general? Do you resist it? Imagine preparing your favorite meal with no time constraints—how would it feel to slow down and enjoy the process? Are there any steps in cooking that feel like a chore? Can you eliminate or reframe them? Which parts of cooking feel meditative or joyful to you? How can you bring more of that into your routine?

Chapter 5: Jazzy Rice

What are the main staples in your diet, and if they've started to feel boring to you, in what ways can you refresh them, make them more "fancy" and worthy of repetition?

Chapter 7: My Hungry Inner Child

What emotions come up when you think about your earlier food memories? Were there meals or snacks you longed for as a child but were told were "bad" or "too much"? Were there foods you were denied? How have those early messages about food shaped the way you cook and eat today? Are there any wounds or similar judgments still lingering? How can you honor past and current cravings in a way that feels joyful and nourishing now? How would it feel to approach food with the playfulness and curiosity of a child?

Chapter 9: Lavish Leftovers

What would happen if you treated last night's meal as a building block, not an afterthought? Brainstorm a few fun ideas for how you can repurpose something you cooked today—a sauce, a side, a protein, a soup—into an entirely different dinner tomorrow.

Chapter 11: Weeknight Desserts

At this moment in your life, what is your relationship to dessert and to "sweetness," literally and figuratively? When you make dessert, do you consider it a joy worthy of savoring, a guilty pleasure, something you must earn? An afterthought? How can you create a more mindful and satisfying experience around sweets, whether often or occasionally?

Acknowledgments

Like so many of the best things in life, this book was born from a place of great pain. At the time, I felt stuck, frustrated, and quickly running out of hope. I was frantic, like a squirrel trying to find a safe place to protect its acorn, angry that the world as it existed seemed determined to destroy it. But in that state, I was able to pause and ask myself: What exactly was this thing that I was trying so desperately to protect?

What I uncovered was the sentiment that life is meant to be joyful, playful, and experimental. That curiosity could guide me forward without the constant shadow of consequence. That my joy wouldn't be buried beneath the heaviness of simply "surviving" life. Especially now, as the world gets darker, that small spark became the ember I wanted to nurture, to protect, and to share—and instead of making me feel victimized, it gave me purpose to realize there was something inside me worth protecting, and so I turned my focus to "how."

To Doris: When you reached out in the fall of 2021 about making another book, you found me in the fog. I remember you saying something like, "I want to catch you while you still want to make cookbooks." I thought I was hiding my weariness well, but perhaps it was already showing. Your words felt like a lighthouse in the darkness. You had suggested another dessert book, but I knew I couldn't keep writing about sugar when my spirit felt so imbalanced. Instead, I pitched a book about preserving the joy of cooking itself.

So much of this book was created in the process. We signed a contract with only an idea and a feeling, and you bet on me. Even when my unconventional ways of working may have tested your patience, you endured. You gave me the space to be myself—even when you couldn't yet see where I was headed. I think that is one of the greatest gifts we can offer someone: a safe space to express both our joys and our grief. Piece by piece you helped me organize the chaos into clarity and that is a rare kind of friendship.

Though this project unfolded in the intimacy of my home, it could've never happened without your motherly care, my agent Nicole's genuine love for cookbooks and knowledgeable suggestions along the way, Jen Wang's undying ability to transform colorless stacks of paper into visually stunning books, and the entire production team at Simon Element. Together, we turned private conversations into something tangible to share with the world—thank you all for working so hard to help preserve this feeling into writing, proof that we need each other and are not here to do this life alone.

To my husband: We have danced together at the depths of darkness and emerged stronger, clearer about how to be our best selves for one another. Our relationship has endured for over a decade and it has taught me the alchemy of true love, how we are simply mirrors to each other, and the richness that comes from betting all your chips on someone and deciding to make life worthwhile no matter the circumstances. Thank you for helping me build a life we both love living. I know I could not have done any of this without a partner as determined, supportive and hardworking as you.

To my son: You arrived as a surprise just as this book was wrapping up. You are the most glorious gift I never knew I needed, living proof that when we commit to treating our lives as extraordinary, they become so. Thank you for making our days brighter, sparklier, and fuller than we could have imagined. You are already doing such a beautiful job being on earth. I'm so incredibly proud of you. And thank you for being mommy's hand model on page 52 so she could have that photo as a keepsake forever, to share with you once you're older.

In the words of Ram Dass, "We are all just walking each other home."

Index

D

E

F

G

Q

R

S

T

U

V

W

Y

Z

SIMON ELEMENT

An Imprint of Simon & Schuster, LLC
1230 Avenue of the Americas
New York, NY 10020

First Simon Element hardcover edition February 2026

SIMON ELEMENT is a registered trademark of Simon & Schuster, LLC

Design by Jen Wang

Manufactured in Canada

10 9 8 7 6 5 4 3 2 1

Library of Congress Control Number has been applied for.

ISBN 978-1-6680-1284-0
ISBN 978-1-6680-1285-7 (ebook)